DATE DUE

12-26-07			

Demco

UNDERSTANDING
TELEVISION

UNDERSTANDING
TELEVISION

AN INTRODUCTION TO BROADCASTING

EDITED BY

ROBERT L. HILLIARD

Department of Radio, Television and Motion Pictures
University of North Carolina

CONTRIBUTORS:

TOM C. BATTIN
BERNARR COOPER
ROBERT L. HILLIARD
ARTHUR HUNGERFORD
WESLEY H. WALLACE
VERNE W. WEBER

A COMMUNICATION ARTS BOOK

HASTINGS HOUSE, PUBLISHERS   New York 22

To My Mother and Father

Library of Congress Catalog Card Number: 64-19074

Published simultaneously in Canada
by S. J. Reginald Saunders & Co., Ltd., Publishers, Toronto 2B

Printed in the United States of America

CONTENTS

PREFACE

THE TEACHING OF television, at one time in the recent past hardly more than a tolerated appendage of some other discipline and even considered in some instances akin to a curriculum-padding, esoteric vocational endeavor, has come into its own. As the educational administrator and the teacher have become more and more aware that the mass media — particularly television — are the greatest potential forces today for reaching and affecting the minds and emotions of mankind, more and more educational institutions have developed television and mass communication courses and curricula. Similarly, more and more people who are not formal students of the mass media have been eager to learn about television, its meaning and techniques.

This is not to say that television is a major field in all of the hundreds of institutions of higher education in which the subject area is taught. In some schools it is part of another program, such as Speech, Dramatic Arts, Journalism or English. The number of institutions in which television is part of a mass communications major — Television-Radio-Film — is growing. In some institutions extensive, specialized study is offered in the several discipline areas of the mass media: history, organization, social impact, studio and control equipment and operation, production, writing, directing, staging, performance, management, research, aesthetics, criticism and educational applications, among others. In virtually all institutions in which television is taught — from a degree program to a single course within another discipline — an introductory course is offered.

The purpose of the introductory course is primarily twofold: to provide a basic understanding of the field to those students who will not go further with a formal study of television but who, as citizens participating in or at least aware of the affairs of the world, not only desire but need a comprehension of the potentials and limitations of the mass media in order to function effectively as thinking human beings; and to provide a basic background in the major areas of television for those who will be continuing their study in the field for professional purposes and who subsequently will take advanced, complete courses in one or more of the basic individual television disciplines. An introductory course in television (or in the mass media, including television) is vital to the education of the college or university student in today's world.

This book attempts to provide for the student and the layman, for the professional and the interested citizen, those areas of television thought and practice that are most meaningful as an introduction to the medium. As you look at the Table of Contents you will note the important subject areas necessary to acquaint the beginner with television background and application — the divisions most often covered in the introductory course and most often expanded into full courses in depth for the advanced student.

There are many comprehensive textbooks of varying degrees of excellence oriented toward meeting the needs of the student of television. Why, then, another? As with other professional fields that have grown in a relatively short time to positions of stature in society, television has become specialized. It is no longer sufficient to have merely a broad overview of the field. Concomitantly, it should not be necessary for the instructor or reader to have to select portions from a large, detailed work that covers in depth all aspects of television in order to effectively have those materials that meet the needs of the beginner. It is no longer advisable to have the ideas of just one or several writers for all major divisions of the medium; in its specialization television has developed experts for its individual aspects. It is no longer efficient to offer the learner solely the ideas and approaches of the professional practitioner in the field — for competent as the commercial practitioner may be, he may not have sufficient (or any) experience as an educator to enable him to write and develop his material for optimum effectiveness and good teaching in the classroom or the home learning situation. In developing this book we have attempted to meet the modern needs of teaching and learning television. Each chapter is written by a specialist in the given subject. Each contributor is not only an experienced teacher and educator, but is also experienced in the professional area of his competency. The material is basic, yet comprehensive; the approach is professional, yet educational.

If the reader gains from this book the knowledge and stimulation to make him or her a person better able to contribute to the goals of peace, understanding, freedom, cultural strength and better living standards through the effective use or perception of the mass media, then the authors will consider their efforts amply rewarded.

We are grateful to Russell F. Neale, publisher of *Communication Arts Books,* for his assistance and patience in the publication of this book.

ROBERT L. HILLIARD
Chapel Hill, N.C.
March, 1964

WESLEY H. WALLACE

Chairman,
Department of Radio, Television and Motion Pictures,
University of North Carolina at Chapel Hill

●Dr. Wallace received the B.S. degree from the North Carolina State University of North Carolina at Raleigh, the M.A. from the University of North Carolina at Chapel Hill and the Ph.D. from Duke University, all in history. He has been active in commercial broadcasting since 1929 as a staff musician, announcer, copywriter, traffic manager, assistant program director, production manager and station manager. From 1943 through 1946 he served first as Officer-in-Charge of Armed Forces Radio stations WVTI, Bougainville, in the Northern Solomons and WVTM, Manila, and subsequently supervised 14 stations as Officer-in-Charge of the Armed Forces Radio Service in the Western Pacific. From 1947 to 1950 he was General Manager of the Manila Broadcasting Company in the Philippines. Since 1952 he has been a member of the Department of Radio, Television and Motion Pictures at the University of North Carolina and is currently chairman of the department with the rank of Associate Professor. He has taught courses in the history and development of broadcasting, station management, broadcasting public relations and promotion, creative programming, social aspects of mass communication and a seminar in mass communication. He has contributed articles to historical journals and is active in various regional and national professional associations.

Acknowledgment is made of permission to use the station organization diagrams: pages 28-29, Jefferson Standard Broadcasting Company, Charlotte, N.C.; page 30, Greater Washington Educational Television Association, Inc., Washington, D.C. For Table 3, page 31: the National Association of Broadcasters, Washington, D.C.

1

GROWTH,
ORGANIZATION,
AND IMPACT

BY WESLEY H. WALLACE

THE MANY-FACETED institution that is television broadcasting plays a number of different and sometimes conflicting roles. These roles are not necessarily inherent in the electronic nature of the device; they are roles assigned by society.

Multiple Roles of Television

For some important voices in society, television broadcasting is a part of the institutionalism of education: a method of transmitting knowledge; a device for spreading cultural richness to culturally arid areas; a mechanism for increasing the effectiveness of the school, the library, and the teacher. For the world of business and industry, television broadcasting is an advertising device, capable of moving goods and services from a few central supplying points to the outermost limits of the United States, capable of popularizing brand names of toothpaste, cereals, cigarettes, soaps and beer. For those who regulate broadcasting, television is seen as a user of the radio spectrum — a natural resource — under a federal license requiring operation in the public interest. To those who see this as television's role, any conflict between private and public interest must naturally be resolved in favor of the public.

For the broadcaster himself, television's role is somewhat confused and contradictory: telecasting is a business, with all of the usual pitfalls of business and some special ones reserved for it; telecasting is also *show* business, catering to the vagaries of public whims and tastes; telecasting is an occupation, a profession, or a source of income from investment, a livelihood, or an outlet for the energies and interests of the frustrated side-show barker or the would-be "con" man, a status symbol, a way to power, an opportunity to serve. To the broadcaster, telecasting is part theatre, part school, part newspaper, part church, and part town meeting — with many of the problems each of these entails. To the broadcaster, also, the television station and its channel are symbols of private property which must be protected from the always-threatening encroachments of government and from the gibes of the critics.

For the critics, television frequently plays the role of the chief criminal on trial for attacking society. The most recent mass communication medium, it is accused of creating mass responses to mass stimuli, of robbing the populace of its will to *do* by persuading it just to sit and absorb, of engendering "bad" social behavior through its power of persuasion. For these critics and many organized groups, television plays the convenient role of whipping boy when social fault must be found.

The role of television which dominates all others through sheer numbers of its adherents is supplying entertainment. It seems clear that the general viewing public expects and demands that television broadcasting amuse, divert, and titillate hour after hour. The public will agree grudgingly that television may sometimes play its other roles, but most viewers insist that the station owner must recognize that his primary responsibilities are to the viewing public which owns the sets and which takes for granted the fact that television entertainment will be *there* when the switch is snapped on.

Americans should not be surprised that the institution of television broadcasting, faced with these multifarious demands, requirements, and expectations on the part of various elements of society, should frequently appear to fall short of portraying any of its roles. The truly remarkable fact, however, is not that television fails upon occasion — in the face of so many and frequently conflicting demands upon it — but that it ever succeeds.

Television's Relation to Radio Broadcasting

Although it is assumed that most of the public is vaguely aware that television and radio are somewhat related — after all, both come into the home without the aid of wires — nevertheless, it is important to understand that television owes to radio broadcasting a very great debt.

The emergence of radio broadcasting in the United States in the early 1920's pioneered such programming concepts as formal time periods for programs (e.g., quarter-, half-, and full-hour), the continuous program operation from morning sign-on to evening sign-off, the brief station identification period at the end of each program as a device for accommodating commercial or public service announcements, and the network concept of a single origination point for programs distributed by wire and radio links to hundreds of stations for national audience consumption. The commercial aspects of radio broadcasting — the sponsored program and the spot announcement advertising goods and services — were transferred intact to television, which followed the example of radio in relying almost entirely on advertising revenue to support its operations.[1] Telecasting took advantage of established radio audience habits that included staying at home to receive entertainment, to absorb information, and to participate vicariously in community affairs, and even rearranging living habits to suit the hours of favorite programs. The patterns of control and regulation — the broadcaster as the trustee required to operate in the *public* interest, convenience and necessity, under the eye of the federal government — were well established for radio broadcasting a decade before television was little more than an engineer's dream or a laboratory experiment. Radio broadcasting conditioned the public to consider that its home entertainment should be free of direct cost once the set was purchased and that the audience had a *right* to be entertained and informed with no admission charge; television continued to cater to these ideas.[2] Finally, from a technological point of view, radio and television have many common antecedents, and in a technological sense it is not wrong to describe television as radio to which electronically dissected, transmitted, and reproduced pictures have been added.

HISTORICAL DEVELOPMENT OF TELEVISION

Scientists in the 19th century were convinced that, since voice could be transmitted over wires (i.e., the telephone), pictures could also be sent.[3] At the same time, other scientists were investigating James Clerk Maxwell's 1873 "ether" theory that something we now call electromagnetic energy traveled through space (i.e., the "ether") in wave-like form and that through the application of mathematical principles man could control and direct these "waves."[4]

Control of electromagnetic energy was achieved earlier than success in transmitting pictures over wires. Work of such men as Heinrich Hertz, Guglielmo Marconi — popularly known as the "father of radio" — Lee DeForest, Reginald Fessenden, Ambrose Fleming, Edwin Howard Armstrong, and many others resulted in rapid development of wireless transmission first in telegraphic and then in voice or telephonic form. By 1920, just a quarter-century after Marconi's first demonstration of wireless telegraphy, development of radio telephony had advanced to such a degree that broadcasting was technologically feasible.[5]

Early Experimentation

The evolution of picture transmission was much slower. Picture transmission, either through the medium of wires or by "wireless," could be done only after the solving of two problems: how to convert varying intensities of light energy into comparably varying electrical currents, and how to "photo-graph" (analyze, "scan," or "read") each minute portion of the picture sequentially and not simultaneously as in the chemical photographic proc-ess. In 1873, Andrew May, an Irish telegrapher, discovered that selenium reacted to light, passing electrical current through it more easily in sunlight than in darkness. A decade later, a German scientist, Paul Nipkow, invented a whirling disc that "scanned" the picture by letting light shine through holes in the disc in a carefully structured sequential pattern. Although the *principles* of television were thus established quite early, the techniques were too crude to be of great practical value.

Experiments in refining these principles made little headway for a number of years. By 1923, Charles Francis Jenkins in the United States and James Logie Baird in England led in transmitting shadows via wireless as a laboratory phenomenon. One writer pointed out: "Rarely in scientific history has success, from known principles, come so slowly and painfully as in television."[5a]

The system of television first developed by Jenkins, Baird and others used the principle of the Nipkow scanning disc, a *mechanical* device. There were limits to the degree of refinement of the whirling disc method; and other American scientists and electronic engineers, including Philo T. Farnsworth and Vladimir K. Zworykin, turned their attention to scanning the picture with an electronic beam. The argument between proponents of the two systems went on during the 1920's. Although those who favored the mechanical system had certain initial successes, such as the transatlantic broadcasting of moving pictures in 1928 and successful color transmission in the United States and Britain in the same year, the decade of the 1930's witnessed electronic television's triumph.[6]

Television was still in the first, or laboratory, stage in the years imme-diately preceding the outbreak of the second World War in September, 1939. The second stage of development, that of experimental operation in which the program interests of the public might be developed, was just beginning, and the third stage, that of full operation on a national scale, was still some years ahead. Part of this slow but relatively orderly development stemmed from a position maintained by the Federal Communications Com-mission. This agency's predecessor, the Federal Radio Commission, estab-lished in 1927 to bring order out of chaos in radio broadcasting, had been interested quite early in the progress of experimentation in visual broadcast-ing. When federal control of wire and radio communication was perma-nently established and the Federal Communications Commission was created by the Communications Act of 1934, the FCC continued to encour-age television experimentation. However, the FCC consistently refused to adopt standards of transmission and reception for fear that equipment manufacturers would cease their experimentation with the result that, in the long run, the public might suffer from a frozen but inferior service.[7] At the same time, the second stage of development — experimental development of program patterns — could not take place until the purchaser of a receiver could be reasonably sure that his set would pick up the signal from the transmitting station, and this required some agreement on technological standards. At FCC urging, the Radio Manufacturers Association cooperated in establishing a National Television System Committee to work out technical standards. The objective was to insure that all receivers could pick up programs from any station within range, and that subsequent technological improvements would not make receivers purchased earlier worthless.[8]

In spite of the lack of standards, stations were broadcasting experimentally. In the middle of 1938, 19 stations had been authorized by the FCC, but only a few were broadcasting programs regularly, and only a few receivers were available for public purchase.[9] Nevertheless, television was on the eve of dramatic developments. As *Fortune* magazine summarized it: "Radio sired it, science nursed it, Wall Street and Hollywood have dandled it — and at last the public is to get it."[10] And the public did get it — when the National Broadcasting Company's experimental television station broadcast President Franklin Delano Roosevelt's speech at the opening of the New York World's Fair, April 30, 1939. As a result, would-be television station operators began to clamor for permission to operate commercially with a regular service to the public, and programming during the next few months included telecasts of a college football game, a six-day bicycle race in Madison Square Garden, a heavyweight boxing match, a visit of Great Britain's King George VI and Queen Elizabeth to the World's Fair, and a major league baseball game.[11]

In the year following the telecasting of the World's Fair opening, interest in television among manufacturers and broadcasters increased greatly. By June 30, 1940, 26 experimental stations were on the air, and the FCC had received 59 applications for new stations. Research and experimentation were going on in the development of coaxial cable and microwave relay systems as methods of network distribution of television programs. The National Broadcasting Company, a subsidiary of the Radio Corporation of America, broadcast portions of the Republican national convention in July, 1940, transmitting the programs via coaxial cable from Philadelphia to WNBT in New York. Manufacturers were developing portable equipment to permit outside or "remote" broadcasts. Color television attracted serious attention from the Radio Corporation of America and the Columbia Broadcasting System. RCA and CBS demonstrated their color systems — which reverted to a mechanical method of spinning disks which employed color filters instead of a wholly electronic system — during 1940 to the FCC and the press; and early in 1941 the National Broadcasting Company began public colorcasting.[12]

The Development of Public Television

All outgo and no income was unattractive to pioneer experimental telecasters, and the Federal Communications Commission was under heavy pressure to permit the new medium to be used — as radio broadcasting had been from the 1920's onward — as an advertising vehicle from which a profit could be made. Thus, at the end of 1939, the Commission granted limited commercial exploitation but, before any commercials were aired, rescinded the permission when it found that one manufacturer was promoting the sale of television receivers in spite of the fact that no standards had been set. The FCC did not want public investment which might subsequently be lost.[13]

A year later, however, the National Television System Committee agreed on an interlacing method of scanning, employing a "frame" of 525 lines.[14] The FCC quickly adopted the NTSC recommendations and commercial television began on July 1, 1941.[15]

WNBT, NBC's New York station, had among its early advertisers and program sponsors Ivory Soap, which offered a television version of the popular radio program of the day, *Truth or Consequences*. Botany Worsted, Adam Hats, Bulova Watch, and a few other companies made up the sponsor list. WNBT's rate card called for a charge of $120 per hour at night, with lower daytime rates. In addition to the time charge, the advertiser had to pay for use of the studios, program talent, announcers, and other production costs.[16] Even these costs — modest by later standards — were high when the advertiser could reach a maximum of perhaps 5,000 receivers.[17]

The active involvement of the United States in World War II halted expansion of commercial public television between 1941 and 1945. No new stations were authorized, and no television receivers were manufactured for civilian use.[18] Nevertheless, during the war six commercial and three experimental stations operated limited schedules of from six to ten hours of programming each week — much of it film.[19] In addition, there was a great deal of anticipation among those who were eager to build and operate commercial television stations when wartime restrictions were removed. On December 31, 1943, midway in the war, 14 applications had been turned in; a year later the number had risen to nearly 100. In January, 1943, station operators and other interested groups formed the Television Broadcasters Association, and the FCC reported that there would be television service in "dozens of cities" when equipment restrictions would be removed.[20]

The Commission lifted its wartime "freeze" on new stations in October, 1945, and by the end of the year 150 applications for new stations had been filed. Yet many applicants began to have second thoughts, and a number of them soon withdrew their requests. Television was a costly business, there were few sets in the hands of the public — for example, there were

scarcely a dozen sets in all of Washington on the eve of commercial telecasting in the capital — station operators were uncertain whether color television would make the black-and-white variety obsolete, and there were
yet no facilities for connecting stations into networks.[21] In addition, standard (AM) radio broadcasting and the newer FM service were growing as
spectacularly as television, and radio seemed to offer an opportunity for a
more profitable operation with fewer problems than did television. (For
growth in AM, FM, and TV, see Table 1, p. 18.)

The lull in television interest lasted only from the middle of 1946 to
March, 1947. The Columbia Broadcasting System sought permission to
operate its own version of color television, but the FCC denied the request
because color was not sufficiently perfected and approval would have resulted in a change so drastic as to make obsolete all receivers in the hands
of the public. The FCC's decision, reassuring to those counting on the
future of black-and-white television, opened the gates to a flood of applications. By June 30, 1947, there were in use approximately 50,000 receivers
serving audiences estimated at 300,000, and by mid-1948, 50,000 new receivers were being added each month. Television networks of coaxial cable
were slowly coming into being, linking 24 cities in the fall of 1949, and
culminating in a transcontinental broadcast of President Harry Truman's
participation in the Japanese peace negotiations in San Francisco on September 4, 1951. Full transcontinental commercial operation began a few
days later. RCA and DuMont Laboratories perfected a method of photo-
graphing television programs directly from the face of the receiver tube — a
process labelled kinescoping — as a means of making popular programs
produced in New York, Chicago, or Hollywood available to outlying
stations.[22]

The upsurge in applications — by June, 1948, the FCC had authorized 109 stations and was faced with another 294 requests — pointed up a
serious problem. There were only 12 channels set aside for television.[23]
With this limited number of channels only the top 140 metropolitan areas
of the United States could expect to have stations, and the FCC soon
realized that demand for channel assignments was quickly outstripping the
supply.[24]

On September 30, 1948, the Commission stopped processing television
applications and in effect "froze" the status of television until it could de-
cide how to provide more channels. The existing 12 channels were located
in the very high frequency (VHF) portion of the radio spectrum and, at
the time of the freeze, the FCC pointed out that any expansion would
have to take place in the ultra high frequency (UHF) spectrum area. [25]

For three and a half years the freeze on new stations remained in effect
while the Commission compiled data, evidence, and opinions on solutions.
Finally, on April 11, 1952, the licensing process began once more to function. Now, however, television consisted of 82 channels: 2-13 were the old

ones, the so-called VHF channels; and 14-83 were 70 new ones in the higher
UHF range. As a result, it was theoretically possible for almost 1,300
communities to have more than 2,000 stations. Nearly one-eighth of the
assignments were reserved for educational, noncommercial television.[26]

In the year following the lifting of the freeze, nearly 400 new stations
were authorized[27] — though most of these did not actually go on the air
until another year had passed. Thus, as Table 1 indicates, between the middle of 1953 and the middle of 1955, television experienced its greatest
period of expansion in the number of stations providing service to the public.

TABLE 1

Twenty-Year Development of Broadcasting Reflected in
Number of Stations Authorized or On the Air

Source: Federal Communications Commission, *Fifteenth Annual Report* (1949),
p. 30; *Twenty-Eighth Annual Report* (1962), pp. 74-75.

As of June 30	AM	Comm FM	Educ FM	Comm TV	Educ TV
1943[a]	912	48[b]	—	6[b]	—
1944[a]	924	52[b]	—	9[b]	—
1945[a]	955	53[b]	—	25[b]	—
1946[a]	1,215	456[b]	—	30[b]	—
1947[a]	1,795	918[b]	—	66[b]	—
1948[a]	2,034	1,020[b]		109[b]	—
1949[c]	2,006[c]	737[c]	34[c]	69[c]	—
1950	2,144	691	62	104	—
1951	2,281	649	83	107	—
1952	2,355	629	92	108	0
1953	2,458	580	106	198	1
1954	2,583	553	117	402	6
1955	2,732	540	124	458	11
1956	2,896	530	126	496	20
1957	3,079	530	135	519	26
1958	3,253	548	147	556	32
1959	3,377	622	154	566	43
1960	3,483	741	165	579	47
1961	3,602	889	186	543	54
1962	3,745	1,012	201	571	59

[a] Stations authorized (licenses and construction permits); no figures available for
number of stations actually on the air. [b] No separation available into commercial and
educational stations in FCC'S figures. [c] Beginning with 1949, figures represent those
stations actually on the air under authority of license or construction permit.

The public responded to this increase in stations by buying receivers
by the millions. Even during the freeze, the increase was great. From an
estimated 1,750,000 sets in the hands of the public at the start of the freeze,
the number increased to 12,500,000 in 1951 and, in spite of shortages
caused by the Korean conflict, 1950-1953, doubled by the year after the
freeze was lifted.[28] The number of homes equipped with at least one television receiver has increased steadily until, in 1964, it was over 91% of
all homes in the United States.[29]

The UHF-VHF Problem

Up through 1963, all of the television receivers manufactured before 1952, and most of those built afterward, could pick up only channels 2-13, the VHF frequencies. Only 7% to 10% of all receivers in use in 1963 were capable of tuning in a UHF station.[30] This was a major factor, though not the only one, which spelled trouble for commercial television station operators on channels 14 through 83. As early as 1954 there were indications of UHF difficulties when 69 authorizations to construct and operate such stations were returned to the FCC in one year.[31] Others who received construction permits from the Commission never completed the stations they had sought; and still others who constructed their stations and actually went on the air suspended operations and either turned in their licenses or held on to them, with FCC permission, hoping for better times.[32]

The lack of receiving sets meant that audiences for these UHF stations were small and therefore less attractive to advertisers. Lack of advertising revenue meant poorer quality, less expensive programming. Less attractive programming was no enticement to a homeowner to pay a premium for an all-channel receiver when he could buy for less a set that would pick up what he wanted to see. And so the circle went: no audience, no advertisers — no advertisers, no revenue — no revenue, no programs — no programs, no audience. In addition, UHF stations offered less geographical coverage than VHF broadcasters — even when the UHF stations operated with 1,000 kilowatts of power as compared with 100 kilowatts allowed a channel 2 station.[33]

From 1954 on, the FCC spent substantial portions of its time in attempts to solve the UHF problem. Among its proposals, either partially implemented or untried, were the "deintermixture" of a few markets — making some areas such as Peoria, Illinois, all UHF or others all VHF so as to even out the competitive factors — and the gradual phasing out of all VHF so as to move all television eventually to the UHF portion of the spectrum, a move which would be expensive to receiver owners and to the station operators because, unless receivers and transmitters were converted to UHF, substantial investments would be lost. Additionally, the Commission authorized higher power for UHF stations — up to 5,000 kilowatts — and it permitted various forms of satellite stations — translators and boosters — to extend the coverage of the "mother" station. The most recent — and most hopeful — step for UHF operators was to persuade the Congress of the United States to enact a law requiring that all television sets shipped in interstate commerce must be capable of receiving all channels from 2 to 83. The Act became fully effective on April 30, 1964.[34]

Color Television: Controversy and Development

Although the Federal Communications Commission had in effect decreed that the United States would develop a black-and-white system when it turned down the CBS color television proposals in 1947, the Commission soon discovered that CBS was not to be put off so easily. Following more experimentation and investigation, CBS demanded and received a new hearing in September, 1949. For 62 days the FCC listened to statements by electronics engineers and others, and the record accumulated 300 exhibits and nearly 10,000 pages of testimony. Just a year after the hearings began, the Commission decided that the CBS method was the best of the three color systems then in use experimentally and ordered that commercial television, using the CBS system, could begin in November, 1950.[35]

One main drawback to the CBS color method was its "incompatibility" with the standards in effect for black-and-white or monochrome telecasting. A standard receiver could not pick up a CBS color program at all — not even in black-and-white — and a CBS color receiver could not pick up programs from regular television stations. Thus a CBS receiver was useless when no color program was on the air, and most viewers who wanted some choice in their program selection would have had to purchase both a monochrome and a CBS color receiver. Another inherent weakness in the system was the use of a mechanical whirling disc with the same intrinsic lack of refinement that had defeated the adoption of the whirling disc method in the 1920's. For these and other reasons a group of manufacturers who opposed CBS, appealed to the courts, challenging the FCC's decision.[36]

The court test, though eventually unsuccessful, delayed the start of commercial colorcasting until June, 1951.[37] Even then commercial color television did not begin in any significant way; in November the National Production Authority forbade color receiver manufacturing because the United States' effort in the Korean conflict was draining the supply of critical materials.[38]

As a result of these delays and obstacles there was no color television programming and no color receiver production for most of the next two years. During the entire period the National Television System Committee continued to work on a compatible, all-electronic system that would permit the growth of color television simultaneously and harmoniously with the older and well-established monochrome method. After re-examining the question, the FCC in December, 1953, reversed itself and gave the NTSC color system its blessing.[39]

The development of color television has been disappointingly slow. In spite of more than $70 million spent by RCA alone in color development by early 1956, the FCC reported an estimate of only 160,000 sets in use by the middle of 1957.[40] The National Broadcasting Company was the only network to program in color to any significant degree. Each year, brave predictions that "this is the year for color" were met by the public's apathetic refusal to buy the color sets. Reasons given included the high cost of the sets, the belief that color was not yet perfected, and the feeling that color sets were both expensive and difficult to maintain.[41] Some viewers commented facetiously that color television receivers were so complicated to operate that an electrical engineering degree was a prerequisite to ownership. Though interest in color television by manufacturers and dealers appeared to be increasing considerably in the early 1960's, color television seemed a long way from sweeping the country.[42]

Television's Economic Growth: From Rags to Riches

The economic status of broadcasting has always been an important concern of the Federal Communications Commission, and the Commission keeps close watch on television's financial condition through annual reports required of all stations and networks.

At the beginning of commercial television, revenue from the sale of time to advertisers did not begin to offset the costs of operation. In 1948 all television networks and all 50 stations on the air reported losses amounting to nearly $15 million.[43] Though revenues increased almost 300% in the next year, expenses increased also, and losses rose to more than $25 million. This was the turning point, however, and in 1950 not only were revenues up more than 200% but losses were under $10 million.[44] As Table 2 demonstrates, television's revenues climbed spectacularly between the beginning of 1950 and the end of 1960. Though operating costs and other expenses likewise grew by large amounts, revenue increased at a greater rate; and, as a result, profits also increased rapidly after 1951. In 1954 television received more money from advertisers than did both AM and FM broadcasting; it experienced its first billion-dollar year in 1958. Expenses exceeded one billion dollars for the first time in 1960. Only in 1957 and 1958 did television's profits fail to increase, and in 1959 the previous high figure was surpassed.[45]

Over-all figures for revenues and profits are somewhat deceptive. Fewer UHF stations made money than did VHF stations; stations located in large metropolitan areas did better financially than those in less populous communities; stations affiliated with networks fared better than their non-network counterparts.[46]

Since television's total profits were both public and impressive, it is not surprising that television stations were considered by those versed in financial matters as valuable properties which could and did change hands for substantial sums. In 1956, WDTV, Pittsburgh (later KDKA-TV), brought $9,750,000; two years later, WCAU-AM-FM-TV, Philadelphia, was purchased by CBS for $20 million. Even a UHF station, KJEO, Fresno, brought $3 million in 1960, and a half-interest in WTAE-TV, Pittsburgh, went for $10,600,000 in 1962.[47]

Pay-TV

Although the pattern of American broadcasting, radio and television,

TABLE 2

Financial Record of Broadcasting
(by calendar years, in millions of dollars)

Source: Federal Communications Commission, *Annual Reports*, 1951-1961

	1950	1951	1952	1953	1954	1955	1956	1957	1958	1959	1960
Revenues	550.4	686.1	793.9	908.0	1042.5	1198.1	1377.5	1461.5	1553.1	1723.9	1866.3
AM-FM	444.5	450.4	469.7	475.3	449.5	453.4	480.6	518.3	523.1	560.0	597.7
TV	105.9	235.7	324.2	432.7	593.0	744.7	896.9	943.2	1030.0	1163.9	1268.6
EXPENSES	491.4	586.0	678.3	785.0	910.4	1001.9	1138.7	1247.5	1343.9	1459.2	1576.3
AM-FM	376.3	392.9	409.6	420.3	407.7	407.4	431.4	464.3	485.8	517.6	551.8
TV	115.1	194.1	268.7	364.7	502.7	594.5	707.3	783.2	858.1	941.6	1024.5
aPROFITS (Losses)	59.0	99.1	115.6	123.0	132.1	196.2	238.8	214.0	209.2	264.7	290.0
AM-FM	68.2	57.5	60.1	55.0	41.8	46.0	49.2	54.0	37.3	42.4	45.9
TV	(9.2)	41.6	55.5	68.0	90.3	150.2	189.6	160.0	171.9	222.3	244.1

a Before federal taxes.

has been one of programs traditionally available without charge to anyone who owned a receiving set and was within range of a transmitter, that concept of "free" broadcasting has been challenged by the principle of subscription television, called pay-as-you-see-TV or simply pay-TV.

On January 1, 1951, the Zenith Radio Corporation, with FCC permission, began a 90-day pay-TV broadcast test of its "Phonevision" system, transmitting programs to approximately 300 homes.[48] The programming fare consisted of three first-run motion pictures per day. The picture on the television tube was "scrambled" and thus was unintelligible; however, the customer wishing to see the film called the telephone company, which made a connection that returned the picture to normal and added a dollar to the viewer's telephone bill.

Zenith's experiment was only the first of several indications of pay-TV interest in the early 1950's, and it soon became apparent that this was a matter which posed several thorny public questions.[49] Was the principle of pay-TV really in the public interest? Was pay-TV, which was transmitted at least in part by means of radio waves, broadcasting as the Communications Act of 1934 defined it? Or was it "common carrier"? What was the FCC's role in regulation of pay-TV? What effects would pay-TV, if developed, have on the established method of free broadcasting?

For more than three years the Federal Communications Commission took no action on requests for a policy decision on these and other questions. Finally, however, in early 1955 the FCC invited opinions from anyone who cared to comment. By this date public argument for and against subscription television had reached substantial proportions. The comments — many of them stated in emotional terms — flowed in to the Commission in such quantities that the material filled 75 volumes, causing the FCC to note that the response had, in sheer bulk, surpassed any previous case within its jurisdiction.[50]

For another two years the evidence was considered, the FCC deciding finally that it had the authority to control pay-TV and to authorize its operation. First, however, the FCC wanted much more extensive tests, and in March, 1959, it set up the rules. A three-year trial was required and the test could take place only in a metropolitan area where four or more television stations had been authorized. Only one pay-TV system could be tested in each area and only one of the stations could be used in the test. Finally, the test applicant had to supply any special equipment to the participating homes to avoid any public investment in equipment which might become useless if the Commission decided eventually not to allow pay-TV.[51]

While a number of pay-TV projects not subject to FCC control — those using coaxial cable — have been inaugurated to serve both home sets and movie theatres, the broadcast method of pay-TV under the FCC's test rules developed slowly.[52] By late 1963 tests were being conducted only in Hartford and Denver.[53] Nonetheless, interest in subscription television

among business interests continued strong, and there were hints that the
new concept might be a "major communications force" by the 1970's and
that the present system of free commercial television would undoubtedly
suffer from such a development.[54]

Community Antenna Systems (CATV)

Although many broadcasters believe "free" commercial television ultimately will face a threat from subscription television, many of them feel
that the growth of community antenna systems, called CATV in the world
of broadcasting, poses a more immediately dangerous threat. The community antenna systems began in areas where mountainous terrain blocked
out the line-of-sight signals from transmitters to receivers. Homes located
in valleys or behind masses of high hills could not receive programs directly,
and in order to bring television service into the community CATV systems
were devised.

In essence, a company or group with sufficient financial resources
constructs a "master antenna" or receiving facility on the crest of the inter-
fering terrain or some other advantageous location; it then "pipes" the television program into the community by means of microwave (i.e., radio)
relay or coaxial cable. In the community itself, the program is distributed to
subscribing homes through a coaxial cable connected to a regular television
receiving set. For this service the customer usually pays a connection fee
and a continuing charge which varies from $2.50 to $6.50 a month.[55]

Starting as a small cloud on the broadcaster's horizon in 1949-50 in
Oregon and Pennsylvania, CATV operations expanded until by 1963, 46
states had one or more CATV facilities. In Pennsylvania alone, 185 communities were served, and more than a million subscribers across the nation
received programs from a thousand such systems.[56]

Expansion of the CATV idea, however, has brought systems into use
in communities which were served by a local station but where the choice of
programming was not extensive. The principal complaint about CATV
operations has thus come from broadcasters who had had audiences to
themselves until programs from some distant station or stations were
brought in via CATV and became competitors. This circumstance was particularly serious if the piped-in stations supplied network programs; the
local broadcaster, especially if he were not affiliated with a network, suffered a loss of audience and consequently a loss of revenue when advertisers
reduced their use of his station. Some broadcasters also complain that
CATV operators pick up programs from their stations without permission
and make a profit from a property — the program — which the broadcasters contend does not lawfully belong to the CATV operator. More distant broadcasters, however, frequently are glad to have their stations' programs fed into a community because their audiences are thereby increased
and their stations become more attractive to advertisers.[57]

What was originally a small enterprise conducted either as a cooperative effort or by an operator willing to risk his capital for a modest return has been modified by the appearance of large firms which buy, sell, build, or operate many CATV properties as a profitable area of investment. For example, TelePrompTer owns systems in Kansas, Michigan, California, New Mexico, New York, Oregon, Pennsylvania, Wyoming, Montana and Hawaii; RKO General, owner of several broadcasting stations, in 1963 operated 19 CATV systems serving 30,000 subscribers. These and many other such companies have moved into communities to offer from four to nine different programs from as many stations and also to provide FM stereo programs. In addition, these systems are ready-made for the advent of subscription television. Having already control over cable connections bringing programs into homes, CATV operators need only to take the additional step of installing scrambling and decoding devices to provide themselves with extra income from special individual programs.[58]

Some broadcasters have long sought to have the FCC regulate CATV operators and, indeed, the Commission first expressed concern about CATV-created problems in the early 1950's. The initial concern was with the possible interference of CATV transmissions with regular broadcast signals. When the CATV companies used microwave relay systems, they came within the authority of the Commission.

The question of economic injury to broadcasters, however, has been a more difficult matter to assess. The Commission would like to require the CATV operators to include the programs of the local station as one of the choices for subscribers, provided the local station wishes it; the FCC would like also to prevent the CATV operator from duplicating a program carried by the local station by bringing in the same program from a more distant source. The Commission's position was strengthened by a recent decision of the United States Court of Appeals for the District of Columbia which held that the FCC properly could deny a license for microwave facilities to a CATV operator as a means of protecting a local television station from economic injury. Earlier, the FCC had sought — so far unsuccessfully — to have the Congress place the antenna systems under its control. The future development of CATV is thus likely to be deeply involved in further action by the Commission, the courts, and the Congress.[59]

Educational, Noncommercial Television

Not all television in the United States is either primarily concerned with entertaining or diverting the public or is supported by money derived from advertising. A substantial portion of telecasting has as its objective enlightenment, instruction and enrichment of many kinds of audiences and derives support from local, state and federal government agencies, from private donors and public foundations, and even from gifts of various kinds from commercial broadcasters themselves.[60]

Educational broadcasting started as soon as any other form of broadcasting.[61] For a variety of reasons, educational radio broadcasting was less than the exciting success its proponents had hoped that it would be.[62] When television emerged after World War II as a potentially great commercial medium, however, educators who had been interested in educational radio or who had had experience operating AM or FM stations on campuses of educational institutions began to exhibit interest in the new medium and its potential for the educational world.[63]

During the "freeze" imposed by the Federal Communications Commission on new television authorizations in the period 1948 to 1952, a number of educators and educational groups combined efforts to plead with the Commission to set aside channels for educational, non-profit, noncommercial use. In spite of bickering and dissent among educators, opposition by commercial broadcasters, and initial apathy and outright reluctance on the part of the majority of the Commission — changed to interest and support by the weight of the educators' testimony and the insistence of Commissioner Frieda B. Hennock — the Commission created a new category of stations — the noncommercial educational television stations — and provided for 242 channels (80 VHF and 162 UHF) for educational use when it issued its allocation plan in 1952, marking — as one writer put it — "the beginning of a new era in American education."[64]

Though beset by problems — lack of money, lack of a clearly articulated operational and programming philosophy, lack of experience, and lack of qualified personnel — ETV, as it has come to be called, has developed into an important phase of American broadcasting. The first station to commence broadcasting under the new plan was KUHT, Houston, which began in 1953, and it was followed by many others so that by mid-1963 the number of stations had grown to 80.[65] These stations were owned and operated by a wide variety of organizations, including universities and other institutions of higher learning, local school boards and districts, community cooperatives formed into non-profit corporations, and private organizations.[66]

Progress has been exhibited in other ways. Educational television networks have come into being — thus far on a state level as in Alabama, Oklahoma, and Florida — and plans are progressing for the formation of other state networks and regional networks to link groups of states. The FCC has set aside additional channels for educational television and has established an office within its organization to deal specifically with educational broadcasting matters. Programs are produced, tape-recorded, and distributed nationally under the direction of the National Educational Television and Radio Center, an organization supported by Ford Foundation money and payments from participating stations. A recent development of major significance is the Congressional authorization of federal grants to all the states if matched by other funds to expand educational telecasting facilities.[67]

ETV has many applications and methods. It is both a broadcasting service, to be received like any other television broadcasting, and also a non-broadcast, closed circuit device. Its program content has been used to enrich and broaden cultural experience for many and to provide both formal and informal, credit and non-credit instruction at elementary, secondary and higher educational levels.

Educational television's potential for use in instruction, for serving innumerable community needs and desires, and for enrichment of the human spirit almost defies comprehension. Not the least of its past and future contributions lies, in many areas, in offering an alternative service to commercial broadcasting fare. The future for ETV is bright indeed.

ORGANIZATION OF TELEVISION BROADCASTING

A television fan, asked about his viewing habits, more likely than not will reply: "Oh, I like to watch channel 4," or, "I turn on WXXX," supplying either the channel number or the station's call letters. The station is identified in the viewer's mind as the source of the programs in his area; yet most viewers have little if any knowledge of how the station is organized or how the institution of television functions.

The Station and Its Organization

Broadcasting magazine reported that in 1963 there were 575 commercial television stations on the air in the United States.[68] The average number of employees per commercial station was 58, while a small number of stations had fewer than 15 full time staff members and 13% of the stations employed more than 100.[69] Since the number of performers whom one sees on the air is rather small, it is obvious that there are many more who work behind the cameras than in front of them.

While every station management organizes its own staff to suit the particular circumstances, there are basic divisions of labor in television which apply no matter how large or how small the staff may be. In commercial television stations, four categories or activities are always present: programming, selling, engineering, and administration. In noncommercial only the sales function is absent. No one function is superior to the others; no station can operate if one of the categories of activities is absent. In the larger stations there is a more formal division of labor; each position is increasingly restricted in scope as the staff size increases. The station organizational diagrams on pages 28-31 illustrate approaches which these particular broadcasting organizations have taken in staff arrangement, lines of authority and responsibility, and the grouping of functions.[70] It is evident that WBTV, a commercial television station in Charlotte, North Carolina, operating in the same studios as its sister radio stations WBT and WBT-FM, has a much larger staff than WETA-TV, the educational noncommercial sta-

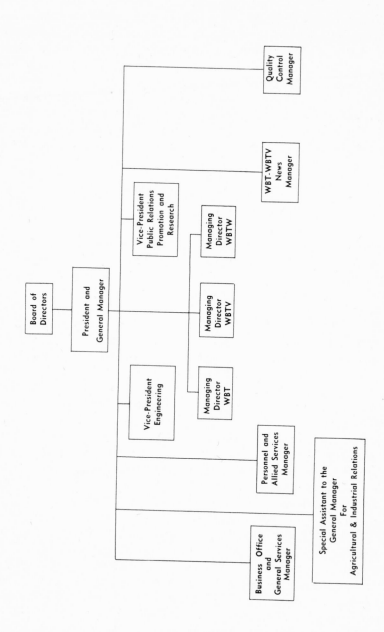

JEFFERSON STANDARD BROADCASTING COMPANY
CHARLOTTE, NORTH CAROLINA

Board of Directors

President and General Manager

Vice-President Engineering

Vice-President Public Relations Promotion and Research

Managing Director WBT

Managing Director WBTV

Managing Director WBTW

WBT-WBTV News Manager

Quality Control Manager

Business Office and General Services Manager

Personnel and Allied Services Manager

Special Assistant to the General Manager For Agricultural & Industrial Relations

BASIC MANAGEMENT CHART

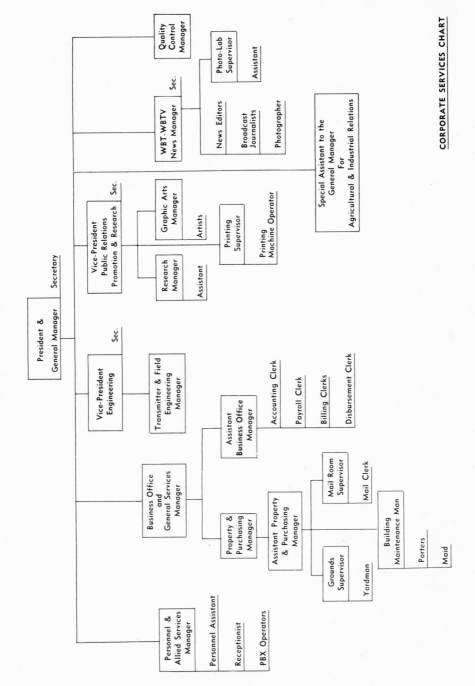

JEFFERSON STANDARD BROADCASTING COMPANY
CHARLOTTE, NORTH CAROLINA

CORPORATE SERVICES CHART

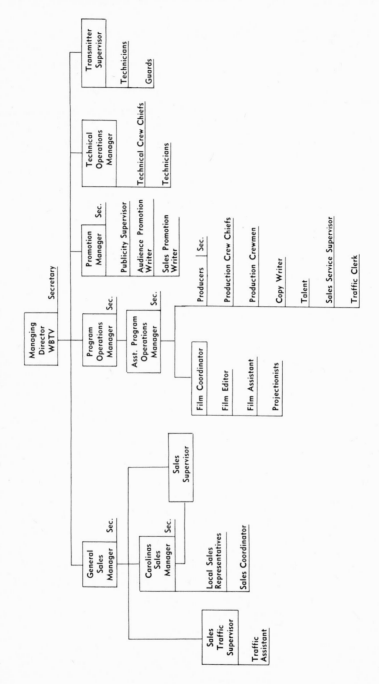

JEFFERSON STANDARD BROADCASTING COMPANY
CHARLOTTE NORTH CAROLINA

WBTV OPERATIONAL CHART

GREATER WASHINGTON EDUCATIONAL TELEVISION ASSOCIATION, INC.

WETA–TV

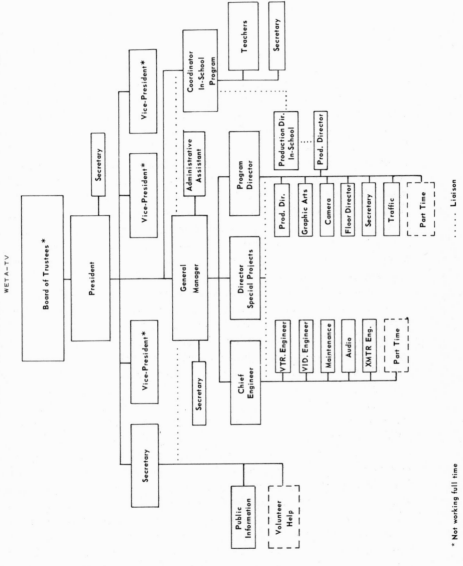

* Not working full time

tion in Washington, D.C. The difference in size is not merely because WETA-TV has no sales staff, nor is it merely because the Charlotte radio and television stations are operated from the same location. WBTV's greater financial resources and its longer operating schedule are more important factors in accounting for its larger size.

Television Networks

Few television stations would choose to operate day after day without the advantages of a network affiliation. From a network, a station receives programs which are commercial — paid for by one or more advertisers — and noncommercial ("sustaining"). Each program supplied by the network reduces the amount of time which must be programmed by the station. The reduction in locally-programmed time permits either a reduction in the size of the staff or a more effective utilization of the staff in other activities. In addition, the network presentations usually add prestige to the station because the artists have national stature and the programs usually meet higher standards of quality in production. Networks are also the best, and sometimes the only, source of coverage of national activities such as political conventions and elections, presidential inaugurations and major sporting events. Networks also pay to their affiliated stations a portion of the money which advertisers pay the networks for originating commercial programs.[71]

The three major national commercial television networks are ABC-TV, owned by American Broadcasting-Paramount Theaters, Incorporated; CBS-TV, owned by the Columbia Broadcasting System, Incorporated; and NBC-TV, owned by the National Broadcasting Company which in turn is owned by the Radio Corporation of America. Unlike radio broadcasting, there are no large separate regional television networks. Both ABC-TV and CBS-TV operate West Coast regional networks, and there are a few small state groups.[72]

Each national television network has several thousands of employees whose activities are grouped broadly into administration, programming, selling and engineering. Since the network organizations fundamentally are program service agencies rather than actual broadcasters, the proportion of programming personnel to engineering personnel is greater than in the television station. Because their staffs are large, networks also require large numbers of executive and supervisory personnel. For example, the programming division of one network includes a senior vice president for programs, a vice president for network programs, a vice president for network programs in New York, a vice president for daytime programs, a director of network programs, an administrative manager of network programs, and a director of program development. The other television networks have similar program organizations.[73]

Since networks seem to represent a pinnacle of "status" in broadcasting, it is not surprising that competition for places on the staffs is keen.

Most commonly, the inexperienced aspirant is employed only as a studio guide or page, working up slowly from there. Even though he may possess experience and talent, an individual seeking network employment opportunities needs a degree of good fortune to establish himself in this rarefied broadcasting atmosphere.

Television and Labor Unions

While no television station or network executive would assign a "box" in his organizational chart to a labor union, the business of broadcasting is influenced by the existence of a number of national labor unions representing a variety of skills and professional areas, and the ways in which stations and networks function are in part influenced by the presence or absence of unionized employees.

Following demands by Chicago musicians for special payments from radio station owners in 1924, labor unions have been organized for many different sorts of broadcasting employees. In the years following the passage of the National Labor Relations Act of 1935 (the Wagner Act), unionization in broadcasting increased rapidly with the principal impact upon musicians, technicians, announcers and actors. What many have called excessive and unreasonable demands by James Caesar Petrillo, then president of the American Federation of Musicians (AFM), were at least partly responsible for the passage of the Taft-Hartley Act in 1947. Broadcasting, however, has been characterized by generally calm and restrained collective bargaining, and broadcast labor-management relations have only occasionally been marred by strikes, lockouts or other labor turmoil. Today organized labor is recognized as a part of the machinery through which broadcasting takes place. Organization of employees is particularly noticeable in the larger metropolitan areas and at the network levels; smaller stations and those in the South are less likely to have collective bargaining agreements with unions.[74]

In television, as in radio, the principal unions are: the American Federation of Television and Radio Artists (AFTRA), which represents many of those who perform before the camera and at the microphone; the American Federation of Musicians (AFM), to which belong most of those who play musical instruments behind the camera as well as in front of it; and two competing unions concentrating principally upon the technicians — the International Brotherhood of Electrical Workers (IBEW) and the National Association of Broadcast Employees and Technicians (NABET). All except NABET, which is independent, are affiliated with the American Federation of Labor-Congress of Industrial Organizations (AFL-CIO).

Television personnel belong, as well, to organizations originally set up in the motion picture and Broadway theatre worlds. Among these are Actors Equity Association (Equity) and Screen Actors Guild (SAG), which compete with AFTRA, and a large number of separate unions joined together in a major group, the International Alliance of Theatrical Stage Employees and Moving Picture Operators (IATSE). Among those unions affiliated with IATSE are make-up artists and hair stylists, stage hands, script writers, set designers and model makers, story analysts, publicists, and scenic and title artists. Independent organizations include the Directors Guild of America, the Television Producers Guild, the Writers Guild of America (divided into East and West groups) and the Composers and Lyricists Guild of America. Altogether, television employees across the nation, at both station and network levels, are represented in collective bargaining with employers by more than 50 labor organizations.[75]

The Station's Sources of Programs

Non-network stations obtain their programs from two sources: non-network program suppliers ("syndicators") and the local studios.[76] A network affiliate has, of course, a third major source — the network program.

Local programs at individual stations may be as varied as the physical equipment and desire dictate. The programming may be "live" (broadcast simultaneously with the creation of the program either in the studio or from a remote point), videotaped or filmed, depending upon the station's equipment, the availability of personnel, the demands of the production schedule and the management's policies and attitudes.

Syndicated programs are normally supplied on film, although more and more program producers are making use of videotape as a recording device. Syndicators supply two types of programs: films made originally for motion picture theatre exhibition and programs made especially for television. The feature films, scheduled in such programs as "Movie Matinee" or "The Late Show," usually are older motion pictures which no longer can be exhibited profitably in movie houses. These films are customarily leased by the television studios for one, two, or more broadcasts within a definite period of time and are used primarily as programs in which commercial announcements for a variety of advertisers may be inserted. On the other hand, syndicated programs produced especially for television generally are series of programs of 13, 26, 39 or more episodes one-half or a full hour in length. These are frequently sponsored on the station by a single advertiser. The syndicated program filmed especially for television more often than not is some form of drama: westerns, suspense, adventure and the like. Industrial films supplied free of charge to both commercial and noncommercial stations are a variation of the syndicated program. Usually these are broadcast as sustaining programs; the station has the benefit of a program at no cash cost and the supplier gains some public relations value from the broadcast.

Network programs closely resemble syndicated programs because each program is broadcast over a number of stations at approximately the same time. However, network programs are distributed from a central point (e.g., New York or Hollywood) to affiliated stations by coaxial cable or microwave relay circuits linking the stations. In addition, networks can produce and distribute programs with greater timeliness than those supplied by syndicators who use film as their method of distribution. Networks have demonstrated their superiority in this field with many documentary programs on social, political, and economic problems; such programs convey a sense of immediacy and urgency.

Television Stations: Their Sources of Revenue

Television stations are costly to operate, as illustrated by Table 3, "Revenue and Expense for the Typical Television Station, Nationwide, 1962." To obtain revenue to pay the more than $800,000 in annual expenses for this "typical" station and to return a profit to those who invested their capital in a financially risky enterprise, the station must persuade many advertisers to spend many thousands of dollars.

Almost all of a television station's revenue comes from the sale of time to various kinds of advertisers. A substantial portion, perhaps one-third in a typical station, comes from advertisers who sponsor network programs. The largest amount of revenue (38.5%) comes from national or regional advertisers whose commercial programs or announcements originate at the station. This form of advertising is labelled "national spot" or "national nonnetwork" advertising because the advertiser "spots" his message in the market or community of his selection, on the station of his selection, and in the form (announcement or program) he wishes. The third source of revenue (28.7%) comes from local advertisers whom the station's salesmen call on directly.

Advertising Agencies and Station Representatives

Most advertisers whose businesses are larger than a single retail establishment do not look after the details of their own advertising but entrust much of the development of ideas and the execution of advertising plans to advertising agencies. Modern advertising agencies employ specialists in the preparation of persuasive visual, verbal and aural messages in all of the media of mass communication. In addition, many advertising agencies have elaborate market and media research departments which seek constantly to insure the most effective use of their clients' advertising money.

Of the two roles played by agencies — the development of the advertising campaign and the execution of the campaign once the client has approved it — the campaign development role is more important to the television broadcaster. It is during this stage that decisions are made to advertise in Market A instead of Market B, to use television instead of or in addition to other media, to choose Station X over Station Y, and to allocate the advertising budgets. All such decisions affect his revenue.

Although many advertisers pay their advertising agencies directly for such activities as special large-scale research, the preparation of brochures

TABLE 3

Revenue and Expense for the Typical Television Station,
Nationwide, 1962

The typical **PROFIT MARGIN** was 16.9%

Revenue and Expense Items	Typical Dollar Figures	Typical Percent Figures
Total Broadcast Revenue[1]	$1,016,700	
Total Time Sales	1,064,500	100.0%
From:		
Networks	349,200	32.8
National & Regional advertisers	409,800	38.5
Local advertisers	305,500	28.7
Total Broadcast Expense	$844,900	100.0%
From:		
Technical	133,500	15.8
Program	295,700	35.0
Selling[2]	109,800	13.0
General and administrative	305,900	36.2
Selected Expense Items		
Total Salaries[3]	$361,200	100.0%
From:		
Technical salaries	84,500	23.4
Program salaries	150,200	41.6
Selling salaries	60,000	16.6
General and administrative	66,500	18.4
Depreciation and Amortization	78,600	
Film Expense	58,900	
Profit (before Federal income tax)	$171,800	

[1] Time Sales plus incidental broadcast revenue minus agency and rep. commissions and payments to networks for sale of time.

[2] Includes all promotion; excludes agency and rep. commissions.

[3] Includes salaries, wages, and bonuses of officers and employees.

Source: *Dimensions of Television* (Washington: National Association of Broadcasters, 1963), p. 6. Data compiled by NAB from NAB Financial Report, 1963. Reprinted by permission.

and catalogues, and the agencies' out-of-pocket costs for completed art-work or photo-engraving, the advertising agencies derive most of their revenue in the form of commissions paid to the agency by the medium which broadcasts or publishes the advertising. For example, if Advertising Agency A on behalf of its Client C contracts with Television Station X for a one-minute spot announcement in a choice time at night between two outstanding programs at a cost of $250 for a single broadcast, the agency would receive from Station X a commission usually amounting to 15% of the cost of the time, or $37.50. Since all newspapers, radio and television stations, and other media of advertising customarily pay these commissions, the agency has no cause to favor one over the other. The recognized ethics of advertising generally prevents the client's going directly to the advertising medium to save the cost of the commission; even without the involvement of the advertising agency, Station X would still charge Client C $250 for the single spot announcement.[77]

In return for its commission, the agency prepares the advertising message, frequently on film or tape, and sends it to the station with all necessary schedule and handling instructions; the station is thus relieved of the burden of production. In addition, the agency insures that payment for the announcement is made promptly to the station.[78]

Since most large advertising agencies and their clients are located in cities at some distance from most of the television stations which seek their business, it is not practical to have station salesmen call directly on advertising agencies. To sell time to these distant agencies, broadcasting has evolved organizations called station representatives. The station's "rep," as it is frequently called, is a firm of broadcast sales, accounting, and research personnel with offices situated in the metropolitan centers where large numbers of advertising agencies are located. A firm of station representatives usually contracts with a number of broadcasting stations widely enough separated so that the stations are not in direct competition with each other. When the salesman from the station "rep" calls on an advertising agency time buyer, he extols the merits of each of the stations he represents. One call thus serves to state the case for a number of stations.

Although there are variations in methods of payments for the services of station representatives, a widespread practice is the payment of commissions by the station to the firm of representatives on all sales of station time made in the representative's city. Frequently this commission is fixed at 15% of the amount paid by the advertiser after the advertising agency commission has been deducted. To continue the earlier example, the station representative would receive 15% of $212.50 ($250 minus $37.50 agency commission) or $31.88. Thus, on most national non-network business the television station receives 72.25% of the amount the advertiser actually pays for time on the station.

Federal Regulation of Broadcasting

Because broadcasting signals cross state lines, almost from the beginning it has been understood that most regulation of broadcasting is the responsibility of the federal government. The Communications Act of 1934, with its many subsequent amendments, is the fundamental law governing broadcasting.[79] The Act established the principle that broadcasting was not a right but a privilege to be enjoyed by those who were selected. The privilege took the form of a federal license of limited duration to be issued only if there was a positive finding that the broadcaster who received the license would operate in the public interest, convenience and necessity.[80]

To administer the Act, to turn its principles into practical regulations and to judge whether broadcasters were indeed operating in the public interest, the Act created the Federal Communications Commission, an independent administrative, quasi-judicial and quasi-legislative agency composed of seven members, each appointed by the President of the United States to serve seven years.[81] To assist the commissioners in the highly technical and complicated regulatory process, hundreds of attorneys, accountants and engineers are employed to carry out the studies, investigations and preliminary work that goes on in great volume day after day.

The license to broadcast is the controlling lever. Every broadcaster is conscious of the FCC's power to grant, to withhold, or to take away a license. The authority of the FCC is clear, comprehensive and well established in the technical and engineering areas of broadcasting. There is little dispute that the FCC has the power to determine the suitability of the applicant's character and financial qualifications. It is in the programming realm, however, that station owners and the Commission disagree on the degree of federal authority. The core of the dispute lies in the provision of the Act which forbids the FCC to censor any program; there is great difference of opinion on what constitutes censorship.[82] The federal courts have held that the FCC is not merely an agency to police the technical aspects of broadcasting but that it must also concern itself with the content of broadcasting.[83]

His entire program schedule is a cause for the broadcaster's concern. He fears FCC disapproval of the amounts of time he devotes to news, education, discussion or religion as compared to the time spent in broadcasting entertainment features. He worries particularly about FCC displeasure with the amount of time he devotes to advertising messages. Political broadcasting is a major concern as well. If he broadcasts speeches by one political candidate, he must make equal time and facilities available to the candidate's opponents. If he editorializes for or against an issue, he must be prepared not only to broadcast opposing viewpoints but on some occasions even to seek out those who oppose in order to maintain balance and fairness in his schedule.

While there is no single document which spells out precisely what constitutes the public interest, convenience and necessity in broadcasting, the broadcaster can turn to the law, the FCC rules and regulations, the various public policy announcements made by the Commission, and the decisions by federal courts as guides to good broadcasting. In addition, he can rely on the codes of practice developed by the National Association of Broadcasters, the principal spokesman for commercial radio and television broadcasting in the United States. A conscientious broadcaster who truly desires to operate in the public interest has little difficulty in determining his proper course of action, and rarely is he in difficulty with the Commission.

TELEVISION'S IMPACT ON SOCIETY

Americans watch television — there is little doubt about *that* — but pertinent data acceptable to most serious students to describe how much, what kind, and with what effects are difficult to obtain.[84] Nevertheless, research by responsible investigators is making clearer some of the unknowns.[85]

The Dimensions of Television

It is generally agreed that the television set in the average American home is turned on between five and six hours per day.[86] But that does not really provide a description of the television audience. A. C. Nielsen Company, a major mass media and market research firm, has studied national viewing habits for a number of years and recognizes wide variations in viewing by substantial segments of the population. At one end of the scale, approximately 5% of homes equipped with a television set used it less than two hours each day; at the other end of the ranking, in 20% of television homes the set was on for 10½ hours daily. In a grouping that divided all television homes into five approximately equal parts according to their viewing habits, the highest two-fifths had sets turned on for seven or more hours daily while the lowest three-fifths had sets on for six hours or less.[87]

There appears to be little except size that is significant in audience description. The television viewer on the average is quite like a cross section of the total population in economic, social and educational status. Almost every one in a television home watches, and many watch a great deal.[88]

The hours of viewing would not be significant if the number of television homes was small, but this is not the case. Earlier in this chapter it was pointed out that more than nine of every ten homes in the nation have one or more television sets.[89] The audience, then, consists of inhabitants of more than 40 million homes.

The Controversy — Television's Alleged Effects

So much exposure to the television picture must result in affecting the viewer and his society in several ways — at least so both critics and defenders of television agree. The agreement stops at that point, however.

The critics on the one hand suggest that television is responsible for many of the ills of society — the rise in juvenile delinquency, a decay of ethical and moral standards, a weakening of critical abilities to distinguish the good in artistic and aesthetic standards from the mediocre, the encouragement of conformity, the subjection of the public to economic exploitation and others. The appealing to the baser elements of human behavior through a superabundance of violence, the manipulation of men as if they were puppets — all these and more are presumed ill effects that come from absorbing the daily fare of the television schedule.[90]

On the other hand, defenders of television hasten to claim that the medium is responsible for an "acceleration in cultural activities," resulting in more and more visitors to museums and increased patronage of libraries. According to these defenders, it elects presidents and is one of the "most powerful forces of social control in the modern world."[91]

A different group, mostly social scientists, raises fundamental questions about the ability of television — or any other mass medium, for that matter — to have serious or even substantial effect upon our attitudes, tastes, and behavior as individuals and groups. This group argues that television and other mass media tend generally to reinforce existing patterns rather than to change them and are only one factor among many affecting the creation of tastes, values and behavior patterns.[92]

There is still another dimension to the argument. In a study of audience attitudes, psychologist Gary A. Steiner discovered that the viewer himself looks upon television among all the mass media as his principal source of entertainment, "a relaxing and pleasant — now an integral — part of his daily life" and worth whatever the costs are in terms of time spent and other activities displaced. The viewer does have some concern about what he feels is excessive commercialization. By and large, however, he is content with the system and the program content.[93]

Some Areas of Social Impact

When all the studies are assessed and all of the areas of the unknown in television's social impact are listed, it is proper to echo the regret of one television professional who wrote that "the large basic problems of how our medium and other media work remain a challenge."[94] Yet that does not really provide the complete framework for thinking about television's impact. If substantial numbers of both average and influential people believe that television has certain attributes or creates certain effects, the belief has its own validity and the public acts upon its beliefs — mistaken though it may be. On the basis of reputable study and on the basis of those beliefs, television does touch society in a number of ways, only a few of which can be suggested.

Television affects other media of mass communication perhaps more than it affects the viewing public. Since the early 1950's the movie industry, rightly or wrongly, has been blaming television for a declining clientele and a decrease in the number of Hollywood-made feature-length pictures. Operating on these assumptions of cause and effect, Hollywood producers have turned increasingly to making films for television at attractive prices, and they have brought in wide screen and other gadgetry to entice viewers back into the movie houses. Theatre owners have gone out of business, started drive-in theatres, flirted with theatre television, or ignored television to struggle along at the same old stand, sometimes relying on the popcorn and soft drink concession to provide the difference between profit and loss, and continuing to be surprised when sizeable and profitable audiences turn out to see pictures worth seeing.

Radio broadcasters seemed to believe in the middle 1950's that there were no more radio listeners and every broadcasters' meeting was filled with gloom at television's inroads. Advertisers, too, were convinced that radio had fallen into bad days. Network radio declined in income; formerly popular comedians, variety programs, dramas, and other program types slipped over to television or went off the air. In desperation, radio sought new formats — each broadcaster hoped that he would find the magic formula — and radio moved into specialized programming, the rock-and-roll, the top 40, the country-and-western, the Negro programming, the good music, and even the all-talk station. The main conclusion seems to be that radio lost its dominance of nighttime audiences but gained new dimensions as the "personal" medium, the source of pastime for specialized audiences.

Newspapers appeared little affected by the advent of television, having earlier made whatever adjustments were necessary to live with radio. But television seems to have hurt the mass magazines which functioned mainly as sources of diversion and entertainment. Both television and the mass magazines were competing for the time and attention of the same general audience.

Television thus seems to have annexed to itself the dominance of the area of mass entertainment and when it has come into competition with another entertainment or diversionary activity has pushed the older competitor into seeking new roles to play or new techniques. The other media have reacted to television rather than to possible changes in the audiences themselves.

In the political world, too, television is rightly or wrongly credited or charged with responsibility for certain major changes. There is little doubt that television has catapulted new personalities into national figures and exposed the clay feet of idols.[95] National and state candidates reach more voters directly and almost personally in a few minutes than they could shake hands with in a lifetime. Whether television appearances change voting behavior is a matter of debate requiring further study. Political conventions have been streamlined to accommodate themselves to the technical requirements of television and to the presumed demands of the viewers: the Democratic party employed an outstanding television executive in 1960 and 1964 to "stage manage" most convention arrangements in order to facilitate coverage by radio and television. Television has taken the audience behind the scenes in various governmental processes: city council meetings, state legislative proceedings, occasional court trials and town meetings. If the public is uninformed, certainly television should not shoulder all of the blame.

Television has not fulfilled the predictions of the prophets of doom that it would ruin the lives of children. There is no reputable evidence that children's imaginations have been stifled, that reading or reading habits have suffered or that other zestful activities have been neglected. On the other hand, children are learning in a different way; through television, children are acquiring information *visually*.

In the commercial world of advertising, marketing and consumption, television has repeatedly demonstrated its ability to introduce new brands of familiar categories of goods, to increase distribution of established brands and to make new products which serve old needs familiar household objects.

When all is said, however, the principal social aspect of commercial television is the supreme place it presently occupies as the main and most sought-for source of entertainment for more people for more hours per week than any other medium of activity.

NOTES

[1] Although educational broadcasting, both radio and television, is generally noncommercial in nature, obtaining its operating funds from a variety of sources, the preponderance of stations and hours of programming are commercial. Educational broadcasting is described briefly on pages 25-27.

[2] Proponents of subscription television (pay-TV) are attacking this principle of "free" broadcasting. See pages 21-24.

[3] John Swift, *Adventures in Vision: The First Twenty-Five Years of Television* (London: John Lehmann, 1950), pp. 21-22.

[4] Maxwell developed his theory between 1860 and 1865, publishing it as a *Treatise on Electricity and Magnetism* in 1873. See J. G. Crowther, *British Scientists of the Nineteenth Century* (London: Kegan, Paul, Trench, Trubner & Co., Ltd., 1935), pp. 301-311.

[5] Swift, *Adventures in Vision*, p. 22. The Communications Act of 1934 defines

broadcasting as meaning "the dissemination of radio communications intended to be received by the public, directly or by the intermediary of relay stations." R. Franklin Smith, in his article, " 'Oldest Station in the Nation'?" in *Journal of Broadcasting*, IV (Winter, 1959-1960), 44, lists five elements required to class any station as a broadcasting station: "(1) utilizes radio waves (2) to send non-coded sounds by speech or music (3) in the form of a continuous patterned program service, (4) intended to be received by the public, and (5) is licensed by the government."

[5a] Swift, *Adventures in Vision*, pp. 20-22.

[6] Orrin E. Dunlap, Jr., *The Future of Television* (New York and London: Harper & Brothers, 1942) pp. 162-164; Swift, *Adventures in Vision*, pp. v, 19, 24, 35-36, 39-40, 61-62. The work of Farnsworth and Zworykin was described in separate articles in the first number of *Television News*, I (March-April, 1931), 48, 58.

[7] Federal Communications Commission (FCC), *Fifth Annual Report* (1939), pp. 5, 45.

[8] National Television System Committee, *Television Standards and Practice; Selected Papers from the Proceedings of the National Television System Committee and Its Panels* (Donald G. Fink, ed., New York and London: McGraw-Hill Book Company, Inc., 1943), pp. ix, 4; Dunlap, *The Future of Television*, pp. 1, 22.

[9] FCC, *4th Annual Report* (1938), pp. 65, 176.

[10] "Television I: A $13,000,000 'If'," *Fortune*, XIX (April, 1939), 53.

[11] FCC, *5th Annual Report* (1939), p. 45; Dunlap, *The Future of Television*, pp 1, 183-184.

[12] FCC, *6th Annual Report* (1940), pp. 39, 70-72; Swift, *Adventures in Vision*, pp. 108-109.

[13] FCC, *6th Annual Report* (1940), pp. 70-72.

[14] National Television System Committee, *Television Standards and Practice*, p. 17. A TV "frame" is a complete cycle of scanning and is the equivalent of a single photograph or "frame" in a motion picture film. The interlacing involves scanning lines 1, 3, 5, 7, etc., in 1/60 of a second and then scanning lines 2, 4, 6, etc., in 1/60. The result is that in 1/30 of a second the entire frame has been "half-scanned" twice, providing for the observing eye the illusion of continuity of motion (frame frequency) and continuity of illumination (field frequency). Thus American television standards are 30 complete frames of 525 lines each per second, half-scanned twice to provide a field frequency of 60 per second. Flicker and jerkiness are thus eliminated. Other nations' standards are different; e.g., England uses 405 lines per frame while France has established 819 lines per frame. An American receiver will not pick up a British or French TV program — an illustration of the need for uniform standards. In general, the more lines per frame, the better the picture definition and the finer the shades of contrast. However, a greater number of lines per frame occupies more spectrum space resulting in a reduced number of stations which can be author-ized. The 525-line frame is thus a compromise between a high quality picture and the maximum number of stations. A channel six megacycles wide is required to accommodate the amount of signal or information transmitted in a 525-line frame. Because of this channel width, the FCC initially could find spectrum space for only 13 channels.

[15] FCC, *7th Annual Report* (1941), pp. 32-33.

[16] Dunlap, *The Future of Television*, pp. 33-34. In contrast, NBC-TV's key New York station, WNBC-TV, charged $10,200 as its highest one-hour rate in January, 1962. See *Spot Television Rates and Data* (January 16, 1962), p. 349.

[17] FCC, *13th Annual Report* (1947), p. 23. At the outbreak of World War II, there were an estimated 10,000 receivers in the hands of the public, half of them in the New York area.

[18] "Memorandum Opinion of February 23, 1942," in *Federal Communications Commission Reports*, IX (August 1, 1941-April 1, 1943), pp. 353-355; FCC, *13th Annual Report* (1947), p. 23.

[19] FCC, *11th Annual Report* (1945), p. 21; *Television*, II (May, 1945), pp. 28-29.

[20] *Television*, II (January, 1945), p. 24; FCC, *11th Annual Report* (1945), p. 21.

[21] FCC, *11th Annual Report* (1945), p. viii; *Television*, II (September, 1945), p. 10; III (April, 1946), p. 37.

[22] FCC, *13th Annual Report* (1947), pp. 23, 26; *14th Annual Report* (1948), pp. 2, 30, 37-38, 39; *15th Annual Report* (1949), p. 6; *17th Annual Report* (1951), p. 13; *Television*, II (October, 1945), p. 32.

[23] The FCC deleted channel 1 on June 14, 1948, because other radio services adjacent to channel 1 (44-50 mc.) caused objectionable interference to television. See FCC, *14th Annual Report* (1948), pp. 39-40.

[24] FCC, *14th Annual Report* (1948), pp. 6, 39-40; *15th Annual Report* (1949), pp. 42-43.

[25] FCC, *15th Annual Report* (1949), pp. 42-43. Channels 2-13 were located between 54 mc. and 216 mc. The Commission proposed the expansion of television in the frequency range 470-890 mc.

26 FCC, *18th Annual Report* (1952), pp. 107-111. The report gives a chronological account of the development of the television issue. The 2,053 assignments in 1,291 communities contrasted with only 400 assignments in 140 metropolitan areas under the old system.

27 FCC, *19th Annual Report* (1953), p. 93.

28 FCC, *15th Annual Report* (1949), p. 41; *17th Annual Report* (1951), p. 113; *19th Annual Report* (1953), p. 113.

29 A study by A. C. Nielsen Company reported in *Broadcasting,* December 17, 1962, p. 85. A. C. Nielsen Company publishes annually results of its studies of listening and viewing. An excellent series of studies on the growth and impact of television on a single community is that of the advertising agency, Cunningham & Walsh, Inc., in its *Videotown* (New York: Cunningham & Walsh, Inc., 1948-1958).

30 The FCC, in *20th Annual Report* (1954), p. 109, reported an estimate of four million so-called "all-channel" sets out of 30 million sets in use. In the *25th Annual Report* (1959), p. 50, the Commission noted that an independent survey indicated only 10% of all television sets produced could receive UHF stations.

31 FCC, *20th Annual Report* (1954), p. 91.

32 Examples of construction permits never activated include: KBIC-TV, Los Angeles, channel 22; WIRL-TV, Peoria, Ill., channel 25; WTLF, Baltimore, channel 18. Examples of stations which were on the air but have since suspended operations include: KVUE, Sacramento, channel 40; KSAN-TV, San Francisco, channel 32; WBLN, Bloomington, Ill., channel 15; WNAO-TV, Raleigh, N.C., channel 28. See *Broadcasting, 1961-62 Yearbook,* pp. A3-A95, for these and others.

33 FCC, *20th Annual Report* (1954), p. 91.

34 FCC, *23rd Annual Report* (1957), p. 106; *24th Annual Report* (1958), p. 102; *28th Annual Report* (1962), pp. 61-62. Examples of all-UHF markets after "deintermixture" were Peoria, Ill., Elmira, N.Y., and Walla Walla, Wash. Translators are low-power transmitters which retransmit the signal from the parent station but on one of the channels between 70 and 83. Booster stations retransmit the parent station signal on the same frequency so as to provide program service to an area blocked by terrain from line-of-sight reception of the parent station.

35 FCC, *16th Annual Report* (1950), pp. 6, 10-11, 103, 105.

36 FCC, *16th Annual Report* (1950), p. 11.

37 *Radio Corporation of America, et al.* v. *United States,* 341 U.S. 412, 71 Sup. Ct. 806 (1951); FCC, *17th Annual Report* (1951), p. 113; *Broadcasting-Telecasting,* June 4, 1951, pp. 23, 62, 70, 76-78.

38 FCC, *17th Annual Report* (1951), p. 13.

39 FCC, *19th Annual Report* (1953) pp. 96-97; *20th Annual Report* (1954), pp. 90-91.

40 *Television Digest,* August 25, 1956, p. 14; FCC, *23rd Annual Report* (1957), p. 105. In comparison with the number of color receivers, an estimated 44,500,000 monochrome sets were in use.

41 *Broadcasting,* August 26, 1963, p. 65. Only RCA manufactured color sets to any significant extent for several years, and the least expensive model was priced at $495.

42 Some experts expected color set sales to reach a total of between 750,000 and 1,000,000 by the end of 1963. Admiral, Zenith, Motorola, and others were getting into color set production and the price of the least expensive model in several lines had been cut to $449.95. As a result of color set sales, profits were higher for RCA and Zenith in the first half of 1963. See *Broadcasting,* May 13, 1963, pp. 76-77; July 29, 1963, p. 50; August 12, 1963, p. 70; August 26, 1963, p. 65. *Television Age,* January 21, 1963, p. 26, estimated that there were 1,220,000 color sets in use by January 1, 1963.

43 FCC, *15th Annual Report* (1949), pp. 3, 54. The four networks were ABC, CBS, NBC, and DuMont. The last-named ceased operating September 15, 1955. See FCC, *22nd Annual Report* (1956), p. 22n.

44 FCC, *16th Annual Report* (1950), p. 118.

45 Radio broadcasting also increased its revenue each year during the same period except 1954-1955, though the amounts of increases were more modest. Radio profits had not by 1963 reached the 1950 figure, falling to a low of $37,300,000 in 1958.

46 *Broadcasting-Telecasting; 1955-56 Telecasting Yearbook-Marketbook*, pp. 367-368.

47 FCC, *22nd Annual Report* (1956), pp. 4, 113; *24th Annual Report* (1958), p. 121; *27th Annual Report* (1961), p. 46; *28th Annual Report* (1962), p. 57. Financial data for individual stations are not open to public inspection; the FCC summarizes the data for broadcasting as a whole each year.

48 *Broadcasting - Telecasting*, January 1, 1951, p. 60; FCC, *16th Annual Report* (1950), pp. 11, 103-104. Other systems use different methods for denying the program to the non-paying public.

49 *Broadcasting - Telecasting*, March 26, 1961, p. 63; FCC, *19th Annual Report* (1953), p. 98. Skiatron Electronics & Television, New York, gave the FCC and newsmen a demonstration of its system on March 20, 1951.

50 FCC, *21st Annual Report* (1955), pp. 98-99; *23rd Annual Report* (1957), pp. 111-112.

51 FCC, *23rd Annual Report* (1957), pp. 111-112; *25th Annual Report* (1959), pp. 63-64.

52 The FCC had no jurisdiction over "wired" (or coaxial cable) pay-TV because electromagnetic signals (i.e., radio "waves") were not involved.

53 *Broadcasting*, July 29, 1963, p. 84.

54 *Broadcasting*, July 29, 1963, p. 5. For a succinct discussion of the whole question, see Robert W. Horton, *To Pay or Not to Pay: A Report on Subscription Television* (An Occasional Paper on the Role of the Mass Media in the Free Society Published by the Center for the Study of Democratic Institutions, [Santa Barbara, Calif:] The Fund for the Republic, Inc. 1960).

55 *Broadcasting: 1963 Yearbook*, p. A135; FCC, *22nd Annual Report* (1956), pp. 98-99.

56 *Broadcasting: 1963 Yearbook*, pp. A135-A150. Only Alaska, Delaware, North Dakota and Rhode Island were without CATV service. *Broadcasting's* summary was drawn from a study in *Television*, in an article published in June, 1962.

57 *Broadcasting: 1936 Yearbook*, p. A135; FCC, *25th Annual Report* (1959), pp. 62-63. The matter of the ownership of the program once it has been broadcast is a knotty legal question to which there are not yet any sure answers.

58 *Broadcasting: 1963 Yearbook*, p. A135.

59 FCC, *19th Annual Report* (1953), p. 98; *20th Annual Report* (1954), pp. 92-93; *22nd Annual Report* (1956), pp. 98-99; *24th Annual Report* (1958), p. 108; *25th Annual Report* (1959), pp. 62-63; *Broadcasting: 1963 Yearbook*, p. A135; *Broadcasting*, May 27, 1963, pp. 64-65; June 17, 1963, pp. 124-125.

60 Educational noncommercial television is a major area of broadcasting and cannot be dealt with in any detail within the necessary space restrictions here. The literature of educational broadcasting is extensive and growing. A very few of the more important books are listed in the bibliography.

61 Claims of WHA, the University of Wisconsin station, to the title of the nation's oldest station are discussed briefly in Smith, " 'Oldest Station in the Nation'?" *Journal of Broadcasting*, IV (Winter, 1959-60), pp. 54-55. An analysis of station ownership made in early 1923 by the American Telephone and Telegraph Company revealed that of 583 stations in existence on January 1, 1923, 72 were operated by educational institutions. See *Radio Broadcast*, II (April, 1923), pp. 522, 524, 526.

62 Harry J. Skornia, "Educational Radio: Its Past and Its Future," in *Educational Television: The Next Ten Years* (Stanford: The Institute for Communication Research, 1962), pp. 354-360.

63 Richard B. Hull, "A Note on the History Behind ETV," in *Educational Television: The Next Ten Years*, pp. 334-345.

64 *Ibid.*; Leo A. Martin, "The Educational Television Stations," in *Television's Impact on American Culture* (William Y.

Elliott, ed., East Lansing: Michigan State University Press, 1956), pp. 197-198.

65 Raymond B. Witcoff, "Educational Television in America: A Review with Some Conclusions," in *Television's Impact on American Culture*, pp. 269-271; FCC, *19th Annual Report* (1953), p. 94; *Education U.S.A.; a Special Report on Educational Affairs*, September 30, 1963, p. 13.

66 Robert L. Hilliard, "The Organization and Control of Educational Television," *Peabody Journal of Education*, XL (November, 1962), pp. 170-181.

67 FCC, *28th Annual Report* (1962), pp. 63-64; L. Keith Tyler, "The Educational Television and Radio Center," in *Television's Impact on American Culture*, pp. 225-266; Hull, "A Note on the History Behind ETV," in *Educational Television: The Next Ten Years*, p. 335; *Educational Television Facilities Act* (Public Law 87-447).

68 *Broadcasting*, August 19, 1963, p. 96.

69 *Dimensions of Television* ([Washington: The National Association of Broadcasters, 1963]), p. 12; *Broadcasting: 1963 Yearbook*, p. 10.

70 These stations were not selected as "typical" of commercial or non-commercial operations; each merely illustrates one way in which commercial and noncommercial broadcasting stations are organized.

71 "Bonus" stations, though contractually affiliated with a network, do not receive revenue from network commercial programs but do gain the other advantages of network affiliation. There are comparatively few "bonus" stations.

72 *Broadcasting: 1963 Yearbook*, p. E21.

73 *Broadcasting: 1963 Yearbook*, pp. E12. E18, E20.

74 There is no good survey of the development and the present state of relations between labor unions and broadcasting. An excellent study of a portion of the story is that by Grover Cleveland Wilhoit, Jr., Labor Union Organization in Radio Broadcasting: The Wagner Act to the Taft-Hartley Law (unpublished M.A. in Communication thesis, University of North Carolina at Chapel Hill, 1963). Nothing significant has been done for the period since 1947.

75 See *Broadcasting Yearbook, 1963*, pp. E30-E31, for a list of union organizations which are active in broadcasting.

76 The syndicator usually has a number of copies of each program, leasing these to broadcasters for use within a specified time. The term was adapted by broadcasting from journalism's term to denote a firm which produced a column of comment or a feature which was sold for publication simultaneously in a number of newspapers.

77 Rates for advertisers vary greatly from station to station, each station having complete authority to set its own. Ethically, a station should not deviate from its published rates to favor one advertiser over another. "Rate cutting" is unfortunately a common practice among some radio and television broadcasters. The business and advertising parts of broadcasting suffer from a number of unethical and even fraudulent practices on the part of a minority of station owners and operators.

78 In all descriptions of agency-station relationships, the theoretical ideal has been set forth. In actual practice, there are many variations from the ideal. The degree of quality and reliability varies among agencies just as it does among broadcasters.

79 *Public Law No. 416*, U.S., *Statutes at Large*, XLVIII, Part 1, 1064-1105. The Act also covers interstate telephone and telegraph communications as well as all other non-broadcasting emissions.

80 The license period cannot be longer than three years in the case of broadcasting or more than five years in all other forms of radio transmission.

81 The United States Senate must confirm the appointment. No more than four commissioners may belong to the same political party. The chairman of the FCC, one of the seven commissioners, is always a member of the same political party as the President of the United States.

82 Section 326, Communications Act of 1934.

83 See *National Broadcasting Company, Inc.* v. *United States*, 319 U.S. 190 (1943).

84 Joseph T. Klapper, *The Effects of Mass Communications* (Glencoe, Ill.: The Free Press, 1960), p. 54, points out that this is true for the whole area of mass communication. He writes: "Many of the data commonly presented are, in fact, of questionable pertinency."

85 Paul F. Lazarsfeld, "Trends in Broadcasting Research," *Studies in Broadcasting; an International Annual of Broadcasting*, No. 1 (March, 1963), pp. 49-64; Wilbur Schramm, "Mass Communication," in *Annual Review of Psychology*, XIII (Palo Alto, California: Annual Reviews, Inc., 1962), pp. 251-284.

86 Leon Arons and Mark A. May, eds., *Television and Human Behavior: Tomorrow's Research in Mass Communication* (New York: Appleton-Century-Crofts, 1963), p. 1.

87 *Nielsen Newscast*, XII (August, 1963), pp. 4-5.

88 Gary A. Steiner, *The People Look at Television: A Study of Audience Attitudes* (New York: Alfred A. Knopf, 1963), p. 234.

89 See page 18.

90 As one of many examples, see "A Last Look at Television," *Esquire* (October, 1960), 114-117, in which one of three critics, Richard Rovere, writes of television's fare as being a collection of "moral and aesthetic absurdities." Daniel Bell, in "Modernity and Mass Society; on the Varieties of Cultural Experience," *Studies in Public Communication*, No. 4 (Autumn, 1962), 3-34, cites (though he does not agree with) a list of charges against television: ". . . there is the argument that most of the run-of-the mill material . . . [on] television . . . is cheap, vulgar, titillating, inciting to violence, amoral, and debasing."

91 Frank Stanton, *Mass Media and Mass Culture; Great Issues Lecture, at The Hopkins Center, Dartmouth College, November 26, 1962* [n.p., n.d.] pp. 7ff; C. Merton Babcock, ed., *Ideas in Process; an Anthology of Readings in Communication* (New York: Harper & Brothers, 1958), pp. 364-365, in his introduction to a section on mass media.

92 Klapper, *The Effects of Mass Communication*, p. 5. Klapper points out, pp. 249-257, that the question of effects of mass media is very complex and that much research lies ahead.

93 Steiner, *The People Look at Television*, pp. 228-235.

94 Norman E. Cash, president of the Television Bureau of Advertising, in a front note, in Arons and May, eds., *Television and Human Behavior*.

95 The late Senator Estes Kefauver became a major figure in the 1956 political arena as a result of his appearances on television while conducting Senate committee investigations of crime. The decline of "McCarthyism" in the late 1950's has been attributed to television's exposure of the late Senator Joseph R. McCarthy to public scrutiny.

BIBLIOGRAPHY

History and General

There is no good history of television in the United States. The student, teacher and broadcaster need many sources to provide adequate background. Only a few are indicated here.

Archer, Gleason Leonard. *History of Radio to 1926.* New York: The American Historical Society, 1938. One of the few serious attempts to write the history of broadcasting, this book is a pioneer work which cannot be overlooked. In controversies between the Radio Group and the Telephone Group, Archer tends to lean toward the former; nevertheless there is a wealth of detail here which cannot be found conveniently anywhere else. The antecedents of modern broadcasting — all except government regulation — are here.

Banning, William Peck. *Commercial Broadcasting Pioneer; the WEAF Ex-*

periment, 1922-1926. Cambridge. Harvard University Press, 1946. More readable than Archer's *History of Radio to 1926,* Banning's work covers much of the same ground. However, Banning leans to the Telephone Group's position in patent and other controversies. The student thus has the opportunity to compare points of view and to realize that there is room for differences in interpretation. *Commercial Broadcasting Pioneer* is an excellent source of information about the contributions made to early broadcasting and to the development of the present day commercial system by the American Telephone and Telegraph Company.

Blum, Daniel C. *A Pictorial History of Television.* Philadelphia: The Chilton Co., 1959. Useful primarily to gain the "feel" of television programming up to 1959. Only a barest minimum of text.

De Forest, Lee. *The Father of Radio; the Autobiography of Lee de Forest.* Chicago: Wilcox & Follett, 1950. If there is doubt in anyone's mind as to the single most important figure in the development of broadcasting, the late Lee de Forest attempts to remove it in his autobiography. In spite of this egocentricity, the work is a source of considerable detail about the development of radio. Even when he is assessed by others less sympathetically inclined, de Forest is still rated as one of the major pioneers in radio.

Everson, George. *The Story of Television: The Life of Philo T. Farnsworth.* New York: W. W. Norton and Company, Inc., 1949. Farnsworth's story is central to the development of electronic television. Here, one can gain some conception of the struggle for patent and power control in a gamble where the ultimate stakes were large. Unfortunately, there is no considerable account of the work of Vladimir K. Zworykin, Farnsworth's contemporary and rival. The student must therefore accept Everson's account as only a part of a larger frame.

Government Regulation

Although there is a substantial literature on government regulation, much of it is old. Selected here is the one indispensible government publication and two others of contrasting approach.

Head, Sydney W. *Broadcasting in America; a Survey of Television and Radio.* Boston: Houghton Mifflin Company, 1956. Students should not avoid the use of this book because of its publication date. This is still the best description of broadcasting in the United States — its origins and growth, technical and commercial aspects, and evaluation — that has thus far been published. The author's balance and judgment on many controversial phases of broadcasting are models to be emulated.

Roe, Yale, ed. *Television Station Management; The Business of Broadcasting.* New York: Hastings House, Publishers, Inc. 1964. A discussion of the practical day-to-day problems of managing and operating a local station, in 17 chapters, each written by a recognized executive in his special field. Includes the independent, network-affiliate and ETV station.

Schramm, Wilbur Lang. *Responsibility in Mass Communication.* New York: Harper & Brothers, 1957. If the student wishes to discover the social roles and responsibilities of all the mass media including television, this book provides a good start. Schramm's judgments and solutions are open to challenge but they are always provocative.

Seehafer, Eugene Fred, and Laemmar, Jack W. *Successful Television and Radio Advertising.* Rev. ed. New York, Toronto, London: McGraw-Hill Book Company, Inc., 1959. The advertising and business portions of broadcasting and radio are well presented. The authors, both advertising agency men, help to bring the commercial aspects into perspective. The organization and management of stations, the nature of the audience, creation of commercial campaigns for national and local advertisers, the organization and role of the advertising agency and the process and requirements of time buying and selling are dealt with. The authors use many examples and illustrations.

Federal Communications Commission.

Annual Reports. Washington: United States Government Printing Office, 1935 —. Though including much more than television, the annual reports summarize governmental actions relating to television, industry statistics, technological development and controversial issues.

Coons, John E., ed. *Freedom and Responsibility in Broadcasting.* Evanston, Ill.: Northwestern University Press, 1961. This is a collection of speeches and comments on broadcasts by twenty leaders from government, broadcasting, law, education and journalism at a conference at the Northwestern University School of Law. Attention focused on problems of broadcasting solutions, and on the nature and optimum extent of regulation of broadcasting by government.

Emery, Walter Byron. *Broadcasting and Government: Responsibilities and Regulations.* East Lansing: Michigan State University Press, 1961. From his experience as a member of the legal staff of the FCC, Emery discusses briefly the background of federal regulation of broadcasting and analyzes in detail the scope and nature of regulation in effect at the time of the book's publication.

Educational Television

Additional weight is given to the bibliography of ETV because this service is in the process of great expansion and intensive self-examination. It is important that the student recognize the many roles, realized and potential, which ETV encompasses.

Elliott, William Yandell, ed. *Television's Impact on American Culture.* East Lansing: Michigan State University Press, 1956. For the undergraduate or graduate student who wants to know something about the Canadian system of broadcasting, how United States noncommercial educational stations came into being and how they function, what the NETRC does, whether commercial television can also provide educational services, and what the place of television is in formal education — this is a useful source of information.

Lewis, Philip. *Educational Television Guidebook. A Service Project of the Electronic Industries Association, Educational Coordinating Committee.* New York: McGraw-Hill Book Company, Inc., 1961. Not for the specialist, the *Guidebook* is designed to help teachers and school administrators evaluate the uses of broadcast and closed circuit television in a variety of circumstances. It is a background and facilities guide; a fairly simple "how to do it" source.

Siepmann, Charles Arthur. *TV and Our School Crisis.* New York: Dodd, Mead 1958. The student will find that Siepmann, though partial to television's many benefits, does not preach that it is a cure-all for the ills and crises of education. Television is there to be used as the situation calls for. No master plot, no over-all blueprint in this book, but some provocative suggestions.

Stanford University, Institute for Communication Research. *Educational Television: The Next Ten Years; a Report and Summary of Major Studies on the Problems and Potential of Educational Television . . . .* Stanford: The Institute for Communication Research, 1962. This is a summary and compilation of 27 articles, statements, and notes on the status and problems of educational noncommercial television. Most of the book looks forward rather than back and is concerned with future financing, programming and use of ETV. What ETV can and should do, its roles in society and the solutions to its problems are examined.

The Year Book of Education, 1960: Communication Media and the School (George Z.F. Bereday and Joseph A. Lauwerys, eds.). Tarrytown-on-Hudson, New York: World Book Company, 1960. The editors note that teachers today have tools — including television and teaching machines — more powerful than any possessed by their predecessors. How these are being used and how they might be used in advanced urban industrial societies and in underdeveloped areas are the questions basic to all the contributions in this book. Almost all of the 49 chapters make important and urgently needed points.

Research and Social Impact

The social impact of television is the most controversial of its many aspects. Judgments in this area must be founded on sound research — too often they are not — and some excellent research is being planned, carried out and published.

Arons, Leon, and May, Mark A., eds. *Television and Human Behavior; Tomorrow's Research in Mass Communication.* New York: Appleton-Century-Crofts, 1963. Certainly not addressed to the undergraduate major in broadcasting, this compilation of proposed research projects reveals to the teacher of broadcasting a number of major areas that must be investigated before we can claim much knowledge of the way television works in its social setting. The teacher will be stimulated by the novel approaches used by many researchers in their proposals.

Bogart, Leo. *The Age of Television; a Study of Viewing Habits and the Impact of Television on American Life.* 2d ed., rev. and enl. New York: Frederick Ungar Publishing Co., 1958. Bogart examines the historical setting for the rise of television, the nature of its appeal to its audiences, the manner in which the audiences use their time before the television set, the effects of television on other media, its impact on politics, its influence on youth, and the future of the medium. To accomplish this, Bogart has studied carefully the research done by others and comments on the findings.

Klapper, Joseph T. *The Effects of Mass Communication.* Glencoe, Illinois: The Free Press, 1960. Klapper analyzes recent research on the effects of mass media on audience tastes, opinion formation and standards of values. His tentatively developed generalizations derived from his study of the research provide teacher, graduate student and undergraduate with a more balanced frame of reference for assessing television's place in society.

National Educational Television and Radio Center. *The Impact of Educational Television; Selected Studies from the Research Sponsored by the National Educational Television and Radio Cen-*

ter (ed. by Wilbur Schramm). Urbana: University of Illinois Press, 1960. Grouped under three major headings — educational television and its place in the community, in the school and in its relationship to children — these studies investigate audience size, composition, viewing habits and attitudes as these are related to educational television.

Rosenberg, Bernard, and White, David Manning, eds. *Mass Culture: The Popular Arts in America.* Glencoe, Illinois: The Free Press, 1957. Although devoted to all the mass media, the book offers sections on mass culture and the broadcasting media. These are in the form of a "dialogue" of contributors who attack and defend mass culture and mass media. The emphasis is upon aesthetics.

Schramm, Wilbur Lang, Lyle, Jack, and Parker, Edwin B. *Television in the Lives of Our Children.* Stanford, Calif.: Stanford University Press, 1961. To the student and teacher who seek to know the effects of television on children, this book gives no precise answers. It demonstrates the complex nature of causes and effects in any social setting. If the student or teacher earnestly wants to rid himself of many myths about television and children, this is the book.

Schramm, Wilbur Lang, Lyle, Jack, and Pool, Ithiel De Sola. *The People Look at Educational Television.* Stanford: Stanford University Press, 1963. Of value to both student and teacher, but for different reasons, this summary of research into educational television describes audience attention to and use of ETV in seven different geographical areas of the United States. For the student, there are answers to questions about who watches ETV and how much; for the teacher, there is a survey of the hard problems of ETV and suggestions for eventual solutions.

Steiner, Gary Albert. *The People Look at Television; a Study of Audience Attitudes.* New York: Alfred A. Knopf, 1963. A report of a study at the Bureau of Applied Social Research at Columbia University, this account does for commercial television what the preceding reference does for noncommercial television. The point of view is that of the audience and the study represents fundamental research into audience attitudes about television.

Periodicals

The field of television is changing so rapidly that books about it are frequently outdated when they are published. Only through the regular use of a few of the more significant periodicals can the student, the teacher and the broadcaster hope to stay abreast of the field.

Broadcasting; the Businessweekly of Television and Radio. Washington, D.C.: Broadcasting Publications, Inc. Weekly. A news magazine of broadcasting, emphasizing the commercial and government aspects. One of the few "musts" in broadcasting.

Broadcasting; Yearbook Issue. Washington, D.C.: Broadcasting Publications, Inc. Annual. The fifty-third issue of *Broadcasting*, it is a compendium of station listings in radio and television and a wealth of other useful reference material.

Journal of Broadcasting. Los Angeles: Association for Professional Broadcasting Education. Quarterly. Wide-ranging articles of scholarly and semi-scholarly nature. Includes both national and international areas. Its objective is to bridge the gap between commercial broadcasting and institutions engaged in teaching prospective broadcasters.

NAEB Journal. Urbana, Illinois: National Association of Educational Broadcasters. Published every two months. It contains short articles and comments dealing with problem areas in educational radio and television broadcasting.

Television. New York: Television Magazine Corp. Monthly. Feature articles on programming, commercial, and management trends in television.

Television Factbook. Radnor, Pa.: Published by *Television Digest,* Triangle Publications. Semi-annual. An excellent reference aid and source.

Television Quarterly; the Journal of the National Academy of Television Arts and Sciences. Syracuse: The National Academy of Television Arts and Sciences in cooperation with Syracuse University Television and Radio Center. Quarterly. Serious articles on many aspects of television with emphasis upon aesthetics and criticism.

ARTHUR HUNGERFORD

Associate Professor of Speech,
Chairman of the Major in Broadcasting,
The Pennsylvania State University

● Professor Hungerford is among those most responsible for the development of educational television in New York City. From 1955 through 1958 he was Executive Director, then Director of Operations of the Metropolitan Educational Television Association in New York, and participated in the establishment of the META Production Center and organized a staff of 40. In 1958 he accepted a Mass Media Award from the Fund for Adult Education for special study at New York University and subsequently served as an assistant to Dean Thomas C. Pollock in determining the feasibility of a College for Independent Study. In 1960 he returned to operate the former META studios as the N.Y.U. Production Center, turning out more than 200 programs, most of which are still meeting education's needs on a national scale. In 1961 he joined the faculty of The Pennsylvania State University, concentrating on the teaching of radio and television production and assisting the administration with special television projects, including the planning and development of an ETV station.

Professor Hungerford received the B.S. degree in Business and Engineering Administration from the Massachusetts Institute of Tec'inology and the M.A. in Education degree from New York University. He began early in the broadcasting field, and from 1933 to 1942 served the National Broadcasting Company in many areas, including market research, sales, engineering, TV programming and production, producing and directing, and films. In 1937 he participated in NBC's planning for expansion, subsequently organized the NBC film section, and in 1941 was named Business Manager of the NBC-TV Program Department. He worked for four years in government service, as civilian head of the Radar and Electronics Section, later as head of the Training Devices Branch, in which he initiated the testing of television's effectiveness in mass training, and finally as Acting Director of Research and Development. In 1950 he joined General Precision Laboratory to organize a national television sales department and he remained there until going to META in 1955. He has also served as Assistant Director, Pennsylvania State University Conference on Educational Television, and as special consultant to the Joint Committee on Educational Television in Washington.

2

STUDIO
AND CONTROL
EQUIPMENT

BY ARTHUR HUNGERFORD

TELEVISION'S ANTECEDENTS are radio, theatre and motion pictures. Some of the early equipment and production techniques were borrowed completely from these senior media. Technically, television has an international genealogy. Nearly every western nation, including Russia, can back a claim of innovation.

Basic Concepts

Television depends upon three basic principles for successful operation: photo-electricity, scanning and the persistence of vision. In addition, television had to await the development of radio transmission techniques before it could be broadcast successfully. Once a television signal is converted into an electronic signal, the techniques of transmission parallel radio very closely, but with considerably greater refinement.

Photo-electricity, the first important principle, may be traced back to a Swedish experimenter named Berzelius who discovered the element selenium in 1817. Many years later an English telegrapher named May noticed that a selenium component in his telegraphic equipment behaved differently when the sunlight happened to fall upon it. Becquerel, a French scientist, noticed a similar effect upon his experimental glass enclosed batteries. Later on other elements, including the element caesium, were found to have similar properties. Caesium has become the photo-conductive material used in television pickup tubes. Thus, photo-electricity has become the basis for the operation of television camera tubes which perform the essential function of changing light into electricity in proportion to the amount of light reflected from various parts of the scene in front of the camera.

The second imporant television principle is scanning. One early system proposed that there be a large bank of photo-cells which would develop electrical currents representing the scene before it and that each photo cell be connected to a light bulb at the other end of a circuit. Each tiny light would glow in proportion to the current in the corresponding photo-cell at the pickup end, thus reproducing the picture. Obviously there would have to be a large number of cells if the degree of detail transmitted was to be at all satisfactory. Literally thousands of cells would be required involving a similar number of wires. This was impractical. In 1884 a German scientist, Nipkow, devised an ingenious system utilizing a scanning disc which consisted of a round plate with a series of holes punched out in a spiral configuration. When the disc was spun in front of an object each hole swung across the picture area in consecutive horizontal lines. Thus the picture was broken down into picture elements along each line and into successive lines. This process is called scanning and is exactly analogous to the procedure by which we read a book. Television scans a picture from left to right and from the top of the picture to the bottom. Many experimenters improved the scanning disc principle. The best known in this country was Francis Jenkins, who operated a laboratory just outside Washington, D.C. But the greatest ingenuity produced only relatively low definition images and it soon became obvious that all-electronic techniques might offer a better solution to this problem. Vladimir Zworykin, a Russian scientist who emigrated to America and continued to work on television development at the laboratories of the Radio Corporation of America, in 1923 produced the iconoscope, an all-electronic invention in which a beam of electrons was the scanning device. A year later Zworykin produced the kinescope, a picture tube very similar to those in television sets today. An all-electronic television system seemed feasible.

Television, like motion pictures, relies upon the principle of persistence of vision to create the illusion of motion. Modern movie technology settled on a standard of 24 picture frames per second. But a typical television picture tube is brighter than even the brightest motion picture theatre screen and the eye detects flicker in a sequence of still pictures more easily as the brightness is increased. Therefore, television settled on 30 pictures per second as a design parameter. This also made the system compatible with the 60-cycle alternating current electrical power which is generally available in America. Actually, television sends out 60 one-half pictures per second, scanning lines 1, 3, 5, . . . etc., down to the bottom of the picture and then returning to fill in lines 2, 4, 6, . . . etc., down to the bottom again. In this way the eye sees 60 one-half pictures, or fields, per second, a rate that effectively eliminates all flicker. This system is known as interlaced scanning.

Television Transmission

Once the television signal has been generated in accordance with the principles just stated, it becomes analogous to an extremely "high-fidelity" radio signal. Television signals involve frequencies in excess of 4,500,000 cycles per second whereas "hi-fi" sound involves frequencies of 15,000 cycles per second. Consequently, the circuits for television are very complex. It is quite remarkable that television sets can operate with so little maintenance over relatively long periods of time. The life of the average television set is in excess of seven years.

Television signals are modulated, that is, superimposed upon radio frequency carrier waves which transport the signals from the television transmitter to the home receivers. The television transmission band includes Channels 2-6 in one segment of the spectrum; Channels 7-13 in another segment; and Channels 14-83 in still another portion of the spectrum. The first two bands are known as Very High Frequency channels, or VHF. The third band is known as Ultra High Frequency, or UHF. These latter channels were not made available to the industry until 1952 and by this time millions of sets had been sold to the public which were capable of receiving only Channels 2-13. As stated in Chapter 1, beginning in 1964 all sets sold in interstate commerce were required to pick up all channels, including UHF channels 14-83.

All television channels are limited in their coverage. Generally it is assumed that a television signal will be received only as far as the horizon (or line of sight) as seen from the transmitting antenna. Consequently, television stations seek to place their antennas on high buildings or mountains to achieve as much coverage as possible. They are limited in this and in other respects by the Federal Communications Commission, which supervises the allocation of television channels in order to eliminate interference between stations. Furthermore, no city can have more than seven VHF television stations. Only New York and Los Angeles have this many. Since channels must be shared between cities which are relatively close together, some cities have only one VHF station, some none. UHF stations have similar restrictions. Up to 1964, Los Angeles had been given the largest total allocation: three UHF channels, in addition to seven VHF stations.

All television signals tend to behave somewhat like light waves. They go to the horizon, but not much beyond, although special antennas at the receiving point can increase greatly the reception distance if the receiving point is also high on a mountain or building. UHF stations require more power than VHF stations to achieve the same degree of coverage. FCC rules permit UHF stations to use more power, in an attempt to make all channels competitive. But higher costs of operation — for electric power and other services — penalize UHF economically and this part of the TV spectrum has not grown rapidly. However, VHF has reached the virtual limits of expansion in cities where there is adequate economic support for television, and any further extension will have to occur in UHF.

Color Television

Color television has gradually assumed the proportions of a new service and the distribution of color television sets has grown rapidly. For a long period progress was slow. Until 1964, most of the effort to develop color television was by RCA and NBC. The Columbia Broadcasting System also experimented with color television at an early stage. The principle which CBS utilized involved a spinning color disc with sectors of red, blue and green. As with the scanning discs of earlier years, there were mechanical difficulties and, although the system was capable of excellent color reproduction, it was not possible to receive these color pictures acceptably as black-and-white pictures on conventional receivers. This need for compatibility was thought to have such importance that the industry, encouraged by the FCC, sought another system. Current color television sets can receive color, of course, but they can also receive black-and-white television. Present black-and-white sets can receive color transmissions in black and white. With this flexibility, color television will grow until it effectively replaces black-and-white television in the broadcasting service.

The current color process involves the transmission of a high quality black-and-white picture together with color information which, in effect, paints in the color on the received images, much as one might tint a black-and-white photograph. The camera in a color studio is very complex. There are three pick-up tubes in each camera: one for the red information, one for the blue and one for the green. These tubes must scan exactly alike and this places very stringent demands upon the engineers and the technical equipment. Similarly, the receiving picture tube has three electron guns producing three beams of electrons which activate the three color phosphors deposited inside the glass front of the tube. As late as 1964, RCA was making all the color tubes for receivers, although it had cross-licensing agreements with other manufacturers.

Television Sound

Television sound is transmitted along with the television picture but by a separate transmitter. However, there is always a fixed distance between the tuning locations of sound and picture of all stations so that when the receiver is tuned for the best picture, best sound is automatically available.

Television sound is transmitted by FM, which provides the capability for high fidelity. But it is difficult to take advantage of this capability because most television studios are considerably more noisy than radio studios due to camera movement, personnel activity and the presence of scenery.

Nor are television sets generally equipped with loud-speakers adequately designed to take full advantage of FM sound.

Summary

Television pictures are produced by cameras which change light into electricity, which generate scanning patterns, and which transmit 30 pictures per second to provide a persistence of visual stimulus and give the illusion of continuous moving images. Television sound signals are picked up through radio techniques and are broadcast by a separate but related transmitter. Color information is incorporated into the television signal in such a way that it does not affect the reception of the picture on black-and-white sets, but does activate the color circuits in color television sets.

TELEVISION CAMERAS

In common with other cameras, television cameras have lenses, a viewfinder and the equivalent of film — in this case, a photo-sensitive pick-up tube. There are two basic types of pick-up tubes: the image orthicon and the vidicon. Each has special characteristics which determine optimum use.

Image Orthicon Tubes

In typical television broadcasting stations, the image orthicon is used in cameras which pick up live action. It is a very sensitive tube.[1] The image to be televised is focused by a lens system on the glass front-end of the image orthicon. Finely divided caesium is deposited inside the glass and has the capability of responding to varying amounts of light in such a way that an electrical equivalent of the scene is created. This pattern of electrical charges is drawn by electric fields to a target plate, and, in the process, these charges are intensified. An electron beam scans the target and is affected by the pattern of charges on the target as a function of the differences in brightness in the original scene. The scanning takes place from left to right and from the top to the bottom of the picture. This beam current signal is further amplified in an electron multiplier[2] and is then delivered to the circuits in the camera proper. The actual size of the image which is focused on the photo-cathode of the image orthicon is comparable with that which used to be typical of motion picture practice. This standard was chosen purposely so that television cameras could make use of the excellent lenses which had been developed for motion pictures.

The image orthicon is a complicated structure and is costly. In the early days of production the rejection rate was high and, if certain specially skilled girls were absent from their jobs, production suffered markedly. Even today each tube costs over $1,000 and has a limited life averaging around 1,000 hours. The tube does not fail abruptly; rather, it tends to become "sticky" when it is near the end of its operating life. Images tend to become "burned in."[3] Although the image orthicon is a complex device, it is surprisingly rugged. There have been occasions when a camera has fallen several feet off a tripod or pedestal and continued to work perfectly.

Black-and-white television cameras use just one image orthicon. Color television cameras use three tubes which are matched very carefully. Image orthicons come in two sizes: 3-inch and 4½-inch (the dimension describes the diameter of the tube at the photo-cathode upon which the image is focused). The 3-inch size was universal until the beginning of the 1960's. The newer 4½-inch image orthicon was first used in England and gives a considerably better picture if all parameters, such as lighting, are controlled carefully. This extra quality became especially important with the expansion of videotape recording, since any recording process benefits from increased quality in the input signal. The newer tube also eliminates one objectionable feature of the earlier image orthicon, namely the tendency for a bright object like a candle to be surrounded by a dark area — not a faithful reproduction of the actual scene.

Vidicon Tubes

The vidicon is a less sensitive pick-up tube but it is also a very high quality device. It is a much smaller tube — typically 1 inch in diameter and 6 inches long. The operating principle is somewhat similar to the image orthicon but the design is considerably simplified. The tube is rugged and very long-lived, with an average life often exceeding 2,000 hours. The vidicon costs about $250. The longer life and lower purchase price recommend the tube for cameras used in industrial situations and in educational television where costs are a vital matter. The principal disadvantage of the vidicon is its lower sensitivity compared to the image orthicon. Light levels in studios using vidicon cameras have to be three times higher than in studios where image orthicons are used. The vidicon is used extensively in television camera chains which televise motion picture film and slides. Usually there is sufficient light available from projection devices so that the vidicon can operate in its optimum range. A new and larger vidicon, which appeared on the market in 1963, is 1½ inches in diameter, and provides increased resolution and better reproduction of the gray scale.

Cameras and Lenses

The television camera is at the heart of all studio operations. Dumont, RCA and General Electric were among the first to develop image orthicon cameras (Fig. 1). Later on, General Precision introduced a version of an English camera manufactured by Pye Ltd. This camera had many automatic features which were just a bit too early to capitalize on the later intense interest in automation. EMI-US, Ltd. developed another English camera which was well received in England and in other foreign markets. In the mid-1960's the RCA 3-inch image orthicon camera predominated. Some chains[4] over 12 years old are still operating satisfactorily. Among those who have produced black-and-white cameras using the 4½-inch image orthicon are RCA, General Electric, EMI-US, and Marconi, another British concern. Color cameras have been distributed in the United States by RCA, General Electric and EMI.

Image orthicon black-and-white camera chains cost about $17,000 and come in two versions — studio and field. The camera is alike in either case but the control apparatus is packaged in portable containers when intended for field use. These cameras are capable of satisfactory perform- ance over a very wide range of illumination and serve equally well in a studio or at an outdoor event. All image orthicon television cameras have viewfinders which enable the cameraman to see what he is framing. Basi- cally, these view finders are small television receivers, but without the need for channel selection they are smaller. The image must be very bright be- cause it must be viewed by the cameraman in brightly lighted studios or, sometimes, in intense sunlight. The size of the picture varies but is gener- ally about 7 inches in diameter. The television camera is made flexible by use of a wide selection of lenses which give different angles of view by merely rotating a turret handle. Generally, at least four lenses are mounted on the television camera turret plate on the front of the camera. Good cameramen can change lenses in a second or less.

Television camera lenses are known by their focal length, which is a measurement of the distance between the lens and the pick-up tube when the lens is as close to the tube as it can get. This corresponds to focusing the lens to view an object at the greatest distance from the camera — in- finity, as it is called. The best known studio lenses are the 50-millimeter (abbreviated "mm"), the 90mm and the 135mm, which are equivalent to 2-inch, 3½-inch and 5-inch lenses. Corresponding angles of view are 35°, 20° and 13°. The longer focal length lenses view a narrower angle and thus can select a close-up view from a portion of a general scene without moving the camera at all. For outdoor work — at sporting events, for example — the cameras may be installed far from the action, in which case very long lenses may be employed. These lenses may be as much as 13 inches, 17 inches, 25 inches or even much more in focal length. Viewers of the orbiting flights by American astronauts will recall being able to follow the progress of the rocket itself for many miles during the initial phase of these flights.

Another specification of a lens is its speed or its ability to perform under adverse lighting conditions. Fast lenses which can collect a large amount of light are generally large in diameter and are expensive. It is desirable to be able to use the same costly lenses when there is ample light. To avoid "over-exposing" the pick-up tube, an iris within the lens assembly controls the size of the hole through which light must pass. When the iris is wide open the lens is accepting as much light as it can transmit; this would

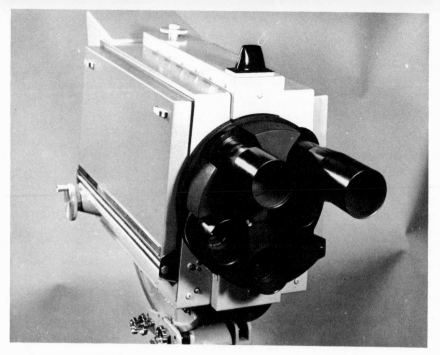

Fig. 1   Image orthicon black-and-white camera of advanced design, type PE 20-A/B.   *Courtesy of General Electric Company.*

Fig. 2   Flexible vidicon camera — useful either indoors or out.   *Courtesy GPL Division, General Precision, Inc.*

be the operating position for poor lighting conditions. On the other hand, in a bright studio scene the iris can be closed down, permitting proportionately less light to reach the pick-up tube. Thus the pick-up tube can run at the same optimum level for both the dark and bright scenes.

Closing down on the iris also has another effect which is often beneficial. The smaller the iris opening the greater will be the depth of field, which means that objects near the camera and those far away will all be in focus. This also increases the depth of focus, making the cameraman's adjustment of focus less critical. This gives him more latitude in following focus changes when dollying. In practice, television cameras are operated with lens openings of about F 8.0, which gives sufficient depth of field for most pickups. The F numbers usually are indicated on the lens barrel and also are spoken of as "stops." The difference of one full stop means that twice as much light (or half as much) is being admitted by the lens. The action of the iris and the meaning of F numbers is the same on a television camera as on a simple film camera.

The focusing of the television camera is accomplished by moving the pick-up tube back and forth with respect to the lens turret in monochrome cameras. Some lenses are provided with focus rings on the barrel for setting-in the average distance from the action area to the camera. Fine focus is then adjusted by moving the tube by means of a knob on the side of the black-and-white camera. Focusing a television camera is much easier than accomplishing the same function on a motion picture camera. The television cameraman can see his picture at all times. The movie cameraman must await the development of his daily rushes hours after the scene is completed.

In addition to the standard and special telephoto lenses used on television cameras, there are zoom lenses which permit changing the focal length continuously by moving a rod or by operating a motor switch. Such lenses are invaluable in covering sporting events or in situations where camera movement is restricted by space limitations. An over-all picture can be used to establish the orientation of the event and then the camera can be zoomed into a close-up without switching lenses. These zoom lenses are very complex and consequently are expensive. Zoomar, the earliest of these lenses, sold for $7,500. Zoom lenses are also available for studio use and make possible adequate coverage of some programs with a single camera. While this economy is not unimportant in black-and-white television, it is much more important in color television where cameras cost about $50,000.

In the early 1960's black-and-white cameras were in a transition stage. The 4½-inch image orthicon gained in popularity. In addition to its improved resolution, better signal-to-noise ratio and better gray scale, it provided simpler operational controls, stability of the circuits and rapid warm-up time.

Color Cameras

RCA and GE have been the principal manufacturers of color cameras in this country. Such cameras are essentially three cameras in one. Light enters through the usual lens system and is split into the red, blue and green components by dichroic prisms. At each of the three focal planes is mounted an image orthicon. These tubes are carefully matched, as are the associated circuit components to assure that the scanning patterns of the three tubes will be in register.[5]

Color cameras are rather heavy — about 250 pounds. Focusing these cameras is accomplished by moving the lens turret. It would be impractical to move three image orthicons simultaneously and still maintain register. The operator views the picture in black and white; there is no special need for him to see a color picture. Color viewing tubes are available in the control room for the quality control personnel and the production staff.

Vidicon Cameras

A wide variety of vidicon cameras has been on the market. Prices have ranged from $500 to $10,000 or more. It is essential that the specific use be defined accurately before purchasing equipment. Some vidicon cameras have viewfinders; others do not. Some industrial television cameras are used to view fixed displays and thus need neither viewfinder nor operator.

Vidicon equipment is considerably simpler to manufacture and consequently there has been more competition than in the image orthicon field. RCA, GE and EMI have offered vidicon cameras for a variety of uses. General Precision Laboratory (GPL) also is widely known (Fig. 2). An early leader and still popular supplier is Dage. Sarkes-Tarzian produced a completely transistorized vidicon camera, a recent technology well suited to vidicon equipment. Still other concerns, including Blonder-Tongue and Sylvania, have been active in the field.

Studio vidicon camera chains cost about one-half as much as image orthicon chains. This factor recommends them strongly for educational use and for smaller stations which are on restricted budgets. Further economies accrue since the vidicon tube itself is cheaper than the image orthicon tube and lasts much longer. Considerably higher light levels are necessary for operating vidicons under optimum conditions.

Since the vidicon is a small tube, most studio cameras using this tube are smaller than the image orthicon cameras. At first this was thought to be an advantage, but practice has shown that good studio camera work is facilitated if the camera is large enough for the cameraman to feel the mass. This avoids over-control. One manufacturer has always packaged the studio vidicon camera on the same scale as the image orthicon. GPL, in the early 1960's, stressed simplicity in operating controls, outfitting one of their cameras with only an on-off switch and one control knob. Automatic compensation for changes in light levels in the viewed scene was developed for some cameras.

All studio vidicon cameras have electronic viewfinders and the trend has been toward bigger pictures for ease in camera work. Vidicon lenses are comparable to those for 16mm film. This assures availability of a wide variety of lenses. The focal length of such lenses is usually given in inches. Typical lenses found on an average four-lens studio vidicon camera would be 1-inch, 2-inch, 3-inch and 4-inch. A 6-inch lens is about the longest one used. The 1-inch lens is comparable to the 50mm lens on the image orthicon camera and views an angle of about 30°. Longer lenses view narrower angles and produce close-up shots without moving the camera closer to the scene.

Camera Mounting Equipment

Television cameras are mounted on panning and tilting devices which permit the flexibility of control needed by cameramen. These devices are called friction heads in some cases and cradles in others. The cradle is the later design and approximates the old rocking chair idea. No matter how the camera is tilted it remains in balance. The camera pan and tilt head is in turn mounted on pedestals or dollies, of which there is a considerable variety. Simplest is a tripod which may be of metal or wood and which is usually mounted on a three-wheel dolly. The principal disadvantage of this type is the lack of vertical movement except by manual adjustment of the tripod itself. More sophisticated pedestals incorporate mechanisms for readily raising or lowering the camera. Some use a hand wheel. Others are so carefully balanced by weights that the pressure of a finger on a large ring is enough to move the heavy camera up and down. Others are activated by electric motors which operate very quietly. Still others are operated by compressed air.

Most dollies operate in such a way that all wheels turn simultaneously so that the cameraman can push the camera easily in any direction by simply turning a steering wheel or other control handle which points all the wheels in the direction the cameraman wishes to go. This design also makes possible smooth dolly shots in which the camera approaches the scene slowly while the camera is on-the-air.

Camera cranes, similar to those used in motion picture production, are found in large television studios. The cameraman rides such cranes in a fairly comfortable seat and operates the camera conventionally. Gross movements are controlled by dolly manipulators who move the camera boom in any desired direction. Such cranes easily elevate the camera to 10 feet or more and can lower it almost to the floor of the studio.

For field work at sporting events and similar remote pickups, tripods with or without dollies are generally used since actual movement of the camera from one position to another is rare. Lenses accomplish the variety of shots needed.

Camera Operating Techniques

Cameras are generally operated by union technicians. Theirs is an important job and the skill which they acquire is considerable. Sports cameramen need to know about the sport they are televising. Studio cameramen need to have a feeling for the dramatic and a sense of good picture composition. The relationship between the cameraman and the director is a close one — and sensitive. It is not desirable for cameramen to out-guess the director. Yet they must be instantly responsive to the director's wishes. Within these limitations on freedom of action, however, the cameraman should display initiative and come up with that unusually good shot which the director may well use once he also sees it.

Cameramen can make a considerable variety of movements. In the studio, the cameras are usually mounted on pedestals which can be raised and lowered. The camera can be panned to the right or to the left, which means that the front of the camera moves to the right or left, respectively. The camera can be tilted up or down. If the whole pedestal and camera assembly is moved sideways, the process is known as trucking. If the camera is moved in or out, the technique is called dollying. Camera movements must be smooth.

Besides moving the camera, the cameraman must select the proper lenses, either on the command of the director or at his own choice when the director merely specifies the type of shot he wants — for example, a two-shot, meaning two people in the shot. Lenses are selected simply by rotating the turret by means of a handle on the cameraman's side of the camera. This can be done very rapidly. The basic concept in lens selection is the minimizing of camera movement. With present lens complements it is feasible to have either a wide angle shot or a tight head close-up of a single performer — all taken from the exact same position in the studio. Once a lens has been racked into the action position on the camera, the operator must quickly find focus which may be considerably different from the previous lens. This he does by moving the focus handle on the side of the camera. Cameramen should allow clearance in their shots. In order to avoid "cutting off their heads," at least 10% at both top and bottom and on both sides should be allowed. Many home sets are improperly adjusted and tend to clip the picture.

Although camera operation is a technician's responsibility in most studios, it is desirable that students of television practice become adept at camera work too, in order that they may be fully aware of the capabilities and limitations of the cameras. This knowledge will enable them to prepare better scripts and produce more interesting programs.

Fig. 3   TV Control room — switcher in left foreground, audio to right. *Courtesy of William Spencer, New York University.*

Control Room Equipment

Control room facilities are needed to provide efficient coordination of the many elements which go into the production of a television program. There are several areas of control. The pictures from the studio cameras must be monitored continuously and the desired cameras switched to the air channel (Fig. 3). Electronic special effects are controlled as an adjunct to the switcher. The quality and amplitude of the audio must be controlled. Controls for projection apparatus for film and slides also are remoted to the control room. Central to all of these functions is a smoothly operating intercommunications system so that all personnel can coordinate their efforts effectively.

Monitors

Control room picture monitors are provided for each studio camera chain and for each film pick-up chain. In addition, there are usually preview monitors and always the on-the-air monitor, which shows the actual picture as it leaves the studio. Where there are few input cameras, the monitors may be quite large — 17 inches to 21 inches on the diagonal. When there are four or more camera chains, however, smaller monitors are often used so that the director can more easily see all of the picture choices without craning his neck unduly. In some studios the monitors are a part of the camera control units and in such cases they are shared between the production director and technicians responsible for adjustments to the camera chains. Separate monitors for the production people permit engineering personnel to utilize the camera control unit monitors for their own critical

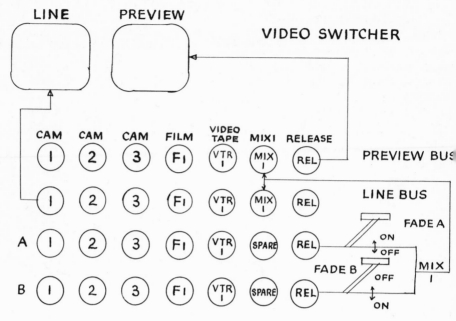

Fig. 4 Preview bus switches any source to the preview monitor. Line bus does the same for on-the-air. When fades, dissolves or super-impositions are desired, they are set up on A and B by pressing the desired buttons — one on each bus — and adjusting the fade handles. Then by pressing "Mix 1" on either the preview or line buses the combined shot can be selected.

adjustments without concern for production needs. Monitors look very much like large table-model television receivers. The quality of the control room monitor, however, is considerably higher than that found in the average television set. Nor are there any channel selection switches on monitors. They receive video signals directly from the live cameras and film chains.

Switcher

The switcher is a very flexible device which permits the choice of any of the individual cameras for the on-the-air channel (Fig. 4). To the layman, a complex switcher such as that in a network studio is a veritable sea of buttons and a complete mystery. Actually, it is simple in concept but complicated by the need for complete flexibility. In the simplest case, a switcher is a row of buttons, one for each camera chain, and a handle to control fading in and out of whichever picture button is depressed. Usually there is also a release button to switch a camera off the air instantaneously. Other than this, cameras are simply switched to the air by pressing the appropriate button.

Such simple switchers are limited in performance. The next more complicated switcher duplicates the simple switcher completely and has one set of buttons immediately under the other set. The fade handles, however, work in opposite directions so that both handles can be operated together if desired and as one switcher fades out the other will be faded in. This is called a dissolve and is a much used special effect. The next refinement is to add another duplicate set of buttons to control the preview monitor. Many directors like to place the next up-coming shot on the preview monitor, which is situated right next to the on-the-air monitor. The preview buttons accomplish this purpose but require of the operator a certain amount of dexterity, rather like rubbing the abdomen and patting the head simultaneously.

If additional facilities are desired, another double set of buttons with opposing fade handles can be added. It is possible to set up combinations of two cameras, known as super-impositions or supers, on the first two sets of buttons, to observe the output on the preview monitor and, when satisfied, take the mixed output through the lower double set of buttons via an addititonal button called Mix 1 — and thus put the combination on the air. The second set of double buttons can constitute Mix 2. Any further complexity begins to seriously tax the operator's capabilities.

Special Effects

Special electronic effects such as wipes, in which one picture seems to replace the previous one by a horizontal or vertical moving line, are created in a special effects generator. This, too, is under the control of the switcher. Literally dozens of different effects are possible. Some of the more familiar ones are corner insertions, split screens (which are really wipes stopped in the middle), circular iris effects and many more. In one manufactured version the special effects are selected by a rotary knob; in another version by more buttons, with the selected pattern indicated on associated self-illuminated tabs (Fig. 5).

Switchers and special effects are controlled by the technical director, or switcher, and his technician is usually the senior technical person present. He serves as crew chief. In some studios he relays all commands to the cameras; in others, where directors talk directly to cameramen, he is still in charge technically and is on the intercom circuit and able to talk to the cameramen as necessary. It is essential that the director and the switcher or technical director work well together. They share the strain of keeping the program rolling smoothly.

Telecine

Telecine (a term derived from television and cinema) is also controlled from the studio control room. Switches select just which film projector or which slide machine will be used. The machines can be started and stopped; projection lights can be turned on or extinguished in individual equipment. Slides can be selected or advanced. In some cases, multiplexer mirrors are also controlled by the switcher or technical director. These mirrors permit several projection devices to share a single television camera.

Fig. 5   Control panel for special effects. Note the pattern identifications on the plug-in modules.   *Courtesy of Radio Corporation of America.*

Sound

The sound control engineer may sit in the control room with the director and technical director or he may be in an adjacent room with glass separating the two rooms. The television control room has been described best as "organized chaos" and it is difficult to monitor audio properly in the din that is present there. Where the sound engineer must operate under such conditions he may resort to earphones. Separate audio control facilities with visual and voice-circuit communication to the director's console provide a solution to the problem.

In addition to the audio console there are turntables, magnetic recorders and automatic tape cartridge equipment. Tape cartridges are plastic containers enclosing continuous loops of magnetic audio tape. The time lengths may be as short as 15 seconds or as long as one-half hour. Commercials, station identifications and other material frequently repeated are pre-recorded and stored in racks adjacent to the audio console operator's position. The latter has only to place a cartridge in the play-back mechanism and throw a switch. After playing, the tape continues to run until it comes back to the starting point, ready for the next play. The engineer is concerned, too, with the sound inputs from the telecine film machines and with any remote sounds which may be piped in from sources external to the studio.

Intercom

The remaining equipment in the control room has to do with inter-communication. There are circuits from the director and technical director, or switcher, to the cameramen and video control technicians; circuits from audio control to the boom operator; engineering circuits which can be isolated so that the video control engineer can talk privately with a cameraman whose camera might be in trouble. There are circuits to telecine and to the lighting director, and between the director and the floor manager who cues the action. In rehearsal, there is a public address system by which the director can speak to all in the studio at once.

FILM AND VIDEO TAPE RECORDING

The television system was designed to accomodate the standards of motion picture film because it was anticipated that film would be used widely. It was believed that programs would be produced on film for later telecasting or that motion picture recordings of live television programs would be made to permit repeat broadcasts. Original film production created no problems because Hollywood had developed all the techniques, and by the early 1960's more than one-third of all evening network television was on previously produced motion picture film. There have always been problems with the process of making a motion picture recording of a live television program. The process is known as kinescoping, or television recording, and consists of utilizing a high quality motion picture camera incorporating special design features to accomodate it to the television rate of 30 pictures per second. This special camera photographs a highly refined television picture tube. The process can be no better than the television image and further quality is lost in film processing, so that kinescope quality has always been marginal. But it was relatively inexpensive, and the resulting film could be shipped easily through the mails and telecast at any television station using 16mm projectors, which are standard at most stations.

Film vs. Video Tape

Film as a medium has many advantages over live television production and some of these advantages appeal strongly to sponsors. Errors in live production may add to spontaneity but not necessarily to the effectiveness of a commercial. Film assures accuracy and the fine equipment available for telecasting film provides virtually fail-safe operation. Film production makes available to the sponsor all the tricks and animation techniques which Hollywood has developed over 50 years. Scene-by-scene production has many advantages in the flexibility it provides for costume changes and for quick changes in locale. Film cameras can be very portable and free from cumbersome cables. Time lapse photography or the reverse, high speed photography, are not possible on live television. Film technology has provided excellent color film which will be an increasingly important factor in the years ahead.

Film has its disadvantages, too. For subjective reasons, at least, it looks like film and not like live television and has tended to be regarded as "canned."

Video Tape Recording, or VTR as it is known, represents one of the most ingenious developments in modern electronics. At Ampex, Charles Ginsburg overcame the principal difficulty of excessive speed of movement of the magnetic tape by the technique of recording across the 2-inch tape in closely spaced magnetic tracks.[6] Using this technique, the tape can be held to a reasonable 15-inches-per-second speed. An hour program can be stored on a single, manageable reel of tape.

VTR has many of the advantages over live television that make film attractive. But there are disadvantages, too. It is more difficult to edit video tape than film. The cuts must be made by looking through a microscope to see tiny magnetic stripes. These are made visible by applying a fast drying solution containing minute iron particles which distribute themselves in conformance with the magnetic pattern of the recording. Except for this technique, nothing can be seen on the tape, whereas film is easily viewed as a series of still pictures. VTR's outstanding advantage is the immediate playback feature. There is no waiting for film rushes. The recorded program can be evaluated at once, and if corrections must be made, they can be accomplished right then before the performers are dismissed. The other principal contribution of VTR is an economic one. Programs can be rehearsed and recorded at the convenience of the principals and staff. Technicians can be scheduled more efficiently than is frequently the case for live television, where rehearsals and final broadcast may be separated considerably by costly staff hours.

VTR Machines

VTR machines are expensive — more than $50,000 for the best quality machine (Fig. 6). Color capability adds still more to the cost. Less expensive machines (Fig. 7) which make video tape available to lower budgeted operations, such as educational closed circuit systems, usually involve compromises with quality. In addition, these machines are not compatible with the broadcast types; therefore, the tapes are not interchangeable. VTR machines also require the attention of skilled technicians and work best in air conditioned dust-free rooms. It is desirable to have at least two machines in any installation. Many stations have more than two and networks install them by the dozens.

Fig. 6 Fully transistorized TV recorder/reproducer for broadcast applications (VR-1100). *Courtesy of Ampex Corporation.*

Fig. 7 Ampex VR-1500 Videotape* Television Recorder. An all solid-state, portable recorder completely self-contained in one unit and adaptable for all closed-circuit television applications.
* *Trademark Ampex Corporation.*

At local stations the VTR machine makes feasible the production of live commercials for local clients. This service is competitive with film producers and provides additional revenue to the stations. Late evening shows can be prepared during the day when manpower is available on regular schedules. Tapes are interchangeable among different broadcast quality machines (i.e. $50,000 price range), and can be shipped from station to station exactly as in the case of film. Furthermore, tapes can be played many times and can be erased and re-used again.

Film Facilities

Film telecasting facilities at broadcasting stations are known collectively as telecine facilities. Included are projectors for film and slides. Many stations make use of film cameras for covering local news stories. These are usually 16mm professional type cameras; Auricon and Cine-Special are good examples. Many stations also have film processors to handle their news films. Television can use the processed negative without the need for making a positive print. By simply eliminating one stage of amplification in the camera chain the negative film picture comes through as a positive television image.

A large amount of program material for television is on motion picture film. Suitable equipment for televising such film is essential to any station. For pick-up purposes, most stations use the vidicon film chain. This chain is very much like the studio vidicon chain except that there is no need for a viewfinder. The camera remains stationary, focused on a field lens which in effect is a tiny motion picture "screen" on which are projected the films and slides to be televised. A system of mirrors or prisms, called a multiplexer, makes it possible to project on the same field lens the pictures from two 16mm film projectors and one or more slide projectors. By turning off the projection light in one of the devices and turning on the light in another, it is possible to select any one of the film or slide projectors as a source of programming. Controls for the multiplexer and the projectors can be local or can be remoted to the control room (Fig .8).

Reliability is of the greatest importance in all television equipment, but in particular for film chains because many commercials are on film. Failure of projection apparatus can be costly in terms of rebates to unhappy clients. Consequently, nothing is spared to make this equipment foolproof and this means higher initial cost. 16mm projectors for telecine uses cost from $3,000 to $10,000; the latter machines incorporate such features as automatic light change, still frame projection and other special capabilities.[7] These machines also incorporate special pull-down mechanisms to adapt 24-frame-per-second movies to 30-pictures-per-second television.

In network headquarters, and in other large and well equipped stations, 35mm projectors also are available. These machines are adaptations from reliable motion picture theatre types and cost well over $10,000.

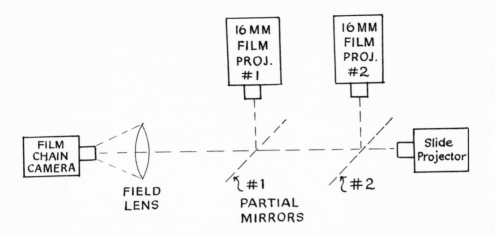

TELECINE MULTIPLEXING SYSTEM

Fig. 8 Light from the slide projector reaches the field lens by passing through two partial mirrors which are capable of both transmission and reflection, in some fixed percentages. Light from 16mm #2 is reflected by #2 partial mirror and passes through partial mirror #1. 16mm #1 is reflected by partial mirror #1. The wattage of the projection lamps is chosen to allow for the differing losses in the several light paths.

Fig. 9 Dual drum 2″ × 2″ silde projector — holds 36 slides. *Courtesy of Radio Corporation of America.*

Since the picture area on 35mm film is four times that on the 16mm frame, pictures from 35mm projectors seem to have greater resolution when telecast. Some part of this improved appearance is due to a higher degree of steadiness in 35mm equipment. General Precision, in cooperation with the Columbia Broadcasting System, developed a high-resolution vidicon film chain based on critical designs for military uses. Though more costly than conventional chains, the results are considerably better and are in keeping with the efforts of American telecasters to obtain the best possible picture within the technical standards set by the Federal Communications Commission.

Slide Projectors

There are basically two types of 2 x 2 slide projectors. One, a relatively inexpensive type, can project a sequence of 16 slides, but there is a momentary break in continuity if the slide is changed when the telecine chain is on-the-air. The projection light goes out; the slide advances and the light comes on again. This limitation can be overcome by having two telecine camera chains with individual slide projectors on each chain.

The second type is the dual drum slide projector which holds 18 slides per drum (Fig. 9). A common projection light is used and slides are switched by a mirror in the optical path. There is no dark time. Still other slide projectors have memory devices built in so that the operator can select any slide by the number of its position and the machine will automatically rotate to the desired position.

Other Projection Devices

The Telop is a device for projecting opaques and works on the same principle as the classroom projector which projects the image of a book page. The size of the opaque card is usually about 4 inches by 6 inches. The optical system is not efficient and there is a requirement for intense illumination of the card to be projected. Strip films, so familiar to the classroom teacher, also are useful in television. Standard projectors with suitable projection lenses are adequate for this purpose.

Film Handling Equipment

Since film is so important to the average station, much thought has gone into methods of logging in expected films, previewing them, cutting in commercials, storing film and shipping prints out. Technical facilities include film viewers which are not unlike those for 16mm home movies. Film counters, based on the standard projection speed of 36 feet per minute, are used for accurate timing of programs. Splicers are used to repair film breaks or to cut in commercials or to make up longer programs out of shorter films. Film handling requires care and, above all, cleanliness. Emulsions are susceptible to scratching and these defects show up as vertical wavy lines which can be very distracting to the viewer.

AUDIO EQUIPMENT

Radio was the parent of television. It provided the dollars for television development. Profits on radio equipment and profits from radio broadcasting were very substantial, and some radio stations were known to have repaid in profits the entire capital investment in a little over one year.

Television has been an unruly child of radio and for a time the latter was in a state of chaos while making long term adjustments to television's more powerful impact on the audience. Radio is now a personal medium. Many people carry transistor radios with them as they go about their daily work. Car radios are practically standard equipment.

Radio involves the conversion of sound waves, which are vibrations in air, into electrical signals which can be made to modify a carrier wave and thus be transported through space to home receivers. This is done in two ways — AM and FM.

AM has been in use since the start of radio. The term stands for Amplitude Modulation and means that the amplitude or height of the radio wave is modified as a function of the electrical signal representing the sound to be transmitted. FM means Frequency Modulation and is accomplished by varying the frequency of the radio carrier signal. An analogy might be the rapid movement of the tuning control on a radio, to and fro. FM service is growing while AM remains relatively on a plateau of full development. Television sound is sent out by FM; television picture signals are sent by AM.

Television sound or audio differs from radio broadcasting, although this is not particularly by choice. Television studios are noisy compared to radio studios. More people are moving about. More items of equipment are in operation. Television scenery introduces hard flat surfaces which may offset the careful sound conditioning treatment of the studio walls, which would otherwise create better conditions for picking up higher quality sound. In many television programs, especially drama, it is not possible to place the microphone in the most desirable position for best sound pick-up. Nor are television receiver audio systems without their limitations. The effort to make the picture in a television set as large as possible cuts down on space for the installation of adequate loud-speakers. Keeping television sets small, as in the case of portables, also works against providing for best sound reception.

Although there are many problems with television audio, equipment is available to overcome substantially most of the difficulties — assuming that production directors give adequate attention to quality audio as well as to quality video.

Microphones

Microphones are the basic devices for converting sound waves into electrical signals. There are several types. In group shows or plays, a boom microphone is usually required (Fig. 10). The boom is a flexible extendable arm which can place the microphone over the action and close enough to the performers to provide an acceptable pick-up. The microphone must be kept just out of picture range. Therefore, on long shots with considerable height showing in the scene, the microphone is necessarily farther from the performer than is desirable from the sound pick-up point of view. For close-up work it can be very near to the performer and still not show in the picture. Compensation for these differences in distance can be made at the audio control console, but the quality of distant and close pick-ups is readily differentiated by the trained ear.

Dynamic or ribbon microphones are used on booms. Generally speaking, the dynamic is somewhat more rugged. Two of the better known ribbon mikes for boom use are the BK-5A and the versatile 77DX. Ribbon mikes usually cost more than dynamic mikes. Electro-Voice 666 is a good dynamic mike used on booms. All of these microphones are directional in that they favor the hemisphere toward which they are pointed. This minimizes pick-up of unwanted studio noises from in back of the cameras. The directivity of microphones can be further sharpened. The extreme example is the rifle mike, which can pick up the sounds of a football huddle hundreds of feet away. (See Fig. 11 for typical mikes.)

Very popular everywhere in television is the lavalier microphone. This is a rugged dynamic microphone and is available in a variety of sizes and shapes. These microphones are small and can be hidden easily beneath the clothing of a performer. They are held around the neck by a light cord and are thus kept in a relatively fixed position with respect to the performer's mouth. This makes the pick-up consistent in quality. When there are but a few participants in the television program, it is convenient to provide each with a lavalier and thus have individual control over the voices of each speaker. This is particularly helpful when one speaker has a louder voice than some of the others. If just one microphone were used there would be a continual need for adjustment of the gain at the audio console.

The principal disadvantage of the lavalier microphone is the mike cable itself. The wireless microphone eliminates this cable altogether. The performer wears the usual lavalier in some inconspicuous manner. The signal is fed to a tiny radio transmitter which is readily concealed about the waist. This unit is transistorized. Elsewhere in the control room or at some greater distance a receiver detects the carrier from the small transmitter and makes the sound signal available at the audio console in the usual way. The quality of this microphone is very good and the reliability is high. Where greater distances are involved, as in the case of sporting events, a booster

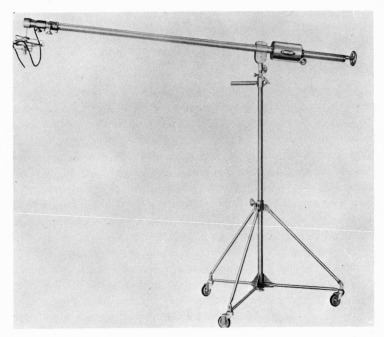

Fig. 10 Small microphone boom, pointing in horizontal plane, controlled by wheel at right. *Courtesy of Century Lighting, Inc., New York– California.*

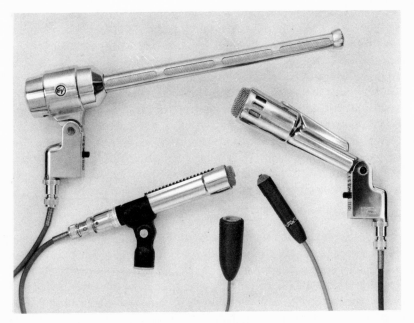

Fig. 11 Typical microphones used in TV. From top left, counter clockwise: highly directional mike, EV-644; cardioid dynamic, EV-676; lavalier dynamic, EV-624; public address lavalier dynamic, EV-647; variable distance dynamic, EV-664. *Courtesy of Electro-Voice, Inc., Buchanan, Mich.*

transmitting unit is employed. But this also is a tiny unit and poses no problem to the performer who wears it.

Other Sound Inputs

There are several other sources of sound in television. Records are primary. The 78 revolutions-per-minute (rpm) discs used to be common as popular records. Sound effects records still use this speed because it is easier to spot exact locations on them than on slower speed micro-groove records. Large transcriptions or platters, 16 inches in diameter, operate at 33⅓ rpm. Several selections or bands are on each side of the typical transcription. Current popular tunes usually are distributed on small 45 rpm records with large spindle holes. Turntables in television studios have provisions for playing all of these types. Some turntables incorporate two pick-ups so that two selections from a single transcription can be mixed together. This is helpful with sound effects records when it is desired to have a continuous effect which otherwise might run out if only one pick-up were used.

Magnetic audio tape is another important source of input sound, particularly for commercials, which may be played against slides or still pictures. The quality of magnetic sound is very high and cannot be distinguished from live sound. The standard tape speed in broadcasting is 7½ inches per second, which corresponds to the higher of the two speeds available on most home machines.

Television relies heavily on sound motion pictures for entertainment and for advertising. Sound is recovered from the usual optical sound track by photo-electric techniques and fed into the audio console for control. Some sound tracks are magnetic, being striped on the side of the film, and are handled much the same as would be the case for regular tape recorders and play-back units. The Bell and Howell 16mm TV telecine projector has provision for picking up either kind of track, simply by pushing the appropriate button.

Live sound effects comprise another sound input, but this source has become less common in recent years. So many excellent effects are now available on records that live effects, which are often more cumbersome, are relegated to the unusual or otherwise unavailable categories.

Audio Console

To many people the audio console is more complicated than the television camera. This impression results from the great flexibility that is built into modern sound consoles. In theory, the operation is quite simple. There are usually keys or buttons which have the effect of connecting certain studio microphones or other sound sources to the console. This connection leads the incoming signal through an amplifier which incorporates a volume control to give the operator control over the gain or level of the

Fig. 12 Two-channel audio console for TV. *Courtesy Gates Radio Company, Quincy, Ill.*

sound. Other keys or buttons route the controlled sound either to the on-the-air channel or to another channel which is used to check the sound without putting it on the air. The latter, the cue channel, is used to cue up such things as records or tapes so that they will be ready to be played on the air when needed. Loud-speakers are available on both the cue channel and the on-the-air channel to monitor the sound. A VU (volume unit) meter also is available across the out-going channel or program channel to help the operator hold constant levels.

Some consoles have two program channels so that if one fails the other can be switched in immediately (Fig. 12). This dual console also provides the flexibility to permit studio rehearsals while at the same time some other sound can be fed to the air through the same console.

It takes considerable skill to operate the audio console and its various input devices. In large installations special personnel may be assigned to cue up and play records to assist the audio engineer. The console operator is also responsible for the quality of sound pick-up and must work closely with the director to achieve needed compromises between the action and the audio requirements, so that the combined effect is satisfactory.

LIGHTING

The principal purpose of all lighting is to enhance the visibility of a scene and to heighten the viewer's appreciation. Lighting also conveys information concerning time of day, locale and mood.

Television has some special requirements with respect to lighting, primarily determined by the limitations in contrast. Ten shades of gray are all that can be distinguished. The system has a limited dynamic range, the extremes of white and black. It is not desirable to have large blocks of bright whites immediately adjacent to large blocks of black, since such extreme variations of large picture areas have a shock effect on the system. Engineers like to have a certain minimum light level which they can use as reference black. Lighting instruments must operate dependably and quietly over long periods of time.

Lighting often is a compromise between the exact artistic desires of the director and the technical limitations of the system. In earlier times the quantity of light needed was so great that there was little room for artistic effect. Today the reverse is true. Nearly any effect is possible. The quantity of light needed is very small in black-and-white television, hardly any more than would be comfortable in the average living room. Too low light levels, however, tend to degrade picture quality.

The design of light plots is the responsibility of the lighting director. In network and most other commercial television organizations he is usually a member of the IATSE or NABET unions (see Chapter 1). Good lighting directors prepare their work on paper, using symbols for different lighting units and indicating the direction of light by arrows. These lighting plots are rendered on scale drawings of the studio area. The lights are hung by other union technicians, and the lighting director and the director of the production approve the final result and order any needed adjustments.

There are two basic types of lighting units: the spotlight and the flood (Fig. 13). Spots can be focused in narrow or wide beams. Floods spread a diffuse light over a very wide angle. Spotlights are analogous to the sun on a bright and cloudless day. Floodlights are analogous to the light on a cloudy day when no shadows are visible.

Spotlights

Spotlights are the most flexible of all lights and if there could only be one kind of light, this would be the most valuable. They are used first to provide the key light, the principal source of light, the "sun." This strong light creates shadows and gives character to a scene. The beam can be narrow or sharp. There is usually just one key in a small scene as viewed by the television camera. There may be several different set-ups on the same stage, however. Spots are also used for back light; beams thrown on the back of the head and shoulders of the performer from overhead to make him stand out from the background. This enhances depth. Spots may be used also to cast sharp shadows on the background, giving a variety of patterns which help create the illusion of depth. Spots are used, too, to highlight close-ups of the face, much as Rembrandt used a tiny daub of white paint to give life to the eye. Spots are even used for modeling or fill light when it is desired to control the distribution with greater care than would be possible with floods.

One of the most popular types of spotlight incorporates the fresnel

Fig. 13   Most commonly used TV lighting instruments —

the scoop or floodlight

the pattern spot or lekolite

the spot or fresnelite

Courtesy of Century Lighting, Inc., New York – California.

lens through which the light is projected. This glass plate, working in conjunction with the movable mount holding the light bulb and reflector inside the unit, permits the generation of narrow or wide beams of light. A control is provided to change the width of the beam. The lighting units are ventilated by means of several openings so that the intense heat from the lamp can be dissipated. Spots come in various sizes, ranging from the 250 watt "inky dinky," often used on the front of a television camera to illuminate eyes or small objects, to 2,000 watts and larger. The other usual sizes found in television studios are 500 watts, 750 watts and 1,000 watts. Except for special effects like the big arc spotlight used to highlight the solo performer on a large stage, all spots use incandescent bulbs which last for several hundred hours. When they are old, they fail suddenly — usually when they are turned on. Once on they are not apt to fail during the show.

Spotlights are ordinarily equipped with barn doors, which are metal vanes mounted on a frame which seats easily on the front of the light and which further controls the light distribution.

Floodlights

Floodlights are large bowl-like units 15 to 18 inches in diameter. They were used first in motion pictures and were known as Hollywood Bowls until the concert stadium of the same name was built. Now they are known as scoops. Many stations light their simple sets just with scoops. Where no artistic effect is needed, this will suffice — but the picture looks flat and lacking in depth. On the other hand, flat light does not produce sharp shadows and often this is an advantage. For example, great care in lighting is required on a dramatic set to avoid mike boom shadows which would distract the attention of the viewer.

Floodlights are used for two basic purposes: to provide the minimum light level which the television camera needs to operate at all, and provide fill or modeling light to get rid of sharp, unflattering or disturbing shadows.

There are, in addition to the conventional spots and floods, numerous special lights which fill out the lighting director's bag of tricks. Strip lights are units of several small internal reflector spots or floods, not unlike automobile headlights or display lights found in store windows. They are used principally to light cycloramas, which are off-white fabric curtains stretched taut around the back of the studio to form a sky background. There is also the Leko spotlight or ellipsoidal spotlight, which has provisions for inserting "kookies" or cut-out patterns which can be projected by the light onto the background — the bars of a jail window, for example.

Color television requires twice as much light as black-and-white television and the visitor to a color TV studio will be impressed with the large number of lighting units suspended overhead. It is believed to be more economical to install many units which can be individually controlled rather than use fewer units which must be repositioned frequently by personnel.

Lighting Grids

Most television lighting is overhead in order to provide maximum room on the floor for maneuvering cameras. There are several ways to install overhead lighting. From the theatre came the batten, a long pipe suspended at either end by ropes or chains. The battens run across the stage area and are often as close together from front to back of stage as the lighting units themselves will allow. The lighting units can be adjusted from a tall ladder, or the battens can be lowered to the stage for easier access. The heavily loaded battens are usually counterbalanced with weights to permit easier movement. Light units are fixed to the battens by means of "C" clamps. Some studios utilize a grid of pipe hanging about 14 feet above the action area. Every few feet there are outlets into which lighting units can be plugged. Lights are adjusted by a technician on a ladder. Some lights are mounted on pantagraphs, accordion extension devices which permit the individual light to be raised or lowered. A special method utilized in studios with low ceilings is a track which fits snugly against the ceiling. Lighting units with special clamps slide readily along the track channels and can be tightened down at any desired point. Some studios install safety chains on each lightning unit as a double precaution against falling, since the units are heavy enough to injure performers seriously.

Lighting Control

The pig-tail, or connecting wire, from each lighting unit is plugged into a convenient overhead outlet. Twist-lock plugs are used to prevent the connections from breaking loose. All of these outlets are terminated in a control board known as a dimmer board. The simplest boards involve patch-cords, one for each light, by which means any light or group of lights, up to some wattage limit, can be connected to a single dimmer circuit — usually a large control arm. By arranging the grouping of lights on the six to eight dimmers provided, the lighting technician is able to control the degree of illumination on any part of the set. Lighting is one of the most rewarding activities in television production. Good lighting has a great effect on the excellence of a television picture. Here is a truly creative opportunity for the artist and technician. Special lighting set-ups for individual programs can be accomplished with a minimum of cost.

For further discussion of lighting, from the designer's point of view, see Chapter 6 of this book.

Summary

The underlying characteristics of all television equipment are flexibility and reliability. Television, in basic form, is a "live" medium and instant coordination of many technical facilities and personnel is a requirement for successful production. Nearly all studios develop special techniques to save production time and to give the directors, casts and crews the maximum opportunities for effective programming.

NOTES

1 When first demonstrated just after World War II, the image orthicon produced an acceptable picture of a person's face illuminated by a single candle held about six inches away.

2 An electron multiplier is an amplifier consisting of a series of vanes upon which the electrons impinge. Each bouncing produces more electrons and hence a stronger signal.

3 Image orthicon life is extended by the use of an orbiter which mechanically or electrically moves the image on the photocathode very slowly and thus minimizes burn-in.

4 Chain is a term that indicates the total facilities required to operate just one camera. Thus, a camera chain includes the camera equipment, the cable and the monitor needed to bring the camera's picture to the control room.

5 The problem of register is similar to that encountered in color printing where the colors must be super-imposed one over the other very precisely to avoid color fringing. It is remarkable that these necessary tolerances can be attained in the television system.

6 The process is analogous to the Palmer method of writing the vertical stroke drills.

7 A single frame of a motion picture can be projected into the television system for viewing on the control room monitor and is further assurance that all is in order. The operator need only start the film transport mechanism when desired and switch the film chain on-the-air.

BIBLIOGRAPHY

Alton, John, *Painting With Light.* New York: The Macmillan Company, 1949. Effective description of lighting techniques, particularly as applied to motion pictures, but generally applicable to television as well.

Bretz, Rudy, *Techniques of Television Production. Second Edition.* New York: McGraw-Hill Book Co., Inc., 1963. Comprehensive description of television equipment and its uses. Profusely illustrated.

Chinn, Howard A., *Television Broadcasting.* New York: McGraw-Hill Book Co., Inc., 1953. For basic understanding of the engineering principles involved in television.

McMahan, Harry W., *Television Production.* New York: Hastings House, Publishers, Inc., 1957. Blending of film and television production techniques with some emphasis on the television commercial.

Millerson, Gerard, *The Technique of Television Production.* New York: Hastings House, Publishers, Inc., 1961. Detailed study of the mechanics, techniques and aesthetics of television production.

Oringel, Robert S., *Audio Control Handbook For Radio and TV Broadcasting.* New York: Hastings House, Publishers, Inc. Rev. ed. 1963. Detailed step-by-step information on audio control procedures, primarily for radio but applicable also to TV.

Wade, R. J., *Staging TV Programs and Commercials.* New York: Hastings House, Publishers, Inc., 1954. Specific information on scenery, lighting, special effects and graphics.

Zettl, Herbert, *Television Production Handbook.* San Francisco: Wadsworth Publishing Co., 1961. Well illustrated handbook covering the important aspects of television production.

New York University Television Production Center. Associate Director
Arthur Hungerford, right foreground. The studios formerly were those of
the Metropolitan Educational Television Association and are now a part of
the facilities of WNDT, Channel 13, the New York City ETV station.
Photo by Irwin Gooen, New York University.

BERNARR COOPER

Chief, Bureau of Mass Communications,
The State Education Department,
The University of the State of New York.

● Dr. Cooper's educational administration and communications experience includes broadcasting and utilization training of more than 165,000 teachers in three countries and in four languages. He has served as an advisor and consultant to the Broadcasting Corporation of Japan on the production of educational, informational and entertainment broadcasts, as an advisor to the United Nations Command on the building and staffing of 12 radio stations in the Korean and Chinese prisoner of war educational program, and as a consultant to the Australian Broadcasting Commission. He has been cited for his work with Military Intelligence and the United Nations Command. He was the general manager of KNME, one of the early ETV stations in the United States. His early broadcasting experience includes all three of the major networks, and he has produced more than 1,200 radio and television programs.

Dr. Cooper received the A.B. degree from Wabash College, where he was elected to Phi Beta Kappa, and he earned the Ph.D. degree from Stanford University. He has taught at Stanford University, Florida State University and the University of New Mexico. In addition to more than 15 articles on communications and broadcast criticism and three monographs in Japanese, Chinese and Korean, he is the author of a text on radio production, written and published in the Japanese language. He was a recipient of one of the first grants to conduct a television utilization training course for teachers in the United States.

Dr. Cooper's activities in professional associations include the chairmanship of the Radio-Television-Film Group of the Southern Speech Association, membership on the Utilization Advisory Group of the Eastern Educational Network, and membership on the National Advisory Council on Foreign Languages for Elementary Schools.

3

PRODUCING

BY BERNARR COOPER

One of the most anomalous terms in all of television is, perhaps, the word "production." The "producer" — who he is and what he is — has been widely and variously described by television personnel. Depending on whether one is talking to the top echelon of administration in one of the networks, an advertising agency media man, or a performer on a particular program, one may run a whole gamut of adjectives and expletives.

To the uninitiate, the producer is *him* — a man behind an invisible and impenetrable mask of function. Precisely what he does or how he does it, or what his production group does, is a kind of never-never, misty, not quite comprehensible matter of not inconsiderable importance. One reads on occasion in some syndicated television column of a change in producers on some program being planned or being produced for airing at a later date. The implication of such reportage seems to be that an important change for that particular program has taken place. Has it? What precisely does such a change mean? How will it affect the final viewer product that 'hits' the air? Indeed, we come the full circle of the original question — the producer, who is he and what is he?

At the outset, let us make one thing clear. The position of a producer is not one in which the novice, the newly-entered-to-the-medium, is likely to begin. The concept of production is based upon a whole continuum of experience, understanding and breadth of undertaking in the television medium. The college diploma may represent the completion of an experience in one kind of learning. It does not represent a passport to the he directs a rehearsal or an on-the-air presentation. At the local level the producer frequently may do his own voice-over-work, his own switching as he directs a rehearsal or an on-the-air presentation. At the local level the producer-to-be may even start as a copywriter, in traffic, in announcing or in graphics work. Eventually, the "future producer" at the local level may move to simple tasks of directing or switching. He may and should move through the "sales" experience. Eventually he will have a total concept experience involving both client relationship and need and the actuality of exigencies of studio potential and application. It is when the individual has come to know the "tools" in an ongoing work-a-day situation and how these may or may not be used — when he has a concept of what the nuts and bolts of studio hardware can be relied upon to do — that he is ready to become the most difficult and tenuous of all of television's contributors, the "producer."

What, then, is a producer? At the highest level of performing function, the producer is three persons in one — a highly imaginative initiator of ideas, an interpreter of desired ends, and an efficient executive. He is an individual of high intellectual achievement, insight, understanding and capability.

In the golden days of radio, the term "producer," "production-man," "director," were used interchangeably to mean the same person. This sometimes occurs even today in a small television station. Generally, however, the producer has several types of directors working under his supervision. The producer is the final coordinator of the work done by such people as the musical director, the dance director, the dialogue director and the like. Frequently, an idea may start with the producer, but there are variations to this procedure, as we shall learn. The producer is called upon to see that one or a combination of the following occurs in every telecast he does: information, education, entertainment.

The producer, then, is the individual who has the over-all responsibility for a production of any kind, any size, any depth, any duration. He may originate an idea. He is always the one who plans and coordinates, sees to it that personnel and material are ordered, planned for, paid for and functioning under all conditions of preparation and final airing. The producer deals with "things" and "concepts." He is distinguished (where distinction is necessary because of organization lines) from a director because the latter deals with performers and the technical aspects of presentation in rehearsal and on the air (see Chapter 5). Thus, if we consider that the producer is the idea man and the coordinator of all aspects of the production, and the director is the interpreter and amplifier of the ideas and coordination, it is not too difficult to understand how both of these persons may be the same individual in a local station set-up.

The authority of the producer is wide, his responsibilities great, and he is always limited by the exigencies of the budget. There is no ideal situation which adequately describes and pinpoints the functions, activities and responsibilities of the producer. All that can be provided is an overview with specific functions in special areas.

THE PRODUCER AS AN INDIVIDUAL

It is important to determine not only *what* the producer is, but *who* he is. The very use of the word "who" implies the characteristics and personality of the human being as related to the particular job.

Influence of Radio

It is generally agreed that much that has formed the pattern of presentation in the television medium has come from radio. This is natural and to be expected. Television began as an experimental offshoot of radio with video portions that accompanied the already known, understood and well-patterned approaches to sound. Indeed, in the early days of television the technique of radio (with some kind of visual accompaniment) was the general method of approach, and the early simulcasts in the two media are proof of this duality of thinking.

One of the most obvious characteristics of the radio medium was its lack of ability to control its audience. Whereas in theatre and movies the audience came to the place of presentation for the express purpose of seeing and hearing the production, this was not true in radio. In radio (as in "free" television) no fee was paid at the time of listening as was typical in movies and theatres. There was no special seat. The listener to the radio program could, often was, and still is distracted by a host of extraneous factors — the newspaper, a book, a ringing of the telephone — any one or a combination of many attention-diverting occurrences. Whereas radio lacked the ability to control its audience, television, the psychological investigator informs us, has its own built-in control. The extent of the control, described below, in many instances depends upon the skill, the ability, the concepts of the producer and, ultimately, of his interpreter — the director.

TV Audience Control

The particular viewer-control influence that seems to be at work in television has been interestingly described with the phrase "the narcotizing dysfunction." This phrase, carefully delineated by Paul Lazarsfeld and Robert K. Merton, aptly describes the influence of television medium-watching upon the individual. (The full delineation of the narcotizing dysfunction is excellently expressed and defined in *Mass Culture, the Popular Arts in America,* edited by Bernard Rosenberg and David Manning White.)

Psychologically, it is known that the human being is incapable of retaining as many sound impressions as visual impressions. Yet the goal of the producer in television remains the same as that of the producer in radio. Both must conceive, plan and implement the purpose of moving an audience, emotionally, to some specific kind of action, to some new or added directions of thought or to a combination of these.

Leadership

It was indicated earlier that the producer is highly imaginative, an initiator of ideas, an interpreter, and an administrative executive. With a host of functions and materials, as well as persons whose work must be coordinated, the producer must obviously be an individual capable of leading others as well as working closely with them. As in all forms of good leadership and administrative and executive acumen, the producer must lead when he appears to be following, must request thinking and action when he is actually initiating such thought and action. If we were to stop with only this aspect, we would be opening the door for the creation of a truly authoritarian monster. Those who have recognized that the producer must have the ability to lead frequently misinterpret that ability for the *need* to lead. The implications involved in considering such a need open a Pandora's box of such psychological proportions that it would take (and frequently has taken) the consultation services of outstanding psychologists to bring about a revision and change in personality. It is necessary to give obvious direction to the phrase "ability to work with others." Too frequently this phrase has been misinterpreted and reinterpreted to mean "working others." The skillful authoritarian uses people rather than encouraging them to make the necessary contribution which must be made if a producer is to function as a superior director and leader of the team. The word "team" has been sorely abused in educational literature; yet it is precisely the original, deep and thorough meaning of "team action" that the producer must bring about to successfully fulfill not only his own function, but the function of the medium and, therefore, the eventual goals of educating, informing, and entertaining. Having organized his team, having brought it to a point where it is making a contribution to the general thought and concept of the program to come, the producer's next necessary qualification is that of being able to delegate authority. Once members of the team have begun to think, to act and execute tasks with imagination and dispatch, the producer must "let go."

Self-Discipline

One of the prime requisites of the good producer is that he be a self-disciplinarian. The producer must be capable of setting all kinds of discipline approaches for himself if he is to be capable of doing so for others. Because of the exigencies of the producer's role, he is always in the position of telling others what to do. If he is to do this, he must himself be capable of being self-directive and highly organized in a work situation. Because he must expect other directors' services outside of the station or the network, suppliers of various equipment, writers and the like to adhere to specific schedules in order to meet broadcasting needs, he himself must adhere to a rather rigid schedule.

Preparations must be made and, in order that all of the contributing services and personnel may make their contributions at the proper time and in the proper amounts for the indicated needs, the all-over director of directors — for this is what the producer is — must himself be highly organized. He must anticipate needs. He must be able to foresee likely pitfalls in the total process of pulling any broadcast together. In addition to working with highly artistic people, he also works with rigidly objective technicians. His engineers, his sound-effects men, his projection personnel, his recorders, his technical director — all of these people are highly skilled, highly organized, and must themselves adhere to the particular requirements of the particular job they do. Because the producer must bring together and synthesize the work of everyone into a cohesive whole that finally makes for a desirable broadcast product, he must be an outstanding self-disciplinarian.

There are other related personal characteristics that must be developed and finely-honed in order that the producer may reach this goal. The producer must have an inborne sense of observation. Everything which occurs in life, and for as long as the producer can remember, will be grist for the mill of his expertise. The sense of observation which the producer carries with him at all times enables him to retain the things which he sees in life. All of these form a basis for judgments, ideas, organizational entities, cost accounting and the visual and oral impact that the good producer must see in his mind's eye long before he even starts to plan a production.

Taste and Mixture

Tied closely to the sense of observation — and hearing and seeing well and remembering accurately for future needs — is the sense of good taste. It has frequently been called showmanship. Precisely what is meant by showmanship is hard to define. In one manner of speaking it is a sense of the dramatic — a sense of the interesting — a sense of that which is complete in accomplishing an all-over effect. Showmanship, like good taste, cannot be taught. It is an inborne thing. It develops with use, it matures with professional aging, but it defies explanation, definition or learning. It is the incredible potential of knowing what is precisely right at the right moment to accomplish the given need. It is for the producer what the selective use of seasoning and flavors is for the good cook.

When we speak of effect, we speak of another personal qualification necessary to the good producer. He must have the ability to take all of the technical and personnel potential available to him and move smoothly to the point of in-studio preparation. Thus, when a director takes over, he is inevitably led to the one resulting effect that the producer had in mind when he first began to assemble the necessary ingredients for the given program. The ability to assemble the proper material and personnel in the proper amount — depending upon the budget — is the one ingredient that the outstanding producer has which can be duplicated by no other member of the total production team.

Temperament

One intermediate conclusion from all of the above is that, with the tremendous amount of responsibility and need to coordinate the efforts of many, the producer has no time for temperament. Temperament, as used here, means those displays of excessive emotionalism and temper tantrums which frequently are the refuge of the frustrated, of those who cannot achieve under given conditions, who find anger and some kind of violence an outlet and replacement for the coordinated action and thought which should take place. The producer has no time to permit an indulgence in temperamental outburst on the part of any member of his team. Within the total production team, emotionally highly-keyed individuals sometimes are found, but one must not mistake the high-keyed individual for the nonsensically temperamental.

Time

Broadcasting proceeds with the inevitable forward movement of a clock. Time is the governing factor of all that is done in the radio and television media. Without a recognition of time as the master of the total direction in which a broadcast moves, one is deluding oneself. It may be argued that if time truly controls all accomplishment in the broadcast media we are indeed slaves to a clock and perhaps these are not the media for truly artistic output. No semantic quibbling can change reality. An examination of the products of the broadcast media will clearly suggest that artistry in almost pure form has existed many times during the history of the development of broadcasting.

Since the producer, like all the members of the team, works under the constant pressure of time, a myriad of detail and seeming confusion constitute the usual atmosphere in which the producer — and subsequently, his director — must work. A careful analysis of what usually constitutes studio confusion will indicate that in the well-planned situation the confusion is only one of simultaneous and seeming unrelated actions. Such actions culminate in a total product, the all-over plan of which may be unknown to any given member of the team. But the all-over *place* in the plan for each member is a matter of well-constructed and agreed-upon organizational approach. Within this seeming confusion, the producer must work calmly, swiftly and efficiently. And as he works at what seems to be breakneck speed against the moving hands of a clock, because of his total pre-planning he is able to handle a multitude of details, seeing that each is completely executed and fitting all of them into the all-over design of the entire broadcast product.

BACKGROUND AND EXPERIENCE

As we review the desirable personal and psychological characteristics of the good producer, it would seem that we have set an impossible level to be achieved by a single human being. We have said that the producer is an interpreter, an executive and an administrator. He has the ability to see many details and handle them in terms of the total broadcast product he is seeking. He must be able to delegate authority and yet be a rigid self-disciplinarian, fitting his working schedule to the time requirements of the broadcast schedule. He must know how to coordinate and inspire the best efforts of the team working with him in order to achieve the best results. He has an inborne sense of observation and an inborne sense of good taste which contribute to a product that must meet the most rigid requirements of a combined scientific and art form. If the producer is to achieve all of the above he needs to bring to his position varied experiences.

Technical

Certainly, if he is to handle and continue to understand a multiplicity of developments in the equipment field which will effect his total planning process, the producer must have some technical background. This is not to say he needs engineering qualifications. He will want to know, at least in layman's terms, the basic function of his amplifiers, microphones, cameras, video and audio consoles, and visual and audio equipment. He must know the principles of operation, limitations and the normal uses of all equipment that he is likely to plan to use on a regular basis. He should know the relationship of one piece of equipment to another. Such general knowledge need not be pursued in depth and can usually be acquired through reading, inspection of the equipment, and by working closely with an engineer when questions arise.

Music

It is helpful to the producer to have a knowledge of the workings of unions such as the American Federation of Musicians, and of music-control groups such as the American Society of Composers, Authors and Publishers. Such knowledge is necessary to the producer in the process of budget-planning. Another aspect extraordinarily useful to the producer is a general knowledge of the *content* of music. The good producer should have some acquaintanceship with the standard classics in the field of symphony, opera and musical comedy. He should be able to work confidently in suggesting theme, cue, background, and fill music. It should be possible for him to suggest the kinds of musical instruments that need to be considered in planning specific musical programs or musical background effects. A producer who would specialize in producing all-musical programs should certainly have a thorough musical background, ability on several instruments, hopefully some conducting experience — in other words, ability to both comprehend and execute some of the requirements of the composer. A strong sense of routining, programming and knowledge of methods of investigation to measure the taste of his potential audience are also needed.

Theatre

There is ample evidence to indicate that a good producer will benefit from some experience in the field of theatre. The opportunities for broad professional theatre background are extremely limited. However, with the development of the off-Broadway theatre in recent years and with the burgeoning of community theatre activity throughout the United States, more and more opportunity for experience is presented to the individual who will eventually be a producer in television.

The broad areas of theatre experience that can benefit the TV producer are in directing, stage-managing and acting. The director in the theatre faces many of the same problems that plague the director in television. His relationships to management, to the producer of a commercial production or to the producing agency of a community theatre are similar to those of the television producer to the advertising agency, to management of the small station or a network. Directing experience in the theatre provides insights for the television producer in determining the ways in which a director's mind is likely to develop a given program problem and product.

Stage managing offers an insight into some of the production problems which the television producer faces. Some directorial problems become clear as the stage manager in the theatre acts as a "leg-man" for the director and his needs. He quickly learns, through practical applications, some of the immediate problems that are met in rehearsal and performance. Both the director and the actor, out of a continuing experience of appearing or preparing for various audiences, learn what different audience reactions are likely to be. The urban audience is not the rural audience. The audience at a high socio-economic level — with college background — is not the audience that has had a terminal high school education. Although many times one must reach both audiences with the same products, one must know when to abandon the undesirable or unnecessary to achieve the total end-product. Most important, the theatre producer, director, stage manager or actor will have had the advantage of watching master craftsmen work over a long period of time, under varying conditions and to various audiences. Learning from such craftsmen who are skilled and knowing provide knowledge that can be procured in no other way, except over a long, intensive time-period of experience.

A valuable complement to experience in practical theatre is a knowledge of the entire field of dramatic literature which provides insights into the history, political developments, manners and morals of periods of time, persuasions of leaders of various cultural and ethnic groups, and the day-to-day problems of the common man of various ages. If one has a solid background of dramatic literature and the times in which outstanding works were written (the influencing factors on the writers of those periods and the sociological implications of what those writers had to say), one may become a true student of the entire panorama of our evolvement from and involvement in both natural and man-made phenomena. Most important, a wide acquaintance with world dramatic literature will give to the producer a knowledge of the works in the field of drama and an understanding of writing techniques. Such knowledge gives almost intuitive information to a producer when he may, for example, compare the precision, the bite, the outlook of a Rose or a Serling with a Fielding or a Chekhov. Such knowledge gives to the producer a basis for judging the content of scripts submitted for consideration, with a view to the type of directorial treatment that will be called for. When a producer takes a practical look at a script, he not only examines the flow of ideas, manner of concept, and the performance qualities required, but he also projects the kind of and even the specific individual whom he would wish to have direct this particular presentation.

Culture and Living

There is no doubt that the good producer also needs a broad cultural background. Solidly based in sociological approaches to various art forms, this will open a whole world of imaginative potential when bringing to production planning a clarification of content for his viewers.

One cannot leave the discussion of the background and qualifications for the producer without making note of the necessity for a comprehensive working and living experience. Nothing can take the place of having planned and produced hundreds of productions with a view to making each presentation a finer product than the one before. We must also take into account that fullness of living and observing life that comes only to those who are aware that all such observations will, in the final analysis, be grist for the mill of thought, of outlook, of breadth which every broadcast shall demand as the full contribution of the producer to his work.

How may we sum up the desirable background for the future television producer? First, it should consist of a basic technical knowledge of the equipment with which he will work. Second, it should include knowledge of the field of music. Third, the producer should have a background in which theatre experience provides a knowledge of the master craftsmen of the drama. Fourth, he should bring to his work a broad cultural background which will contribute insights and goals of desirable production achievement not otherwise possible. Fifth, there should be a breadth of working and living experience not required of or usually attained by any other member of the production team.

RELATIONSHIP TO NON-STATION AGENCIES

The Producer and the Advertising Agency

The function of the advertising agency in the actual production of television programs has varied over the years. At one point in the historical development of the medium it was considerable. It is now negligible insofar as the actual total programming and packaging concept is concerned, although advertising agencies work closely with production firms in creating particular types of programs desired. An agency now usually concentrates upon a carefully selected buying of available programs, and station or network time. The particular time of day during which a program is to be aired and the viewer for whom it is being aired will determine what the actual content will be. The producer of such a program may enter into the planning concepts early or after the idea has been firmed up. He may be given the job of creating everything necessary for the total production package or he may be brought in at the point at which a script has been pulled together for a series or for a special program.

At whichever point he enters, it is the producer's job to consider, in the light of total agency and client needs, the abilities of personnel, the equipment, and other services he may require in order to accomplish the task at hand. The final production team usually includes individuals in the following categories: artists who create visuals and who design sets, photographers, carpenters and, frequently, specialists in the creation of product displays. Often, when there are special problems involved in a production and when the resolution of these problems may depend upon the writer, the latter, too, is part of the total production team.

It must be borne in mind that when we speak of the relationship of the producer to the advertising agency, distinctions are made between the large advertising agency which services the network and the local advertising agency which specializes in rendering service to a smaller client. The large advertising agency is not usually a production agency. It may designate talent; it may designate the producer; it may designate many different areas of personnel that it wishes to employ to accomplish a particular task. For the most part, however, it will leave such matters in the hands of the production organization or the network.

The local advertising agency may perform one of a number of different services. It can, for example, provide not only the producer but the writer; it may provide "live" program scripting; it may provide the entire message in "canned" form, such as a film or video tape. In many instances the local advertising agency provides photography for slides and telops, films, jingles and animation; sometimes it jobs out these various functions to a local station or other organization with adequate facilities.

The Producer and the Station "Rep"

The function of station "reps" (sales representatives) is to get advertising placed on stations that they represent. There are between 80 and 90 such agencies throughout the country. Their effect is considerable. They handle promotional advertising and determine the stations and the markets in which programs and commercials are to be placed. It is the function of the station rep to have available at his fingertips all matters of information related to the market of the station or stations which he serves. Frequently, the producer called upon to do a new, unusual or different kind of production job overlooks the potential value of the station rep. Insights which the rep can supply into the market, its kinds of people, its size, its mean socioeconomic level, its major interest, can have meaning for the producer and may frequently supply him with an approach that will make the difference between success or failure in marketing a given product or meeting a given client's needs, particularly where such needs are clearly sectional.

Music and the Producer

Earlier in this chapter we mentioned that the producer is responsible for all of the elements which go into the total program, that he is responsible for the excellence of the product which is finally conceived in the studio and emanates in the form of a program. Not the least part of the program product is music. However, music presents special problems to the unwary. The producer with accumulated experience in other aspects of programming, in both television and radio, is particularly careful of music copyrights. Music to be used in programs must be carefully planned, accurately logged, and scrutinized for copyright control.

Where new and original music is to be composed for a program, it may be contracted for. The one-time use of such music presents no special difficulties, since a contract will adequately protect the composer as well as the conductor of the score. If the composer is a member of the American Society of Composers, Authors and Publishers (ASCAP), his rights will be protected under the usual contractual arrangements with radio and television stations that are subscribers to the ASCAP list. The same is true for music controlled by Broadcast Music Incorporated (BMI). The contracts for the continued use for such music are standard and clearly spell out the conditions under which music is controlled, the amount that is to be paid, and the way in which payment is to be made. ASCAP, BMI and one other controlling agency — the Society of European Stage, Authors, and Composers (SESAC) — are the agencies with which most stations will hold a music-use license.

Unions and the Producer

In large cities most good stations are unionized, and there can be no question of unionization at the network level. But in many of the less-than-large areas, the union situation can be complicated. How do unions affect the work of the producer? The first concern is when the producer begins to draw up his budget requirements for a particular program. The standards of salary and working conditions established by the union must be taken into account in all-over budgeting. Not only do unions define minimum salaries, but producers must also budget time around the number of rehearsal hours permitted any individual before overtime pay goes into effect. If the prestige of a name performer is required, it will have to be budgeted and paid for. The frequency with which such stars appear in many programs and the all-over efficient professionalism that they bring to a presentation may be thought necessary for maximum impact. Sales must justify the employment of such high-priced talent.

In markets where unions, talent agencies, and basic minimum conditions of work, employment and salaries exist, sufficient information by the producer new to that area can be elicited either from the union representative, union headquarters, or the lawyers of the particular station or network.

PRODUCING THE NEWS PROGRAM

Perhaps the most anamolous program of all is the news program. In approaching the problems of newscasting, particularly the problems of the producer, it is interesting to note that we begin with a commonly aired product, a type well known to the viewer, and yet one which is more complicated in its association with the producer than perhaps any other program type on the air. News is one program type in which there are few clear-cut divisions between the producer, the director and the newscaster.

Multiple Local Station Role

In the local station the producer-director and newscaster are frequently one and the same person. Top-level management at the local level will frequently exercise some of the prerogatives of the producer. Management may dictate to the newscaster the type of programming approach it wishes. Indeed, frequently it may dictate what the editorial policy of the station is. In the most desirable situation it will permit the newscaster a freedom in interpretation of the news that need not necessarily be the policy of the station. Since the producer is frequently the newscaster, and, therefore, the one who determines the content of what shall be presented, we have an interesting dual role. Selection of news items, determination of which are important, which shall take precedence, and which shall be "fill" are made not by one man and executed by another, as they frequently are at the network level, but are made by one individual, alone. The responsibility of the newscaster at the local level is a heavy one.

The newscaster-producer must be a well-read individual. Where a news summary is more than a five-minute precis of headlines, singular importance must be attached to the kind of individual who shall be responsible for this particular program. There must be a keen sense of rapport between the newscaster-producer and the director of the program. Having determined what the news item shall be and having begun the necessary writing before airing the news, the newscaster-producer must now work in close coordination with his director. He is entirely at the mercy of the director for the camera shots that shall be called for, and for film, tape, or still inserts at the proper moment.

Visuals

One of the most important determinants of a news item, apart from its news importance, is the available supporting video material. Without consideration of visual contributions and their impact upon the viewer in terms of news value, there would be no reason to use the television medium for news reporting. The director must ask himself at the outset such questions as: is a video tape recording available on such-and-such particular news story? Is film being flown in from abroad? Do we go by direct wire or do we go by microwave to some distant point for a particular news pick-up? How many remote switches are involved? Are stills being used in the studio? Will slides be used? Will video be from the slide and film chain, or will it be from a rear screen projection (a large, translucent screen background to the set on which a still or motion picture is projected from the rear)? How many commercials must be inserted? Where do the appropriate places for these inserts come?

It is clear, then, that not only is understanding of news activity necessary, but the producer of the news program is closely tied to the skill and the precision of the supporting technical team responsible for the split-second timing of the video. If television news reporting is to be simply a voicing of the kind of verbalization that appears on the pages of a newspaper, then it would be less expensive, more expeditious, far less costly, and far less time-consuming to prepare a news broadcast for radio rather than for television.

Some of the basics in news coverage of the international front have not changed very much from the early days in which these were first conceived. When stations in New York City were still experimental before World War II, the early international news broadcasts were largely supported by and dependent upon good maps. In June 1942, to all intents and purposes, news broadcasting by television came to a halt. Skilled technical television personnel went to work for special projects in war research and it was not until the end of 1946 that television news broadcasting resumed its development. Put in the position of meeting a challenge for news coverage from abroad, it began to formulate a distinct method of approach and presentation peculiarly its own. During the Korean action, from 1950 to 1953, television provided a visual effect of what was being experienced, through films quickly flown to this country. This was not a period when television news reporting was held in particularly great repute. But because television had begun its first experiment with 15 minutes of news, five days a week in 1949, by the time the Korean crisis of 1950 arrived, it was ready to meet its obligation to the viewing public.

The true effectiveness of television news reporting depends to the greatest extent on the technical potential of the medium to meet the requirements of factual reporting that is no longer once-removed from participation by the viewer, as in newspaper reporting. To make a viewer a true participant through use, in the early days, of film and, later, of video tape was and still is the hallmark of the good news broadcast.

Planning and Personnel

What must the producer plan for? What personnel will he need? What additional materials and sources must he take into account? Let us separate the role of the producer from the role of newscaster and writer. When these are different persons in a large station or network situation, the television news producer must take into account an expanded list of needed personnel and extended functions of a production team. Not the least of the group will be the film cameraman. Sometimes the film may be sound and motion, sometimes silent film. The kinds of facilities available in a given news coverage situation will affect the kind of material the cameraman can obtain, and in turn affect the planning of the producer.

The producer's staff also includes a good film librarian. The film library

is to the telecast what the "morgue" is to the newsman. The film cameraman's ingenuity determines not only what will be captured on film for
the immediate telecast, but also for permanent acquisition by the film
library. The good film library serves the same purposes as the rich resources
of a print library. Nothing which is news happens in isolation. The story
does not begin now and end in the next few minutes, nor did it begin yesterday, nor will it end tomorrow. There is a continuity of history that runs
as a thread through all of newscasting. The news library must be a reposi-
tory of all which is likely to be meaningful.

In some stations, the film crew — made up of a cameraman, sound
man and light man — may be large and well developed. In other stations,
it may be a two man operation — including the newscaster-producer himself. The one person in any news situation closest to performing the ideal
function of "leg-man" for the producer is the man known as the "contact"
man. He decides what represents a news item. He is completely responsible
for content. He decides on the over-all approach. He suggests the shots but,
of course, in technical matters defers to his most skilled technician, the
cameraman, who must judge lighting, distance, and the like. In addition to
a cameraman, a contact man, and a sound and light man, the producer
must also have a film editor. The film editor must be provided a cutting
room in which he can project a 16mm "hot" print, and he must be familiar
with and have tools required for editing, such as a sound-reader and
splicers. The producer must have an arts and graphics staff that will include all-purpose artists capable of quickly producing charts, graphs, cap-
tions, still photographs, and other visuals. The production team also includes
special engineers and technical personnel, cameramen who go out on location, projectionists in telecine, the audio and video control personnel. In
large operations there may be numerous assistants to the producer. The
director is a member of the staff. There are traffic specialists, office personnel, and representatives of sales, the sponsor and the agency. The mis-
cellaneous personnel that the producer has under his command may, in a
large station or network situation, include messengers, clerks, typists,
mimeograph operators and teletype operators; where special services are
needed one can frequently include a helicopter pilot. All kinds of miscel-
laneous supporting personnel, depending upon the sponsor of the program
and the product being exhibited, may evolve in relation to newscasts.

Organizing the program

It is the responsibility of the producer to preside at that most important determining session known as the "line-up." This is the meeting at
which all members of the news production team, including the newscasters,
editor, producer, director, film, arts and graphics personnel, and writers
appear. Line-up time in large television news centers is usually two to four

hours before presentation. The purposes of this session are to examine a suggested routining of the presentation of stories, to choose a lead story, and to determine the appeal of particular stories by discussing, examining and listening to an evaluation of the picture material available for each of the news items to be presented. The usual ratio estimate of video to audio material is approximately one-to-one in a 15-minute commercial news program. For example, six to seven minutes will be devoted to film and other visuals and the remainder will be devoted to the "shooting" of the newscaster himself.

Individual film stories may vary in length. On a 15-minute program, six to seven minutes of film may break down into four to as many as eight video periods. These periods, properly distributed throughout the entire program, will hold the live camera portions of the program to no longer than 30 seconds or a minute at any one time. A decision to include or exclude specific materials for specific purposes is up to the producer. For example, an unusual news story of above average running time, on film or video tape, may be substituted at the last moment on the decision of the producer made in conjunction with his newscaster and director.

It is not the purpose of this chapter to discuss in depth methods of news selection. Suffice to say, among the most important decisions made by the producer responsible for the allover newscasting policy of the station will be those of coverage for *particular audiences* at *particular times* of day. For example, the early morning adult audience is in a hurry. It will do more listening than watching. It needs quick, concise coverage. The daytime audience is different. On weekdays, it is largely feminine and is interested in a slackened news pace and in more features. The early evening family audience desires broad coverage of all the news that has happened within the past 24 hours. As many stories as possible should be covered, and shock and horror stories avoided. Late evening news coverage can be more relaxed in pace. The audience is presumed to be mainly adult and wants news reviews and indications of what may occur the next day — including weather predictions.

Thus, the responsibility of the producer of the news telecast includes the direction of all personnel and elements of the program, intimate involvement in everything from writing to projection, and a tight control over the line-up period.

THE DISCUSSION PROGRAM

The discussion program is one of the most common types which the producer will be called upon to organize, either at the local or network level. The characteristic of the roundtable discussion is "informality." Do not confuse informality with lack of organization. The word informality, as used here, means a free discussion in which there is an orderly exchange of ideas, in which content is organized, and in which participation by the members of the roundtable is controlled by the moderator.

Choosing participants

The informal roundtable may be either person-centered or problem-centered in its content approach. Where person-centered, it revolves around the availability of a famous personality in a given field of endeavor. For example, the discussion topic may be on tropical diseases and their treatment. The discussant might be Albert Schweitzer. We might add a panel of qualified men in the field of communicable tropical diseases, hospital administration, or the like. Where the discussion is problem-centered, equally qualified persons in such fields as cancer research, heart disease, diabetes and polio might be participants.

Preferably, there will be four members on the panel plus a moderator although, frequently, it is perfectly acceptable to have three panel members plus a moderator. Never, only two participants and a moderator. When you have only two participants what you have is a kind of "dialogue" discussion which is simply an exchange of ideas between two qualified persons who may or may not have different points of view on the problem being discussed.

Although all members of the panel should be qualified in relation to the content, there are degrees of qualification. It is the producer's obligation to find persons who fit categories that can provide a discussion in depth. What categories of qualification are there? First there is the *authority* — the person qualified in both training and experience in the particular problem or area under discussion. The second panelist is usually an *informed* person in relation to the content. He will have some training or some experience, but rarely both. The third person represents an audience point of view and is intensely interested in the content areas being discussed. He may have some general knowledge of the problem and may have some training, but usually will have no experience. He may have a great deal of independently investigated knowledge. This person, working with the moderator-producer, helps to elicit the kind of information and reaction that would be of interest to the viewer.

If the producer is also the moderator of the program, he must acquire some background on the subject of the discussion. He must also have necessary background information on each member of the panel and, in presenting them during the broadcast, must make clear the level of their competency and authoritativeness. The producer-moderator must be capable of abstracting ideas from the members of the roundtable, organizing the discussion, routining the presentation, and summarizing the ideas presented. If the producer is not the moderator but the director of the program, then a moderator acts for the producer-director, maintaining organizational control over the discussants through agreed-upon signals conveyed through the floor manager of the program.

Procedure and Organization

A discussion program is not organized in the haphazard manner that sometimes seems all too apparent when we view such shows on television. Too frequently, discussion programs are organized loosely, planned at the last moment, and if any preliminary warm-up with the participants does take place, it is usually in a very cursory and off-the-cuff manner. Whether or not the producer is also the moderator does not change his primary responsibilities. These include:

1) Locating the participants and determining levels of authoritativeness.
2) Interviewing each member of the panel in preparation for a preliminary discussion, to fix areas to be included in the content of the broadcast.
3) On the basis of individual preliminary talks with the participants on the program, tentatively suggesting what shall be the high points of discussion.
4) Planning the first meeting of all of the participating discussants, making sure that each has received a proposed preliminary content outline of points to be included in the broadcast.
5) Taking ample notes during the first group run-through, thus being able to return to the second preliminary broadcast session with the discussants to effectively finalize an agreed-upon content-approach to the problem under discussion.
6) Determining with the participants the art and graphics materials needed to heighten the visual effectiveness of the program. It must be noted here that most discussion programs, as done today, would be equally effective if aired by radio. One major point of TV effectiveness is the visual impact of the personality of the discussant on the viewer. To simply turn a camera on a discussion, because the place of origin is a television studio, is to make less than complete and adequate use of the medium for heightening understanding.
7) Preparing for the final "warm-up" discussion period — which should desirably take place immediately before the broadcast — and planning a ten-minute period between the warm-up and the actual on-the-air discussion.

Routine sheet and visual materials

The producer must prepare the following materials for use by the director:

1) A complete routining sheet. The routining sheet, which acts as a guide to the director and is used in annotated form by the moderator, will have the following form and parts:

THE ROUTINING SHEET FOR A DISCUSSION PROGRAM

INTRODUCTION to the program. This should be fully scripted and accurately timed.

OPENING This is fully scripted and accurately timed. It introduces the subject, *briefly*. The opening provides for an introduction to each member of the panel. *Don't* (as is the usual practice) have your panel member sit there, saying nothing, staring vacuously into the camera, while an overvoice describes how outstanding he is because of what he has done or accomplished. *Do* try to involve the discussant in helping to give some of the background about himself. *Don't* concentrate on the past too long. *Remember,* the good producer wants to get to the discussion as soon as possible.

SEGMENT 1 Note that most discussion programs will conveniently break into three segments — the usual number of segments to be found in most communications, whether good letters, stories, dramas, public addresses, classroom presentations by teachers, or well-organized broadcasts. This should be semi-scripted and in outline form for the points to be covered. SEGMENT 1 should conveniently lead to a . . .

LINK This should be fully scripted. It may be:
(a) a summary of SEGMENT 1, or
(b) a transitional statement leading to SEGMENT 2, or
(c) a combination of both, an internal summary as
described in (a) above, and (b) above.

SEGMENT 2 Again, semi-scripted and outlined as in SEGMENT 1. SEGMENT 2 differs from SEGMENT 1 in that it represents a high development or exploration of points introduced under SEGMENT 1. SEGMENT 2 leads naturally to the next . . .

LINK In form, this is the same as the first LINK, above. Its purposes are also the same, namely, to summarize SEGMENT 2, to act as a transition to SEGMENT 3, or both.

SEGMENT 3 This is semi-scripted and outlined, as are the previous segments, and the points covered are the major points of the discussion. In this segment we bring the discussion to its highest point and conclude it. This leads to our last . . .

LINK which is a transitional statement, only. The transitional statement (*fully* scripted) leads to a . . .

SUMMARY AND CONCLUSION This is the final wrap-up summary, or an internal summary, or a concluding statement for the entire content of the discussion, or all of these.

PROGRAM CLOSE This concludes the program, thanks the guests, contains a statement preparing for the next discussion program, and gives the credits.

2) The producer should indicate, clearly, the places in the routining sheet

in which art, graphics, visuals, stills, clips — visual inserts of any kind — are to be incorporated, and should see to their execution.

3) At least one part of a discussion can advantageously use multiple graphics to aid the understanding of difficult statistical points. A variety of stills, slides or a combination of these may be used in well-organized succession.

4) There should be at least one three-dimensional artifact used in the program. This lends visual variety and can provide a focus for carefully delineated consideration and clarification through visualization.

The above requirements for visuals for a discussion should be regarded not as a definitive list, but as a listing to stimulate the thought and outlook of the producer. With such a list in hand the producer will consciously seek, throughout the pre-broadcast discussions, to find ways to more effectively use the television medium to disseminate the information and philosophical attitudes of the panel.

Production Techniques

Just as one cannot legislate good citizenship, one cannot dictate the production level to be sought by the honest, thorough-going, involved and concerned producer of the discussion program.

Certain standard methods of physical juxtaposition of panel members in a studio setup have evolved over the years. Most panel discussions are two camera presentations. One camera must be used as a "cover" camera. The other must be kept completely mobile and, at the discretion of the director, able to go to individual panel members or to the moderator as they move from content point to content point. An aid to the director in predetermining the shots he will take is the routing sheet and its indications of a particular panel member's contributions on a particular point.

An important aspect of graphics preparation is identification boards or slides used for each member of the panel; customarily there is a small name-identification visual on the table area in front of each discussant. Usually, a last name is sufficient. Frequently, it will be preceeded by the abbreviation of a title such as "Dr.," "Prof.," or the like. It is usually advantageous to prepare a slide which can be "supered" in a medium shot over the discussant, identifying him at key points in the panel discussion. At the beginning of the program, as the camera goes from one member of the group to the other during the introduction, the name is supered over the lower part of a medium shot of the guest. During key points in the discussion itself, the name of the discussant is supered over a medium shot of him — particularly when he may be presenting more than two or three points on the topic under consideration.

Finally, the routing sheet should contain an estimated timing of each segment and a specific timing for all fully scripted portions of the program.

The timing elements for the "wrap up" at the end of the program will give the director an opportunity (by means of hand signals or an intercom voice signal to the floor director) to convey to the moderator precisely how much time he has left to finalize his discussion, make adequate identification at the end of the program and insert promos or commercials.

Summary

The obligations of the producer in relation to a discussion program are, then, the following:

1) He must identify the particular content to be discussed, its timeliness, and its application to the interest of his viewers.
2) He must identify and commit to both preparation and broadcast, the authorities to be used on a discussion program.
3) He must hold preparatory individual conferences with his participants to elicit from them information expressing their attitudes on the content to be discussed, and background related to each discussant and his expertise in the subject area.
4) He must prepare, first, a rough outline; second, a more detailed outline; and third, a routining sheet of points to be covered, indicated timings for the discussion, the links between segments, internal summaries, final summary, introduction and wrap up of the program.
5) He must work closely with his art and graphics people on conceptions of photographic, three-dimensional, slide, film and other material that may enhance the content presentation as well as provide as much visual interest as can be achieved by such a program.
6) He must work closely with his engineers in seeing to it that there is adequate in-studio preparation and set-up for the broadcast, taking into account close association with the director in the lighting, camera angles, and microphone coverage problems of the broadcast.

THE DRAMA

Before we can arrive at a full understanding of the total range of the television producer's responsibilities, one more primary program type must be considered: the television drama.

Contrast with other types

Because of its very nature, the drama presents more possibility for imaginative and interpretive production skill than any other program type. It may be argued that the "variety" or "magazine" program type has the advantage of greater latitude in conceiving various portions of the program. One might plan a dance presentation in one part, a specialty act in another.

But once the determination of a particular act or performing artist is made, little interpretive latitude or production skill remains to be exercised. The director of the variety program plans the creative aspects of sound and picture. In the musical program much depends upon the ability and musical training of the performers and the conductor or upon the compositions that form the content of the program. In the discussion program the personalities of the discussants, the expertise they have in relation to the subject-content, and their general enthusiasm in conveying information and insights determine the success of the broadcast. The producer of the drama, however, has the opportunity to mold each element of the presentation, changing interpretation, controlling the elements of bridge music, picture and sound, and working with the writer until over-all desired effect is achieved.

As in the news and discussion program types thus far discussed, the drama broadcast product is frequently affected by whether the producer of the drama is also the director. For the purposes of this chapter, let us assume that the producer and the director of the drama program are *not* the same individual.

Procedure

What are the responsibilities of the producer of the drama broadcast? In this respect we are not discussing the daily drama serial, but the full-length original script or dramatic adaptation, usually the once-a-week presentation, a half-hour or an hour or more in length, and a story or dramatic unit that is completed at the time of broadcast with no carry-over of story line to a subsequent broadcast time.

The producer's first step is either to read the script under consideration for broadcast, or to commission an original or adaptation script to be written. If the script is to be commissioned, the producer must determine what type of play it shall be — comedy, drama, deep tragedy, or possibly a dramatic semi-documentary. The answer to this question will depend very much upon what audience the producer has in mind, the time of day of the broadcast, and the sponsor — if there is sponsorship. In educational television broadcasting the answer will depend upon whether we are trying to do direct instructional programming, general informational programming, broad cultural programming, or presenting part of a total series that offers a continuity of insights to a particular event (or events) in a period of history — as does a semi-documentary or documentary.

Once we know the kind of drama, we can determine who shall be asked to write the script. Like skilled artisans in any art or craft, writers, by disposition, outlook, ability and opportunity, tend to specialize. The skilled documentarian will have a highly developed sense of research ability and (frequently) training in one or more aspects of historical scholarship, and an intuitive sense of characterization analysis for the important and common personalities of the past.

Once the script is completed, the detailed work of production planning begins. If the producer of the dramatic program is not the director, the determination of who shall direct the program will have to be made almost at the same time that the writer has been assigned to script the presentation. The producer and the director will work closely together as determinations are made as to who, how many, and what kinds of support shall be needed on the production team to back up the director in the studio.

Analyzing the script

What happens when the producer finally has his script in hand? First, he gives the script a quick, complete, uncritical reading. In this first reading, the producer is interested in one thing and one thing only. He is seeking the same reaction he would expect from a viewer who will see and hear the drama for the first time. When the first reading is completed, only one question should occur to the producer: "will the listener *appreciate* it?" This is a little different from the question, "will the listener *like* it?" Depending upon the nature of the script, it is not always important that the viewer *like* it. Does the drama capture the viewer's interest? Does it hold his attention from beginning to end? Does it fulfill the objective for which it was written — that is, does it move the viewer to action, to a new point of view, or does it attract attention and bring about a phase of new consideration and ideas in the viewer's mind?

Now the producer is ready for the crucial question, "shall the script be produced?" If it is to be produced, are changes needed? If so, what kind? To arrive at a determination of whether the script shall be produced and if so, with or without changes, a critical analysis is important. The following are questions the producer could well raise as a basis for determining the desirability for producing the script in hand:

1) Can the entire drama be produced as written? Is there complicated action which cannot be readily understood by the viewers? Should any of the dialogue be rewritten? Are all the scenes necessary? Do all the scenes contribute to the over-all structure of the drama? Does the drama fit the allowed broadcast time?

    At this point, the individual who will direct the script on the air should be brought in to read it, to discuss it with the producer, and to aid in making determinations on further questions, below.

    If the script looks like it is precisely right in timing, yet should subsequent rehearsals prove it overlong, where shall cuts be made? The writer should be consulted as to suggested script cuts. Are any of the speeches too long to be handled by an actor?

2) Are time and place in all scenes clearly delineated? The delineation must be in the form of readily identifiable sound effects, visuals, graphics, and/or scenic execution. Scene settings must be clearly defined in terms of visuals, music and/or sound.

3) Is there sufficient visual, sound and music support of reaction? Is there too much?
4) The plot, characters, dialogue, exposition, motivation for entrances and exits, and immediate presentation of the interest-holding conflict at the beginning of the drama must reflect the principles of writing the good and effective television play, as delineated in Chapter 4 of this book.

At this point, the producer and director must minutely examine all places where transitions are needed — from scene to scene, from character to character. Indeed, the transitions from a scene to a commercial announcement are of particular importance in commercial television. Although commercial transitions are frequently considered the province of the writer, ideally they should be decided upon jointly by the director, the producer and the writer. If an advertising agency is involved and has indicated that it wants commercials in specific number and in specific places during the time sequence, such request should be honored wherever possible. Much of the time, slight rewriting for timing or for making a smooth and integrated transition with the drama can be readily achieved.

The producer does exercise certain prerogatives over script changes. He may make these without consultation with the writer if he wishes. They should always be made in consultation with the director so the director will understand precisely what the producer has in mind. Sometimes the addition of music, sound or visual support or the subtraction of these are made by the producer to fit his all-over production idea and concept. Sometimes changes are dictated by budget limitations. For all of these reasons, the producer, in consultation with the director, may make certain transitional changes or small cuts when necessary for timing purposes — or he may delegate the making of such cuts entirely to the director. First option for script changes must go to the original writer, but if he refuses, rewrites may be done by the producer or director or whomever they designate.

Analyzing the production needs

The producer's answers to major questions concerning the program provide the bases for understanding the approach to solving the drama program's production needs.
1) What is the aim of the program? The purpose of most dramatic programs is either to inform, entertain or educate. Sometimes drama programs will attempt to do more than one of these at the same time; in any event, entertainment in the highest sense is always included.
2) What type of drama is this? The producer's answer to this question leads to several considerations.

Characterization. A delineation must be made between characterization in tragedy — which is thoughtful and slow and must be developed in greater detail for the audience — and in farce, in which the character approach is in terms of a rapid tempo and broad interpretation rather than thoughtful depth. Characterization determines the type of actor the producer and director will look for in casting any given part.

Production treatment. If the drama is tragedy, not only will characterization be more thoughtfully and slowly developed than in farce, but the director's entire pacing will be more deliberate, building to a climax that resolves all the tragic implications indicated in the plot. This very pacing will determine the type of scene-setting, the kind of incidental and background music, the types of transitions, the whole artistic approach to visuals. Conversely, farce will be at a fast pace and the entire production slanted toward rapid exchange of dialogue — in many instances, for gag value — and very much in the manner of farce techniques so well known in the theatre. The important influence in determining production pacing relates directly back to budget considerations. The kind of artistic approach necessary for drama, the kinds of settings this will produce, the entire way in which music shall be composed or sought for in transitions or for backing sequences — all will be directly influenced by the budget for the program.

Interpretation. Although the final on-the-air interpretation of any drama script lies, for execution, wholly within the hands of the director of the drama, the producer must nevertheless indicate clearly, succinctly and with no equivocation to the selected director, precisely the kind of interpretation he has in mind, why he has this in mind, and the way in which he sees this influencing the whole dramatic outlook that the director will bring about. To the extent that the director understands precisely what it is the producer wants, interpretation in terms of taste, good sense and cohesiveness will be achieved. Where the producer and the director are in disagreement as to interpretation, these disagreements must be resolved before rehearsals get under way. Should these disagreements develop during rehearsals, they must again be resolved on a mutually professional basis of understanding. In all cases, the final arbiter of what the interpretation shall be must be the producer. It is up to the director to deliver this. It is also up to the director to have a depth of understanding of the producer's interpretative desire. Only with such interpretation and depth can the director properly motivate his actors to produce the results sought.

3) What is the setting of the play? On the face of it, this may seem like an ambiguous question. However, determining the exact locale is a matter of agreement between the producer and the director. On the determination of such locale will depend the budget allocation for the particular setting desired. For example, it is not enough that the producer, working with the director, shall have as a setting "a street cor-

ner." It must be a particular street corner in a particular city before the exact locale can be achieved in scenic design and construction. Once the locale is determined, the next question is, "where precisely is the audience's place in the scene?" Is the viewer with the main character in the scene or does he have a perspective of what is going on from, for example, the vantage point of a traffic policeman in an outdoor setting at the corner of, let us say, 5th Avenue and 42nd Street. The director is responsible for the details of clarity which will move an audience within a scene from one point to another, or from one scene to another. On transitional devices — whether these are visual, or in terms of sound effects, music or dialogue, or some combination of all of these — will depend the quickness and clarity with which the viewers will move from one locale to another.

4) What methods of transition will be used? Naturally, the methods of transition will depend upon the type of drama and the kinds of scenes involved. Budget, too, will be a factor in deciding upon the transitional device. On a low budget program, for example, it might be necessary to dissolve to a still shot, with background music and background sound effects making the transition. It might be necessary to go to an in-limbo (a non-representational background) presentation to achieve the transition. In any case, the transitional device must be clearly established and followed through in execution, in terms of music, sound, narration, arts and graphics.

5) How shall the drama be cast? Factors such as the following will influence the decisions: the number of characters in the drama; whether a "name" actor is to be used; whether, because of the large number of parts or the peculiarity of character types, auditions must be held. Until the main characters are cast, minor or supporting roles should not be. Much will depend upon a balancing of acting talents, voices, physical types, and contrast of such types.

6) What are the production staff requirements? For the most part, dramatic programs require the following: engineers; an announcer or narrator; a music director and orchestra, or organist, or record engineer — depending upon the music to be used and whether the budget will allow for original scoring; sound effects personnel; arts and graphics personnel; studio construction personnel; and other standard studio and technical persons. If the program is part of a regular series, it will usually have a fairly fixed cast with permanent leads, and with only minor characters changing.

7) What are the studio needs? At this point, based on budget, the producer must make his decision on the following: How many microphones and cameras will be used? What kind and amount of sound equipment is needed? What are the accommodations for the size of the cast? Do the director and the engineer have line-of-sight to all

studio elements from the control room? If not, are studio elements placed in such a position that these are readily controllable and viewable through the use of monitors in the control room? In setting up his studio plan, the director working with the producer must be ready with alternative plans should changes be necessary because of budget, because of set construction, or because of the non-availability of specific kinds of studio space.

8) What are the special effects problems, if any? For example, there may be video or sound effects never before used which require special experimentation. Frequently, such experimentation must be carried out in conjunction with the Engineering Department in order to achieve the effect desired. Occasionally, the special effects problems may involve special orchestration or require a highly specialized original underscoring. Whatever the problem may be, it is frequently up to the producer, in conjunction with the director, to work with the particular departmental chief or chiefs under whom the total effect needs to be worked out.

9) How much rehearsal time is needed for this broadcast? Naturally, the amount of rehearsal time required is entirely in the hands of both the producer and the director. Only one stipulation needs to be made. The broadcast must be prepared so as to hit the air at the scheduled broadcast time on the scheduled day. We must recognize that the producer and the director of the drama program, who work for a product of superiority, will never believe that the rehearsal time has been sufficient. Apart from striving for this ideal, however, the following factors determine the amount of rehearsal time that should be planned: If a cast is large, it will take more time to rehearse a program than if the cast is a small one. The complexity and amount of sound and visual patterns sought are determining factors for the amount of rehearsal time needed. Video and sound routines employing standard materials, however, are not difficult to rehearse nor do they necessarily require a great deal of time. Original background music will take more time to rehearse than music which is standard. It is generally conceded that the amount of required in-studio rehearsal time for the average well-produced drama program is roughly 15 to 20 times the length of the broadcast. Each program presents its own time complications, however, when it comes to setting a rehearsal schedule. It is frequently better to overestimate rather than have a production suffer because of insufficient amount of rehearsal time.

Summary

What may we best say about the producer of the drama program and the way in which he approaches his production needs? In reading the script, he looks for particular things — interest aroused at the opening, whether all characters are necessary, whether time and place are clearly delineated, whether all audio, video and music references in the script are necessary to the action, whether there is a definite progression from minor to major climaxes, whether the drama should be produced as written, whether entrances and exists are properly motivated and whether transitions satisfy the producer's and director's script treatment. The producer must then do the following:

1) See to the duplication of scripts in sufficient number to take care of the cast, engineers, announcing, production, video, sound and music, filing and publicity.

2) Requisition the staff. Final contracts must be drawn where these are necessary. As the producer gathers his studio staff, engineers and cameramen, he must also requisition audition and rehearsal space, as required.

3) Requisition studio equipment, including numbers and kinds of cameras, microphones and special effects devices. All of this must be planned well in advance, against a carefully worked out time schedule.

4) If one of the rehearsals is to be video-taped for analysis before going to the final dress rehearsal, this must be arranged for.

5) Set up the rehearsal sequence, including reading rehearsals, blocking rehearsals, the first microphone and dummy camera rehearsal (if required), the music cue rehearsal, the technical and camera rehearsal, the dress rehearsal, the spotting rehearsal.

6) Whenever possible, a second dress rehearsal should be scheduled. Under most conditions this is a luxury that is not often attainable.

As the producer approaches air time, there are a number of things he must do:

7) Check his script for last minute changes and confer on those changes with the personnel involved, including cameramen, floor director and video engineer.

8) At the last minute, rehearse the opening of the program to make sure that all of the elements are ready and in place. Make a final check with the floor director, the video engineer, the musical director or the music man, and the sound effects personnel.

9) Make a final microphone check.

10) Provide the announcer or narrator introducing the program with a last minute run-through.

OTHER PROGRAM TYPES

By-and-large, all that has thus far been described as the producer's duties and responsibilities, his pre-planning requirements, and detailed anticipation of in-studio and on-the-air needs, is applicable to all other program types. Some interesting variants that the producer is likely to meet, however, suggest a brief overview of other major program forms.

The Documentary Program

Documentaries generally fall into two major categories: the semi-documentary and the straight documentary. The semi-documentary allows greater latitude for creative approaches in concept and writing. It gives the producer, the director and the writer an opportunity to enlarge, in an imaginative way, on circumstances and persons of the past. It allows more freedom in interpretation — within the limitations of basic fact — and provides a means for bringing alive what could be factually dull if done as a sheer recital of researched material. The producer's responsibility is to provide, within budget limitations, the facilities and writing support necessary to accomplish the pre-determined objectives of such a program.

The pure or straight documentary requires ingenuity in researching files of known visual and audio materials of the past, accurate examination and cataloguing of such available materials, and a planned concept for use. All other production needs and requirements remain generally the same.

The Variety and Magazine Types

The variety and magazine types of programs may contain elements of news, discussions and interviews as well as featured performers, such as singers, instrumentalists or others. Many such programs include circus acts and similar types. The problems of the producer, while essentially the same as those previously discussed, may be minimized, depending upon the length of each segment of the program. One of the difficulties the producer faces with the variety or magazine type is that, if his budget is more or less standard, he may in many instances be forced to settle for other than "name" talent. He must learn how to find and judge new talent from night clubs, off-Broadway theatres and other sources.

Women's Programs

Women's programs tend to follow the magazine format. They usually contain special features, a cooking insert, a fashion segment, and special news materials. The fashion segment may include interviews with outstanding women in the field. Special and news features may relate to the Red Cross, Community Chest, local public service campaigns and similar efforts. Women's programs can frequently have dramatic inserts. Sometimes these are filmed in advance, sometimes not.

Children's Programs

Children's programs present altogether different problems and indeed would require a separate chapter for comprehensive analysis. The producer of these programs requires special background, experience and training. A perusal of *Television and the Child,* by Himmelweit, Oppenheim and Vince, and of *For the Young Viewer,* by Garry, Rainsberry and Winnick (see bibliography) provide special insights into this problem.

The Dramatic Serial

Some differences between the handling of the regular drama program and that of the serial-drama permit a shortening of time in preparing the latter. In many instances there is a continuity of cast, crew and other production personnel and facilities, reducing the amount and kind of pre-rehearsal work. First rehearsals are usually a combination of blocking and reading. Frequently, these may take place before dummy cameras and either dummy or live mikes. On the serial-drama program, sound and music are brought together in the rehearsal immediately following the blocking rehearsal. Sometimes these elements are not combined until the final "dress," just before video-taping or going on the air. There should always be a run-through for timing of the announcer's opening and close, as well as for any commercials that may be used. Basically, the producer makes no distinction between the regular drama and serial-drama when it comes to an adherence to principles of organization, pre-planning, budgeting and the like.

One may end this chapter on a note of unwholesome gloom, looking through the crystal ball of impossibility at the tasks that the television producer faces. One might shrug and say that the whole thing is impossible; that surely, there must be a better way to earn a living; surely, one has the right to enjoy a professional existence that doesn't lead to ulcers — the long-accepted hazard of the television profession — fallen arches, prematurely graying hair, sippy diets, or the early collapse of the lungs from the overuse of tobacco and hard liquor as professional tranquilizers. But if we pass this professional way only once in our lives, we have a right to expect something more than the mundane, the utterly and reliably dull, dependent things in life. If professionalism cannot bring an air of excitement and constant inconsistency — if we cannot each day turn a new corner and find a whole new set of challenging and interesting circumstances to cope with, what are we doing in broadcasting to begin with?

The maturation of the whole man — or woman — through professionalism is in itself a growth in learning along a continuum of constant education. Let us not hold a flag-of-cause for the Alice-in-Wonderland way of professional life. We must remember that the way for the producer can be one of excitement in outlook, fullness in accomplishment, and rich in personal satisfaction for each positive goal achieved.

BIBLIOGRAPHY

Barnouw, Erik, *Mass Communication.* New York: Rinehart and Co., 1956. The portions on the history and the psychology of mass communications are necessary basic information for the television producer.

CBS News Staff, *Television News Reporting.* New York: McGraw-Hill Book Co., Inc., 1958. An excellent analysis in depth for organizing the news program and staff.

Garry, Ralph, F. B. Rainsberry and Charles Winnick, editors, *For The Young Viewer.* New York: McGraw-Hill Book Co., Inc., 1962. Contains examples of children's programming and basic information on planning.

Himmelweit, A. Hilde T., N. Oppenheim and Pamela Vince, *Television And The Child.* London: Oxford University Press, 1958. A definitive study, well researched and documented, on children and their reactions to television.

Krulevitch, Rome and Walter Krulevitch, *Radio Drama Production: A Handbook.* New York: Rinehart and Co., 1946. A detailed text spelling out methods and procedures in producing the radio drama.

Lazarsfeld, Paul and Robert K. Merton, "Mass Communication, Popular Taste and Organized Social Action," in *Mass Culture, The Popular Arts in America,* edited by Bernard Rosenberg and David Manning White. Glencoe, Ill.: The Free Press, 1957. Pp. 457-473. A must for insights to the many aspects of communication theory, practice and psychological investigation.

Lewis, Philip, *Educational Television Guidebook.* New York: McGraw-Hill Book Co., Inc., 1961. A definitive compilation of information on all aspects of preparing the educational telecast. Contains good, basic technical information and case studies.

Millerson, Gerald, *The Technique of Television Production.* New York: Hastings House, Publishers, Inc., 1961. Informative, and with detailed diagrammatic illustrations. Thorough analyses of why production decisions are made.

Stasheff, Edward and Rudy Bretz, *The Television Program.* New York: Hill and Wang, 1962. Excellent illustrations and charts; emphasis on camera techniques.

"Theatre on Television," in *World Theatre,* Vol. IX, No. 4 (Winter, 1960). A compendium of international thought and reports on producing and directing the drama for television.

ROBERT L. HILLIARD

*Associate Professor of Radio, Television and Motion Pictures,
University of North Carolina at Chapel Hill*

●Within six months of its publication by Hastings House in 1962, Dr.
Hilliard's *Writing for Television and Radio* became the leading work of
its kind — as a text in colleges and universities, as a reference book for
professionals and laymen, and in circulation throughout many countries in
other parts of the world. *Understanding Television* is Dr. Hilliard's third
book, and he has published more than 20 articles on communications and
education in professional journals and is co-author of a monograph on
educational television in New York. He has been active in both the commercial and educational mass media fields as a writer, director and
producer, has been the recipient of several playwriting awards and has had
his plays produced in university and community theatres. His newspaper
background includes five years as drama critic for the *Brooklyn Daily*.
Dr. Hilliard received the B.A. degree from the University of Delaware,
where he majored in philosophy and political science, the M.A. and
M.F.A. degrees from Western Reserve University and the Ph. D. degree
from Columbia University. He began his teaching career in 1950 at Brooklyn College, subsequently taught at Adelphi University, and is now Associate Professor and Director of Radio and of Closed-circuit Television,
Department of Radio, Television and Motion Pictures, University of North
Carolina at Chapel Hill. He has been active as a speaker and panelist on
the communications media and prominent in professional associations.
His offices include those of Chairman of the Radio-Television-Film Group
of the Southern Speech Association, Chairman of the Educational Television Committee of the Southeastern Theatre Conference and past Chairman of the Television Project of the American Educational Theatre
Association. In 1963 he was on leave from the University of North Carolina to serve as a consultant on television in higher education for New
York State.

etails

ction to broadcasting. Edited by Robert L.

play

4

WRITING

BY ROBERT L. HILLIARD

THE MASS MEDIA of television and radio are potentially the
the most powerful forces in modern civilization for communicating ideas
and impressions to the minds and emotions of the people of the world. The
most important element in the mass communication process is the script.
The writer who has something to say and knows how to put his ideas into
the proper and most effective form can have great influence and, if he
wishes, make a contribution of infinite value.

From a vocational point of view, relatively few job opportunities exist
today for the serious television playwright. The jobs available in the broadcast media for writers are most frequently found among the program types
which exist on local as well as network levels, including news, sports, talks
programs of various kinds, panel-games-audience participation shows, wom-
en's and children's programs, music and variety shows, special features and,
sometimes, documentaries. The writing of announcements and commercials
offers probably the widest employment channel. That is not to say that there
is not drama in television; there is and some of it is good. All potential television writers should learn the art of dramatic writing, for it provides a base
for all other forms of writing.

In order for the writer to know what he can or cannot do in any given
script, he should understand the potentials and limitations of television, including time, space, audience, subject matter, and audio and video effects
possible with cameras, including sound, music, visual devices, control room

119

techniques, and other mechanical and electronic forms. Careful study and critical evaluation of programs seen on television are invaluable to the writer.

Audience

The audience of the mass media is as varied as is the population of the United States. To make any single piece of material effective, the writer often is told that he must find a common denominator which will reach and hold as many as possible of the groups and individuals watching television or listening to radio. The sponsor and producer usually search for and often find the broadcast common denominator, which frequently turns out to be the lowest. Because of the disparity of the mass media audience, its lack of selectivity, its distraction by the everyday surroundings of the home, and the constant presence of competing programs, the writer must make every word in his script purposeful and pertinent so as to gain and hold the attention and interest of the viewer and listener as soon as possible. Television is unique in that it may combine many of the best techniques of radio, the theatre and the film, including radio's ability — through complete control over what stimulus the audience receives — to orient the audience to any setting or to a specific physical relationship to a given character; the ability of the theatre to present the sustained, rising intensity of a live, continuous performance; and the ability of the film through electronic techniques to emphasize close-up and other subjective aspects of the script's content. The television writer is limited primarily by time, both in program length and rehearsal, and by space, in terms of the comparatively small viewing screen and the sizes of most television studios. Television may provide subjective orientation for the audience through the use of the close-up to direct it toward a specific stimulus; at the same time, television can achieve non-illusionary or objective relationships by having a performer address himself directly to the audience.

Subject Matter

Censorship is an issue of critical importance to the writer. In almost all instances program content is controlled by the sponsor. Most sponsors will censor any given piece of material if they feel it may in any way displease any potential customer anywhere. Material that is of a controversial nature, whether it pertains to political, religious, social, economic or other problems, usually is censored. Many sponsors not only object to material that they believe may in some way alienate a customer or damage the image of their product or company, but they frequently censor material because of personal prejudices. Another form of censorship relates not only to controversial material, but to material that is considered in bad taste. Profanity, for example, falls into this category. Many networks and stations have their own codes. Many subscribe to the Television Code of the National Association of Broadcasters. Although the practical considerations of keeping a job in television may require the writer to conform to the censorship restrictions of the industry, it is hoped that conscience will permit him to maintain his responsibility to the public at large.

Production Elements

In order to write effectively, the writer must know the elements of production that directly affect writing techniques. Chapters 2, 5 and 6 of this book present various technical and directing techniques with which the writer should be familiar. Camera movement, including the dolly, pan, tilt, follow shot and boom shot, may change the position, angle, distance and amount of subject matter the writer can show. In order to designate the amount of subject matter to be seen on the television screen, the writer must indicate the kind of shot to be used, including the close-up (CU), medium shot (MS), long shot (LS), and combinations and variations thereof. The writer must also be prepared to state the kinds of transitions or special picture modifications necessary in his script, including the fade, dissolve, super, wipe and split screen. He must remember that in this visual medium the designation of a visual effect and what it suggests to the viewer is as important as the writing of dialogue. The writer should also know, to a lesser extent, the advantages and restrictions of studio size, camera lens openings, special video effects such as titles, miniatures and projection machines, and television adaptations of sound.

ANNOUNCEMENTS AND COMMERCIALS

Word counts sometimes may be used to determine time lengths for straight verbal messages. Approximate counts are: 10 seconds—25 words; 20 seconds—45 words; 30 seconds—65 words; 45 seconds—100 words; 60 seconds—125 words; 90 seconds—190 words; 120 seconds—250 words. Where visual action takes up time, a word-count scale is difficult to apply. Although the ID, or station identification, is literally simply an announcement of the call letters of the station, it frequently includes, in its 10-second length, an 8-second commercial spot. Public service announcements — provided by health organizations, educational associations and welfare groups, among others, to stations that may have some unsold station time when these announcements may be inserted — do not, in the strict sense, sell a product. Nevertheless, they do attempt to persuade the viewer to support some cause and, in that sense, must follow the purposes and principles of writing good commercials while at the same time being in good taste and appealing to the audience's highest attitudes and feelings. Some public service announcements may be oriented toward specific types of programs or around special occasions, such as holidays, but most are general in nature, such as the following:

20-SECOND TV ANNOUNCEMENT

VIDEO	AUDIO
SLIDE NO. 2 (BE HEART-SMART)	The Lost Colony's population in 1587 was 118, before it vanished mysteriously. In North Carolina last year, 21,000 persons died from heart disease—"a Lost Colony of Heart casualties every 48 hours." The North Carolina Heart Association urges regular "Health and Heart Checkups" for you. See your physician.
	Courtesy of North Carolina Heart Association.

Writing Techniques for Commercials

At one time the art of persuasion was practiced primarily in speech-making. Today it is effected largely through the writing of broadcast commercials. The relationship between the two can be found in the application of Aristotle's principles of rhetoric. Aristotle noted three appeals: logical, ethical and emotional. The three, particularly the last one, emotional, apply to the writing of commercials today. An emotional appeal is not used to make one laugh or cry; rather, it plays on the basic needs and wants of the person or persons to whom it is addressed. Analyze the next few commercials you hear or see. You will notice that in all probability they will appeal to the non-intellectual, non-logical aspects of the prospective customer's personality. The automobile commercial, for example, most often appeals to the need for power and prestige. Most commercials are not so overt, however, and the good writer uses subtlety in making his appeal. Other basic emotional appeals are self-preservation, love of family, patriotism, good taste, reputation, religion, loyalty to a group and conformity to public opinion.

In order to use appeals effectively, the writer must know his audience as intimately as possible. Because the audience of the mass media is so diverse, accurate analysis is almost impossible. However, depending on the content of the program being sponsored and the location and coverage of the station, the writer can come to some conclusions concerning the needs and wants of his audience. Before writing the commercial, the writer should attempt to determine, as far as possible, the following about his potential audience: age, sex, size, economic level, political orientation, primary interests, occupation, fixed attitudes or beliefs, educational level, knowledge of the product, and geographical concentration.

The five steps in persuasive technique (Dewey's, Borden's, and those of any recognized authority who has examined the subject are similar in almost all instances) are found in the organization of the well-written commercial. These steps, in chronological order, are: a) get attention, b) hold interest, c) create an impression that a problem of some sort exists, d) plant an idea of how the problem may be solved, and e) get action — in this instance, the purchase of the product. An analysis of the commercial script below delineates the five steps of persuasion. Attention is achieved through a combination of humor, a novel situation and a startling statement — when Bud Collyer indicates that he is going to play the part of a housewife and has an apron tied onto him. The visual picture continues the interest of the audience, as does the statement which describes the meal. The impression that a problem exists (the picture and statement also contribute to the holding of the audience's interest) is made clear by the appearance of the dirty, sprouting potatoes and Collyer's discovery that the entire bag is sprouting, making preparation of the dinner impossible. The question "So, *now* what do we do?" leads into the step in which it is disclosed that the problem can be solved by the use of the sponsor's product. The film clip demonstrating the use of the product, with Collyer's voice-over explanation, confirms the value of the product. The final step in persuasion is made with the display of the package and the appeals in Collyer's concluding statement. (The Roman numerals I through V designate the five steps; this is not done, of course, by the writer or director, but is used here for illustrative purposes; the Arabic numbers 1 through 6 on the original commercial script refer to the video sequences for production purposes.)

VIDEO	AUDIO
COLLYER STILL WITH CONTESTANTS. AS HE CROSSES OVER TO TABLE SET UP FOR FIP COMMERCIAL.	COLLYER (ON CAMERA) And now — let's have a little real-life Sunday dinner drama. I'm playing the part of the housewife. I
- -	- -
I 1. COLLYER AT TABLE. MADELINE II OR BETTY TIES PRACTICAL, COVER-UP APRON ON HIM. III TABLE HAS TWO SACKS ON IT. ONE CONTAINS SPROUTING POTA-TOES (DIRTY). THE OTHER (WITH BOTTOM CUT OUT) CONTAINS BOX OF FIP.	COLLYER: We're having roast beef II and brown gravy for dinner. And at <u>our</u> house . . . that means <u>mashed potatoes</u>! So . . .
2. REACHES IN BAG AND PULLS OUT SPROUTING POTATO. POTATO IS DIRTY SO THAT DUST OR DIRT CAN BE BRUSHED OFF WHEN COLLYER HANDLES SPUD. THEN ANOTHER.	What's this??? A potato tree! Oh, III no! The whole bag's sprouting! So, <u>now</u> what do we do?
IV 3. TAKES OFF APRON. BETTY OR MADELINE PUTS CUTE, HALF-APRON ON HIM.	We <u>change aprons</u> and be a <u>smart</u> IV housewife who . . .

4. YANKS OFF SACK TO REVEAL BOX OF FIP.	uses New French's Instant Mashed Potato! Because French's are made from perfect, selected <u>Idaho</u> potatoes. No waste! No storage problem! Just delicious mashed potatoes <u>every time.</u> Watch!
5. FILM CLIP - 20-SEC. #20070- "DEMO-FINISHED FIP." DEMON- STRATION SHOWING MILK BEING POURED INTO BOILING WATER. FIP POURED FROM FOIL ENVEL- OPE INTO LIQUID WHILE FORK STIRS. MASHED POTATOES FORM BEFORE YOUR EYES. DISH OF MASHED POTATOES. HAND COMES IN AND PLACES PAT OF BUTTER.	COLLYER (VOICE OVER): All you do is add milk to boiling water — stir in French's Instant Mashed Potato . . . and whip 'em up! Like that—you have fluffy, Sunday-dinner mashed potatoes. In <u>seconds,</u> they're creamy-smooth and ready to serve. Enough for 8 hungry people.
V 6. COLLYER WITH BOX. POINTS TO POTATO ON BOX.	Let your family just <u>taste</u> New V French's Instant Mashed Potato and you'll never peel another potato for Sunday dinner!

<u>Courtesy of the R. T. French Company</u>

It is important for the writer to try to keep the commercial in good taste. It should be sincere, direct and simple. It should fit the personality of the performer delivering it. It should be grammatically correct. In persuasion, action words are very effective. Important ideas should be repeated, usually in different words or phrases unless the writer wishes to present a slogan. Avoid false claims and superlatives; in some instances pressures are put upon the writer to write in that manner. Commercials follow trends and fads, as do program types. For example, in the late 1950's and early 1960's satire, sophisticated humor and the family-type commercial were popular.

The Story Board

The TV "story board" shows the sponsor what the commercial will look like on the screen. Along with the script the advertising agency develops a series of sketches which show, step by step, what visual picture will accompany each item of dialogue. The story board (pp. 126-127) of the Piel commercial with Bob and Ray is an example of the combination dramatization and humorous-satirical commercial format and of the non-realistic action physical form.

Types of Commercials

The *ID* or station identification is a 10-second time period, within which may be the actual station identification and an 8-second announcement. A service announcement is a commercial which presents information of a public service nature, such as the time or weather, along with an advertising message. The 8-second announcement may also be a straight commercial. A *chain break* refers to the time available between the network identification and the local station identification; 20-second commercial films for television usually fill this spot. *Station breaks,* 42 seconds for television for a half-hour program and 72 seconds for an hour program, permit the insertion of the ID and one or more commercials. 20-second, 30-second and 60-second commercials are the lengths most often used. *Participating announcements* are those on programs which are unable or unwilling to get just one sponsor, and will use a number of participating advertisers who jointly share the cost of the entire program and whose commercial time varies in direct proportion to their share of program cost. *Program announcements* comprise the most frequently found type of commercial. When a single sponsor has an entire show, his commercials are called program announcements. Although there is great variation, depending on the sponsor and program format, a show usually has three program announcements — at the beginning, in the middle and at the end. Occasionally there are four commercials, divided into short opening and closing "billboards" and two insertions within the body of the program. *Cowcatcher* and *hitchhiker* are commercials for other products of the sponsor of a show, and are inserted just before the beginning of the program (but after the station break) and just after the program (but before the ensuing station break). *Co-op announcements* are sold by a network program on a local basis, with regional or local sponsors inserting their commercials through the local stations carrying the program at given time breaks within the program.

Formats

The *straight-sell* format is a simple, direct statement about the product. The straight-sell frequently uses a slogan or a gimmick that is repeated for a relatively long period — weeks, months and even years. The *educational* commercial usually uses logical, rather than emotional appeals, and reflects institutional as opposed to product advertising. The *testimonial* varies from the endorsement of a product by a celebrity to the asserted use of the product by ordinary people with whom the audience can most readily identify. *Humor* may vary from gentleness to outright satire. *Musical* commercials have long been popular. From the early jingle, musical commercials have developed in some instances into presentations by entire orchestras. *Dramatizations* are very effective, particularly if they can be incorporated into the action of the program itself. Through the use of the dramatization the writer can easily apply the five steps of persuasion by the solving of a problem by one or more of the characters involved in the action of the commercial.

SOUND: LAUGHING & JOKING OF GROUP

SOUND: BELL RINGS. THEY REACT WITH A
WHOOP.

BERT: Harry, if you've ruined this delicate
mechanism with your tom-foolery,
I'll...

HARRY: Gee, Bert, we just --

BERT: Well, that's about as well as Brand X
ever scores.

LIVE ACTION
_____

BERT: Don't see why--why, Harry, don't you
want folks to know how delicious our
beer is? It's the beer with the barrel
of flavor! Why, this machine proves
beyond a doubt how much more refreshing
Piels is!

HARRY: I still don't think people will believe
it till they taste it for themselves, Bert

BERT: I know, but-- (THE BELL RINGS AGAIN)
What the --

HARRY: I guess that's one piece we forgot
about, Bert.

BERT: Harry! What the devil are you doing!
Where did that toast come from?

HARRY: (EMBARRASSED) From your
Refresherometer, Bert.

BERT: What?! Why, this machine measures
the refreshment qualities of beer!

HARRY: Well, it seems that it makes pretty
good toast, too.

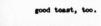

Here, here's the Piels. (BELL-
RINGING)

BERT: Seems to be all right, Bert. All
we did was...

BERT: Fortunately for you, Harry, we can
still prove that Piels is the most
refreshing beer of all time!

HARRY: Well, I don't see why you need the
machine for that, Bert.

BERT: It's burnt toast at that.

[REPRINTED WITH PERMISSION OF PIEL BROS., BROOKLYN, N.Y.]

Physical Forms

In radio the commercial may be either live or recorded (on record, tape or cartridge). In television, however, there are a number of approaches combining various potentials of the live, taped and filmed presentation. These are: live, with realistic action, talent in view and being heard; live, with voice-over narration; film, with realistic action; silent film, voice-over; film, with non-realistic action (such as animation); electronic and mechanical effects; and combinations of the preceding.

NEWS AND SPORTS

Any real happening that may have interest for people is news. In some instances the television and radio newswriter has to actually gather the material; in most instances he rewrites the material as it comes from newsgathering sources. Writing television and radio news is basically the same as writing newspaper news: the five W's, Who, What, When, Where and Why apply. Special considerations of the mass media, however, necessitate important modifications in their use.

Sources

In the networks and larger stations, news is obtained from the wire services and from special reporters and correspondents. The writer need only adapt and rewrite in terms of the special needs of the given news program. The television news writer must consider the availability of visual material, such as film clips and photos, to integrate with the written reports. In local stations a news writer may seek, write and deliver the news. In some instances a staff writer may do no more than prepare a basic format and leave the actual newswriting to a special staff.

Styles

The writer, in utilizing the 5 W's, must remember that the audience does not have an opportunity to go back and re-hear or re-see. The newspaper reader, of course, has the chance to re-read. News broadcast over the mass media must be presented concisely, clearly, simply and directly. Transitions between news segments should be smooth. The material should be thought of in terms of dramatic action, but at the same time should be scrupulously accurate. The nature of the mass media permits presentation of news almost as it happens, something that newspapers cannot do. The broadcaster is entering the home at all hours of the day, and the selection of material should be in keeping with the composition of the audience and their actions as far as can be determined by the writer. The criteria in the NAB codes concerning the treatment of news provide a good guide for the writer.

Broadcast Types and Content

The 5- and 15-minute straight news broadcasts are the most common. However, the writer may be required to prepare the same news material for other broadcast types, including the news analysis, the personal opinion of the news, the news in depth technique and the editorializing approach. The writer should be aware of whether he is really writing straight news or whether he is coloring it or orienting it toward a special purpose. In addition, there are special categories of news broadcasts, such as financial reports, garden news, women's news, campus news, and so forth.

Organization

The proper organization of the television news program is as important as an effective layout for the front page and the placement of stories on subsequent pages of a newspaper. No matter what special organization is used, the writer should be certain that it is clear and logical. News broadcasts are developed around one or a combination of several major organizational forms. In a geographical grouping, stories occurring in the same geographical location would be put together. Another grouping is in terms of size: international down to local, with the stories usually presented in that order. In a topical organization stories with similar subjects would be put together. Sometimes an entire news broadcast is organized around one major story of the day. The most commonly used approach is to put the most important story first and the others in descending order, as does the newspaper, and to divide the remaining stories of equal importance into international, national, state and local groupings.

Techniques

The physical setting as well as the news content is important. Television news may incorporate photographs, videotape, film, slides, inanimate objects or live guests. The visual aspects should be given as much importance as the aural, especially if the event reported is an action one and can be seen happening, rather than being described. Scripts usually have rundown sheets or time outlines of the stories and the visual effects to be used. Note, in the following rundown sheet and news script, the organization of stories, the style of writing, the time breakdown and the visual techniques used. The script included here on the next two pages is just a short excerpt.

Douglas Edwards with the News

October 17, 1961

1. Edwards	live	:40	:40
2. Goodyear	35/7	:15	:55
3. Kalb Congress scene setter	16/4, 16/2	1:35	2:30
4. Edwards	live	:15	2:45
5. Pierpoint and Lapp	RR/WTOP	2:30	5:15
6. Mudd and asst. civ. def. chief	RR/WTOP	1:30	6:45
7. Edwards	live	:10	6:55
8. Goodyear	35/7	1:30	8:25
9. Edwards	live	1:40	10:05
10. Ike politicking in Jersey	16/4	:40	10:45
11. Edwards	live	:10	10:55
12. Barker and Camel driver	VTR	1:15	12:10
13. Stox	live	:25	12:35
14. Goodyear	35/7	1:00	13:35
15. Edwards	live	:20	13:55
16. Goodyear	35/7	:15	14:10
17. credits	T/3	:05	14:15
18. system	T/3	:10	14:25

VIDEO	AUDIO
1. EDWARDS	Good evening everybody coast to coast, Douglas Edwards reporting.

Two weeks remain till the largest explosion ever set by the hand of man.

The hand will be that of a Russian.

And the decision is that of Nikita Khrushchev.

He announced today—the Russians will end their current series of nuclear tests by exploding a 50 megaton bomb on October 30th or 31st.

Fifty megatons—a power almost indescribable—equal to a force of 50 million tons of T-N-T.

Imagine—if you will—the first atomic bomb dropped on Hiroshima—a bomb that killed more than 78 thousand persons. Then imagine two and a half thousand Hiroshima bombs combined into one. There you would have the power of 50 megatons.

Khrushchev boasted the Russians can double that power. He declared: "We have a 100 million ton bomb, but we do not intend to explode it." Because—he said—"we might break our own windows."

The Soviet premier spoke at the opening of the 22nd Communist party congress.

Tonight—a look at Moscow—as that Communist meeting begins—and a study of the meaning of the big bomb.

Details of those stories in a moment.

2. GOODYEAR 35/7	COMMERCIAL
3. KALB 16/4, 16/2	CBS NEWS CORRESPONDENT MARVIN KALB FILM REPORT ON MOSCOW CONGRESS
4. EDWARDS	In some respects, Khrushchev's opening speech to those delegates was milder than many westerners had expected. Khrushchev did back down on his deadline for signing a German peace treaty. He said the deadline could be extended past the end of the year, providing the west is willing to negotiate.

The most spectacular news, though, was the announcement of that 50 megaton bomb.

Some reaction today in this country. Atomic scientist Dr. Ralph Lapp told CBS news correspondent Robert Pierpoint that Russians within a one million square mile area would have to be warned not to look at the explosion—or they might suffer eye damage. Lapp answered other questions in Washington. |
5. PIERPOINT RR/WTOP	PIERPOINT IN WASHINGTON INTERVIEWS LAPP.
6. MUDD RR/WTOP	DIRECT TO CORRESPONDENT ROGER MUDD INTERVIEWING CIVIL DEFENSE OFFICIAL.
7. EDWARDS	The X-15 rocket plane streaked its way to a new speed record today. That story in a moment—after this message from Goodyear.
8. GOODYEAR 35/7	COMMERCIAL
9. EDWARDS	Civilian test pilot Joe Walker regained his world speed record today. He flew the X-15 rocket plane at 3,920 miles an hour. Walker said later he could have flown even faster— but he followed instructions and lowered the tail flaps to act as a brake on the plane.

Former President Eisenhower stepped into a new controversy— while invoking an old image—in New Jersey. |

Sports

The straight sports news program is much like the straight regular news program except that in sports broadcasting one can use more colloquial phrases and technical terms, which are probably familiar to sports fans. Most sports news programs are of the recapitulation type which give results of contests. The most-important-to-least-important story approach usually is used, presenting the results first of the most important sport of the particular time of year and gradually working down to the coming events of the least important sport. Local sports news is coordinated with national sports news on most local stations. As with all news broadcasts, however, the most important story, regardless of the sport or season, is the lead story. The sports feature program is one in which interviews, anecdotes and background stories on personalities and events are incorporated. The live broadcast is the most popular form of sports program and although the on-the-spot presentation is essentially a special event, it will be discussed here. The writer for the live sports broadcast is more concerned with transition continuity than with a regular script. He must prepare all opening, closing, transition and filler material. This includes information relating to pre-event color and action, statistics, form charts, the site of the event, the participants, and human interest anecdotes. More and more broadcasters provide their own filler material. Where it is prepared by the writer, the writer's function is primarily that of a researcher, and his script may be little more than an outline and/or a series of statistics, individual sentences or short paragraphs.

SPECIAL EVENTS AND FEATURES

Special Events

These broadcasts are usually under the direction of the news department of the station. The special event is essentially something that is taking place live and is of interest — critical or passing — to the community. These on-the-spot presentations are similar to the live sports broadcast in that they are narrated rather than announced, and the writer must prepare continuity accordingly. Frequently, films or tapes are written and prepared beforehand for insertion at proper times during the reporting of the event. The station does not ordinarily set up special events. They originate independently and include such situations as parades, dedications, banquets, awards, political conventions and the opening of new supermarkets. In order to have available all the possible opening, closing and filler material that may be needed by the broadcaster, the writer must study news stories, maps, press releases, photographs and other material that may be pertinent. Because the form of the special event is extemporaneous, the material, though prepared, should be simple and should sound as though it were ad-libbed. In some instances the writer may have to prepare only an outline.

Special Features

The special feature differs from the special event in that the former is planned beforehand and is controlled by the station as a planned program. In addition, the special feature usually is pre-recorded on tape or on film. The writer prepares a complete script, much as he would prepare a documentary. Special features usually are either two or fifteen minutes in length, the former for fillers and the latter for full programs of a public service nature. The subject matter for the special feature varies. Some of the types of programs possible include the presentation of the work of a special service group, an examination of the local school system, a tour of the firehouse, a trip to some point of interest, a how-to-do-it broadcast, and a behind-the-scenes broadcast relating to any subject — raising chickens to electing public officials. The special feature offers the writer the opportunity to create a program of high artistic quality closely approaching the documentary. Although the script is of a public service nature, it does not have to be purely informational or academic. It may include forms of variety and drama, as well as the more common news and discussion materials. Special features customarily are oriented around a person or thing or situation. Sometimes — as, for example, when preparing materials for an expert who will do a demonstration — the writer needs to prepare only a detailed rundown sheet rather than a complete script.

Talks Programs

"Talks" is an all-inclusive term that covers such diverse program types as interviews, discussions, quiz, panel and audience participation shows, and speeches. Most of these programs do not use complete scripts, partially because the program is represented as being extemporaneous and partially because the non-professionals who appear on many of these programs cannot make a script sound ad-lib as can the professional performer. However, in order to make certain that the program is as good as it can be, as much of it is prepared beforehand as possible. The job of the writer, in most instances, is to write a detailed routine sheet, that is, scripts which are written out as fully as possible with as much of the dialogue and action as can be prepared. Frequently, a key phrase or descriptions of routines suffice, and these are filled in extemporaneously during the program by the master of ceremonies and principal performers.

The Interview

The completely prepared interview is too risky because the interviewee, unless he is a performer, may sound too stilted and be embarrassing. The completely ad-lib interview is also too dangerous and is rarely used except for the man-in-the-street kind of situation. The most frequently used form of script or routine sheet for the interview consists of carefully and fully prepared questions and, through pre-interviewing, general lines of answering. The writer of the interview, after research on the subject and on the interviewee, prepares preliminary questions. A pre-interview conference is held with the interviewee, during which time the preliminary questions are discussed and general lines of answering are set. On the basis of this information, the writer can then prepare a detailed rundown and routine sheet. The interview program itself may vary from strictly questions and answers to discussion. In many instances a pre-interview is not possible. In that case, the producer will try to get the interviewee to the studio before the program for a rehearsal or at least a warm-up session. In any case, the writer must prepare the opening and closing, introductory material about the interviewee and, in some instances, transition material between program segments for lead-ins and outs for commercials. Because the interview, whether on radio or television, is oriented toward the interviewee's words, visual material on television sometimes can be distracting. Some visuals may be used, such as films or photographs of the interviewee's home town, of past highlights in his career, or of the place where he works. Such use should be in moderation, however, and should not tend to detract from the main purpose of the interview.

There are three major interview types. The opinion interview is exemplified by the man-in-the-street ad-lib approach, for which the writer may prepare only an introduction, a question and follow-up questions. When the opinion interview is with a prominent person, the personality interview may be combined with the opinion type. The information interview has as its purpose the eliciting of factual material of a public service nature from relatively unknown or well-known persons. Because the presentation of information is the object, the routine sheet may be more detailed than for other types of interviews. The personality interview is perhaps the most popular kind in the mass media because of its orientation toward the human interest or feature story. In all cases, the writer should obtain full background information on the interviewee and in addition to the usual opening, closing, introduction and transition material, should have ready a series of follow-up and probe questions developed in light of the possible answers educed during the pre-interview. An interview may take place with one or more interviewees and with one or a panel of interviewers.

Discussion Programs

Discussion programs, which are aimed toward an exchange of opinions and information, should not be confused with the interview in which the purpose is to elicit and not to exchange. The writer of the discussion program has to walk a thin line between too much and not enough preparation. It is not possible to write a complete script, partially because the participants frequently do not know exactly what material is to be presented by the other persons in the discussion. No preparation at all would permit the participants to ramble and to present the moderator with the impossible task of getting someplace without anyone knowing where they were going. A detailed discussion outline, distributed to all participants some time prior to the program and altered as they respond to it, is the most effective kind of script. In addition, the writer should prepare opening and closing material, introductions of the participants, and general summaries for the moderator, based on the outline.

There are several types of discussion programs. The symposium presents several persons who have prepared solutions to a given problem. Each participant is given equal time for an opening statement and a final summary. Within the program a set time is arranged for questions from the audience. The issue should be controversial. The routine sheet or outline contains the moderator's opening remarks, introductions of the participants, and time limits for the various sections of the program. The panel discussion — not to be confused with the quiz-type panel — is not so structured as is the symposium and ordinarily presents a number of people in a more or less informal discussion about some topic of interest. The participants may do as much or as little preparation as they desire. A moderator attempts to keep the discussion on the track and frequently summarizes. The routine sheet consists of the moderator's opening remarks, the introduction of the panel members, a statement of the problem by the moderator, a flexible outline of topics to be discussed (usually this has been revised after the participants have seen a first draft), and the closing. Two other forms of discussion — group discussion and debate — are infrequently found on commercial television, although sometimes presented on educational television. Group discussion, in which the participants come to mutually agreeable conclusions within a problem-solving format, requires from the writer an outline containing the opening, introduction of participants, some basic factual information under each step of the organization, and the closing. Debate has many forms, and with its inherent sharp conflict provides a base for dramatic program interest. The writer usually prepares the opening, introduction of participants, explanation of procedure, introduction and time limits for each phase of the debate, interviews, if desired, presentation of the decisions and the closing.

Quiz, Panel, Audience Participation Shows

The goal of each of these kinds of programs is for someone to solve a problem, stump an expert, or successfully perform some action, such as hitting one's spouse in the face with a pie. The writer does not prepare a full script, but because these shows communicate an extemporaneous quality, he prepares routine sheets. Since the programs must seem spontaneous, but yet professional in quality, as much material must be prepared beforehand as possible. As far as the non-professional participants are concerned, however, the material cannot be in dialogue form. The routine sheet should consist of the opening and closing, the introductions of the participants, the presumably ad-lib gags, the questions and similiar material, and the transitions between program segments. Before each stunt or question, the routine sheet should include detailed continuity. Action portions of the program must be timed beforehand and the writer frequently prepares different closings, depending on whether the show is running short, long, or on time. Obviously, television permits an emphasis on stunts, charts, costumes and other visual factors. The writer also tries to find a "gimmick" which will involve the audience in the proceedings, such as being phoned to share in a prize. The following routine sheet provides an indication of the material needed for a quick-witted, flexible M.C.; many routine sheets are far more detailed than this one.

"TRUTH OR CONSEQUENCES"

BOB BARKER

1. Bring on contestants.

2. Interview and question.

3. Now, I know it probably never happens in your family, but every once in a while you hear about some member of a family putting a little money away for a rainy day, so to speak . . . and the interesting thing about some of these deposits is that only the person who put the money away knows where it is.

4. Tell me, Mrs. _____, do you think your husband has a few bills tucked away that you know nothing about?

   (HEH HEH)

   And, M·. _____, do you think that Mrs. _____ might have a dollar or two hidden in a teapot that you know nothing about?

   (ANSWER)

5. In any event, when such a thing does happen the money is put in a secret place known only to the one who put it there. Now, today we want to conduct a little experiment.

6. Reveal table and props.

   (WE NEED ONLY THREE PROPS . . .
   A COOKIE JAR . . . A PIGGY BANK,
   AND A COPY OF PLAYBOY FOR THE
   COFFEE TABLE)

7. I want you to notice that we have on
   display a cookie jar . . . a piggy
   bank . . . and there on the table, a
   man's type magazine.

8. Now, here's what's going to happen.
   Mrs. _____, I want you to
   take these bills.
   You'll note there is a one dollar bill . . .
   a five dollar bill, and a one hundred
   dollar bill.

9. Now, Mrs. _____, I want you
   to hide one of these bills in the cookie
   jar . . . one in the piggy bank, and one
   in the magazine. We'll close the curtains
   so not even the studio audience will
   know where you put the money. The
   first one Mr. _____picks
   is the bill you take home.

10. Play act.

11. Award winnings and consolation, if necessary.

      A variation of the audience participation sequence may be noted in the fol-
lowing excerpt from a "Truth and Consequences" program of an earlier format. Here the
script preparation is a little more detailed.

         STEVE DUNNE

And now, ladies and gentlemen — as you
can probably well imagine, TRUTH OR
CONSEQUENCES is not exactly what you
might call a well rehearsed show. In fact,
we very rarely have any idea of what's
going to happen right up to and including
the time we go on the air. Well, tonight is
no exception. During our pre-show warmup,
I met one of the cutest young fellows we've
ever had in our studio audience. Anyway —
I thought you folks at home might get as much
of a kick out of seeing this youngster as I
did. And so, I'm going to ask that same
youngster along with his mother and grand-
mother to come down here on our stage if
they will, please.

(TURN ON HOUSE LIGHTS AND FOLLOW
FAMILY DOWN ON STAGE)

1. Establish that mother's reason for bringing
   child to show tonight is that she couldn't
   get a baby sitter.

2. Ask camera to get closeup of baby.

3. Comment on the fact that there are three
   generations.

        Courtesy of Ralph Edwards Productions, presented on NBC-TV.

Speeches

Inasmuch as most speeches are prepared outside the station, the staff writer need have no concern with them except for the opening and closing of the station's part of the program. In some instances, usually on the local level, speakers unfamiliar with television's time needs may have to be advised how and where to trim their speeches so that they are not cut off the air before they finish. In other instances it may be necessary to help the speaker rewrite in terms of legal, FCC or station requirements concerning statements made over the air. Speeches which are developed into more than a verbal presentation through the use of film clips, slides and other visual material are in actuality illustrated talks or lectures and are prepared as special features.

MUSIC AND VARIETY PROGRAMS

Music comprises the bulk of radio programming today — almost exclusively on what has become known as the disc jockey show — through records, transcriptions and tape. Although there are many programs with music on television, most of these are not devoted primarily to music, but fall into the classification of variety shows. The job for the writer in the area of music is essentially in the writing of continuity for the radio music show; it is infinitely more difficult to be a successful writer for television variety programs.

Music types and formats

The writer must find a central theme for any given music program in order to achieve some kind of organic unity within his script. The theme can be oriented around almost anything: a holiday, an event, a composer's birthday, a new film by a singing star. Transitions, from number to number, must be clearly developed throughout the script. The musical program should build to a climax, moving from a good opening selection through careful variation of selections to avoid repetitiousness to a high point of interest. The writer of the television music show should concentrate on a type of performance. Physical types include vocalists, combos, instrumental groups, orchestras and choral groups. Straight musical programs have been singularly unsuccessful on television, probably because music itself is essentially aural and not visual. The writer can help overcome this problem by supplementing the music with visual material that relates either to the music itself or to the central theme of the program. For example, film clips of a locale can sometimes add to the music of a particular country. Interesting shots of the musicians, audience participation such as dancing, actions of performers such as the antics of a hillbilly band, and abstract representations through electronic effects are other methods of adding a visual dimension to televised music.

Variety Shows

The term variety implies a combination of two or more different kinds of performances. The basic variety program types are the vaudeville show and the music hall variety — which are essentially the same, both oriented around specialty acts and frequently including musical and dance numbers; the revue, which is composed primarily of music and dance; the comic-dominated show, which may be centered around one performer or may tend toward the variety program type; the personality program, which is in essence a review centered around one person; and the musical comedy type, which requires plot continuity, no matter how thin, with the music and dance. The vaudeville show, as represented by the Ed Sullivan program, has been most successful on American television. The writer must find something to hold the continuity of the show together, either a theme or, in some instances, the strong personality of the master-of-ceremonies. The audience must be held from one number to the next. The writer must determine the orientation of the various facets of the show: what kind of music, dances, comedy. The term variety implies contrast, and the writer must make certain that numbers adjacent to each other are not too much the same. Unless a particular program is oriented toward one type of performance, such as juggling, there should be a differentness among acts throughout. The final number should have two versions, short and long, so that the proper one may be used depending on the time left in the program.

WOMEN'S PROGRAMS

There are many programs aimed at women as judged by the time of their presentation: mid- and late morning and early afternoon. In a strict sense, however, the women's program is one which, at any time of day, has its content oriented primarily toward that which especially interests women. On the network level, if we exclude soap operas, the women's program varies from the catch-all, or magazine format, to the non-magazine format in which the material is oriented towards one area, such as cooking or fashions. (The magazine format ordinarily is that in which different advertisers sponsor different portions of the program as they relate to the product being sold; for example, the cosmetic firm might sponsor the section of the program dealing with beauty hints.) In the magazine format the writer sometimes deals more with a demonstration than with a dialogue-type show and may prepare a detailed routine sheet rather than a traditional script. The local women's program is usually in a magazine format, with the writer frequently preparing the program in terms of the available sponsors. On the local level the women's program can make important contributions to public affairs while at the same time being commercially successful in nature. Local news, fashions, personalities, social and civic events and problems can comprise much of the content of such programs. The material should be written simply and directly, although technical terms relating to the item under consideration may be used, provided these are terms known to all women. The material should be informal, but never condescending.

CHILDREN'S PROGRAMS

Children's imaginations, not yet stifled by the restrictions and formalities of the adult world, are keen, alive and boundless. Children are creative and, provided you give them a believable base to begin with and develop it logically, can enjoy characters, situation and environment that the adult is not free enough to identify with.

Approach and Format

Most children's television programs are neither written nor oriented for children. Series of old cartoons, with little meaning for children other than a visual representation of aggressive and anti-social action, take the place of what could be material developed especially for children. Programs ostensibly for children but directed as well, if not principally, toward the adults who have the money to buy the products make up much of children's programming. Although parents are ultimately responsible if they permit their children to watch television at the child's whim, it is the writer who creates the program that is tasteless or dull. The writer might use the following as a guide: if the program is tasteless and dull to him, then it will most assuredly be so for the child. The section, "Responsibility Toward Children," in the National Association of Broadcasters Television Code has laudable principles, especially those concerning violence and related to the "healthy development of personality and character" of the child. A look at the so-called children's programs on the air, however, will clearly show that the Code is not very fully adhered to or enforced. Ethical program content depends in great measure on the writer. The kinds of children's programs possible, vary: the learning experience in a variety of friendly and enjoyable situations, as exemplified by "Captain Kangaroo," probably the best continuing children's program that commercial television has presented; the widening of horizons as in the "Discovery" series; the observation of important phenomona as presented by "Mr. Wizard." There have been others of this nature, but, unfortunately, most children's programs have been of the cartoon variety or the pseudo-kindergarten participation type on the lowest level of imagination and stimulation. Some general standards may be applied to age-level interests. For the pre-school child: activities, some elements of fantasy, and things familiar to his environment. For the early elementary school grades: beginning elements of logical thinking such as plots, fairy tale stories with basic action, and activities. For the child over eight or nine years of age: activities and accounts of the outside world, such as adventure, individual action and aspects of reality. However, the best children's program is not written for a certain age level, but should be of a high quality, the best representation of that kind of program, and on a level on which everyone may enjoy it and be stimulated. A dramatization of *Winnie the Pooh,* for example, might fall into this category. The writer who has no respect for children is not a good writer of children's programs.

Techniques

Children respond well to the presentational approach. The ideas should be simple and clear, but not condescending. Action is important, too much dialogue sometimes dull. Children do not have the attention span of adults and not too many ideas should be presented at once or for too long a period of time. In drama the material can be light but, if serious, not tragic or morbid. Remember that the child identifies strongly with the characters in a program, and for effective identification the characters should be part of the child's real world. Educational materials should not be unduly repetitive of what the child may be learning in school, and if a moral is to be presented, it should not be ambiguous. Several techniques have been successful in children's drama, including suspense, a good conflict, a secret that the viewers know but characters in the play do not, and an exciting and perhaps humorous chase. Television permits the writer to broaden the child's experiential horizons, particularly those of children who do not have the opportunity to take advantage of the many learning experiences available only in large metropolitan cities. Visits and demonstrations are helpful in this regard. Special visual devices such as electronic techniques, film and puppets can enhance the children's program. Most non-drama children's programs are not written out in script form, but are developed as detailed routine sheets. Sources for children's programs are unlimited and include storybooks, fairy tales, poems, folktales, playground and party games and creative dramatics. All of the arts can make contributions to the good children's program.

THE DOCUMENTARY

The documentary is considered by many to be the highest form of the television and radio art, combining as it does news, drama and music, and presenting them in a highly organized manner stimulating to both the mind and the emotions. In recent years, especially following former Chairman of the Federal Communications Commission Newton N. Minow's assumption of that office, the documentary has gained in importance on television. There are several forms for the documentary and within each form special procedures and techniques possible for the writing of a good documentary.

Type and Form

Television documentaries grew out of the principles developed in film documentary making. Robert Flaherty, considered by many to be the father of the modern documentary, explored the strength and courage of man in a hostile environment; Pare Lorentz used the documentary as a means of presenting a social problem and offering solutions to it; John Grierson stressed the ordinary, everyday life of man and his environment, although he did incorporate some of mankind's societal problems. The television documentary may be any one or a combination of these basic types. A documentary is essentially a presentation in depth of something newsworthy: an event, a person, an idea, a thing. It goes further than an ordinary news story in that it attempts to explore more thoroughly the motivations behind the story and the effects of the occurrence upon society. Technically, it is a true story. In practice, because editing is such an essential part of documentary making, the selection and combination of materials may sometimes result in an accidental or deliberate distortion of fact. Yet, the purpose of the documentary is to present a point of view. The manner in which it editorializes is the pertinent point. Some documentaries combine fact and fiction, that is, use fact as a base for what is essentially a dramatic script; these are called semi-documentaries or fictionalized documentaries.

Procedure and Technique

Since documentary material is gathered essentially in the field, the writer must be sure that the real words of real persons and the real sounds and real pictures of real events can be obtained. The writer must first have an idea; frequently the idea is determined by the producer; in many instances the producer and writer are the same person. What subject of public interest is worthy of treatment? What documentary type and form will be used? After the decision has been made, the writer must spend vast amounts of time doing research, not a little of it in libraries. After he has gathered what seems to be sufficient material, he can prepare a preliminary outline. As the actual recorded, filmed and taped material is gathered, the writer revises his outline. Through a continuous process of revision he arrives at a final script at about the time he knows what material has been obtained and what is still available. He may incorporate stock film, old newsreels, recorded radio interviews from an earlier date, and other non-live materials to fill out his documentary plan. In brief, the procedure is determination of available source material, preliminary research, revision of subject and purpose, tentative outline, field work, additional research, final script, and editing. Human interest is the keynote of the good documentary. Although the facts must be presented, they should be presented in terms of people. Even when the subject may be an event or an inanimate object, endow it as much as possible with human qualities. Keep in mind the elements of good dramatic writing. Organize the material in terms of an initial conflict, rising action through complications, and suspense before the climax or crisis is reached. Production elements of the drama, such as background music and special settings, are important. A narrator almost always is used. Avoid the possibility that the documentary may turn out to be nothing more than a series of lectures or interviews. Keep in mind television's visual needs and think in terms of films, photos and graphics. The following excerpt from *The Twentieth Century* documentary series is an example of the combination of two techniques, interview and travelogue, to present an understanding of a country. This documentary utilizes the three classical approaches: the presentation of a problem of society, the special analysis of the life of a man or of a people, and the showing of the everyday, ordinary existence of a part of the world.

CRONKITE:

I'm Walter Cronkite — and this is Stockholm. What is it like to live in the world's most highly developed welfare state? Today in democratic Sweden — a unique experiment is going on. Social benefits extend literally from the cradle to the grave. Some call it a paradise on earth. Others see it as beset with problems — juvenile delinquency, alcoholism, suicide   Today we present the first of two episodes filmed by THE TWENTIETH CENTURY in this land of many paradoxes — "Sweden" — Is there trouble in Paradise? as The Prudential Insurance Company of America presents THE TWENTIETH CENTURY.

(MAIN TITLE)

(COMMERCIAL)

CRONKITE:

Town hall	Stockholm — a city built on islands and spanned by bridges — sometimes called the Venice of the North. This is the capital of the Swedish Welfare State — the center of a homogeneous nation of seven and a half million people who enjoy the highest standard of living in Europe today.
Train thru countryside	Here, old tradition lives side by side with the development of one of the most progressive societies in the world — under a government which has delivered to its people an ever increasing number of social benefits that have aroused both skepticism and envy throughout the world. (BEAT) Stockholm is overcrowded and many of its one million inhabitants commute daily from suburban centers. Prosperous,
People in train	well fed, well clothed — the Swedes are well provided for — by a benevolent, paternalistic, democratic government — aiming to banish poverty and provide a sense of security for all the people.
People in street	What is it like to live in the Welfare State — where few are wealthy and fewer are poor — where practically every basic need is anticipated by the State? Does the levelling of society and all this security lead to the loss of incentive and initiative? We asked the Swedes themselves.

Bergmann   A worker.

MR. BERGMANN:

"I need not worry so much about my parents and relatives as I
had to do under other circumstances. I need not fear from being
ruined by sickness and unemployment. When I am old and cannot
work any longer, I know I have a pension I can live on. This gives
me real liberty."

CRONKITE:

Browaldh   A banker.

BROWALDH:

"Well, I've heard a lot about this problem about what makes Sammy
run, I mean, what is the incentive for me and other executives to
work as hard as we undoubtedly do — running around in a square
wheel in fact. And I don't believe that Swedish executives have such
pronounced economic incentives as maybe our American colleagues
or our English colleagues. I and my generation of executives, we
feel that being an executive in charge of a very interesting job is
sort of reward enough."

CRONKITE:

Heckscher   A Conservative leader.

HECKSCHER:

"In many respects I think public life in Sweden and even private life is
becoming a bit dreary. You do everything by organization. You live
in a house which is established by one organization. You buy your
food in a coop established by another organization. Your salary, your
wages, are fixed by collective contract. You take your pleasures in a
society which is again part of a large organization and the only un-
organized thing is sleep."

CRONKITE:

People   Despite divergent opinions the fact remains that the people of the
Welfare State have lived under the same Social Democratic, or Labor
Government, almost continuously for the past 29 years — repeatedly
endorsing it in parliamentary and municipal elections.

Govt House   In the Chancery — Government House — we spoke with Sweden's
Prime Minister for the past 15 years — Tage Erlander.

CRONKITE:

Erlander   Mr. Prime Minister, what is the ultimate objective of the democratic
government? Are you striving for total state ownership of the means
of production and of real property?

PRIME MINISTER ERLANDER:

"Now, the ultimate goal is the happiness of the citizens and the
nationalization cannot be more than a means to reach that goal. We
have in Sweden a mixed economy. I should think that only 10% is
owned by the government, by the State, and 90% are private industry."

THE TWENTIETH CENTURY — Sweden: Trouble in Paradise? Part I. ⊙Columbia
Broadcasting System, Inc. 1962. Written by Wilfrid Fleisher.

The Play

Playwriting is an art on a plane of creativity far above the mechanical facets of some of the craft phases of continuity writing. The genius and inspiration of playwriting cannot be taught. An understanding and application, however, of the proven principles of good dramaturgical technique can provide the playwright with the tools to utilize effectively whatever talent and insight he may have. The principles of dramaturgy, continuously modified from Sophocles to Shakespeare to Brecht, contain universal applications to all forms of drama. Further modifications occur according to the special requirements of the individual medium.

Sources

The writer may find the motivating ingredient for his play in an event or happening, in a theme, in a character or characters, or in a background. Although all potential playwrights have witnessed or experienced events that seemingly contain the elements for a good play, it is important to remember that drama is not life. Drama is heightened life, a compression of those elements that may seem exciting in the everyday world. The playwright must interpret, condense and reorganize. A theme or idea may serve as the germ for a play, presenting the writer with such concepts as loyalty, independence, self-realization and so forth. The writer must remember, however, that the ideas must be expressed not as entities in themselves, but as manifestations of the dramatic action of his characters. A significant reason for television's inability to generally fulfill its potential as a medium for fine drama is the fact that themes or ideas which may be considered controversial are almost always censored or altered. Some drama programs of recent years, notably "The Defenders" and "East Side, West Side," have put the good play above censorship. Backgrounds — the slum society, the high society, the business society, even the campus society — provide another source for the play. Inasmuch as the motivating force in any good play is character, character is a major source for the drama. As with an event, the writer cannot transfer a character from real life, but must heighten and interpret and frequently develop an entirely new character as a quintessence of many from the actual world.

Play Structure

In modern drama character has become the motivating factor. The psychological make-ups and stimuli of the characters determine what they will do and, consequently, determine plot; their special personalities govern what they will say and how they will talk and therefore determine dialogue. These three major elements in the play structure — character, plot and dialogue — must be coordinated into a consistent and clear theme. The coordination of all elements toward a common end results in the *unity* of the piece, a unity of impression. All elements in the play should relate in a thorough and consistent fashion to the purpose of the playwright. There should be no distracting elements. The *plot* structure of a play is based on a complication arising out of the individual's or group's relationships to some other force. This is the conflict, where two or more elements come into opposition. The conflict should be introduced as soon as possible. A series of complications enhance the conflict, building it into a rising crescendo to the crisis or climax. When the two forces meet head on and one wins and the other loses, the climax has been reached. The play may end at that point, or through the resolution the audience may learn what happens as a result of the climax. *Character* is the prime mover in the play. The character is revealed through what he does and says and not through arbitrary description. The most effective delineation is — as is true in real life — at moments of crisis. The individual character must be consistent throughout the play in everything he does and says, and must be plausible in terms of — though not a copy of — life and reality. *Dialogue,* as is drama itself, is heightened and condensed from that of real life. It must conform to the personality of the character speaking it, it must be consistent with the character and with itself throughout the play, and it must forward the situation, the revealing of the character and the movement of the plot. *Exposition* is the revelation of the background of the characters, the situation, and the clarification of the present circumstances. It should be presented as soon as possible, but must not be obvious or contrived. It should come within the action of the play. *Preparation,* which also must be presented subtly, is a foreshadowing of what will happen later. It prepares the audience for subsequent events or actions of the characters, making their occurrence logical and not arbitrary. The *setting* is determined by the form of the play and the physical and mechanical needs of the play structure. It serves as a locale, background and environment for the characters and is a psychological and aesthetic representation of the author's purpose.

After the writer is certain that he understands and can be objective about the various elements in his play he can begin to create each of them in depth. He must research as fully as possible and literally psychoanalyze every character, providing each with a complete case history. After the characters have been created, the plot line is done in skeleton form. The conflict may be between individuals, an individual and a group, between two groups, between an individual or individuals and nature, between an individual or individuals and some unknown force, or between an individual and his inner self. A scenario or detailed outline, carefully constructed and analyzed, can help the writer eliminate the bad points and strengthen the good points even before the actual line by line writing of the play has begun.

There are, of course, many procedures in writing, some of which may not overtly include case histories, research, scenarios or other accepted methods of preparation. Some writers literally seem to sit down at the typewriter, write "Act I, Scene I" or "Fade In" at the top of a page, and the play ostensibly writes itself. Keep in mind, however, that inspiration is only a small part of successful playwriting; regardless of the method used, incisive preparation and hard work are intrinsic to the good play.

Television's Special Characteristics

The television medium presents special potentials and limitations for the playwright. One potential is its ability to create a purposeful direction of the viewer's attention toward subjective, intimate, inner manifestations of the character's actions or thoughts. The use of the close-up is, of course, significant in this respect. Another potential is that of opening up the action through the use of film or tape and making possible many transitions and complete fluidity of time and place. Even in live or live-type taped television, mechanical and electronic techniques permit fluidity even while the consistency of continuous performance is maintained. Perhaps the greatest limitation for the television playwright is that of time. The hour drama is really only about 51 minutes long, the half-hour drama 24 minutes in length. Even the one and one-half hour program permits only about 75 minutes for the play itself. Therefore, the television play must be extremely tight, with no irrelevancies. It must have few characters and one main simplified plot line if it is to be truly effective. The writer sometimes may concentrate on plot at the expense of action — a frequent approach which results in the stereotyped figures seen on most television dramatic series today — or on character without including much valid action. Neither approach is satisfactory. Space limitations are of two kinds: the physical size of most studios and the relatively small size of the home television screen. It is difficult, in a studio shot drama, to put many characters on the screen at one time and, frequently, to call for a large number of sets. Exteriors and nature effects, such as floods and earthquakes, are limited. The space and time limitations and the potentials for subjective orientation combine to indicate a special approach for the good television play: probing of a short span of the intimate life of a character. And, indeed, this kind of play, exemplified by the Chayesfskys and Roses, reflects the high point of drama in television's short history thus far. A final important limitation, already mentioned is censorship. Yet, although the artistic bases have changed from the live to the filmed play, and although the broad base of censorship continues, in the middle 1960's plays were being produced on television dealing with controversial topics that were rarely, if ever, seen a decade before in the so-called "golden years" of TV drama.

Dramaturgical Concepts for Television

The earlier analysis of play structure indicates some universal dramaturgical concepts stemming from the basic medium for all drama — the theatre. While the television play utilizes, in effect, all of the principles noted, television's special characteristics require some modifications that should be applied by the playwright in the newer medium. The *unity* of action or impression is as vital to the television play as to any other form of drama. Fluidity of time and place, however, is much more flexible in television than in theatre. Television can transcend boundaries of place and time in a twinkling. The *plot* line for television is more restricted than that for the stage. It should be oriented around a single action and should exclude sub-plots. It should concentrate on a single, simplified action. Because television is restricted in time, the plot must be even more the essence of reality than the plot of the stage play. The writer should aim for the short, terse scene. Because of the limited running time, the conflict must come much sooner in the television play — in fact, the exposition may be cut virtually to nothing and the script may open with the conflict in full view. Fewer complications are required, the final complication being the climax. The plot structure must build, however, and the climax should be the result of consistent, intensified rising action. Because of the lack of time, the resolution is usually dispensed with in the television play. The subjective nature of television suggests that conflict between individuals or between man and himself is more effective than those between man and a larger force or between groups.

Character must be even more heightened in the television play. Any character used must be essential and must contribute to the main conflict and the unified plot line. The ability of television to present the depth of character is both an advantage and a disadvantage. The writer cannot present the group as protagonist as effectively as he can in the theatre. However, he can present the individual more effectively and orient the audience, through camera and control room techniques, toward the character's intimate, inner feelings. The time limitation makes it difficult to develop good characterizations for more than one or two persons; if the play has too many essential characters, then it must be re-thought. *Dialogue* is modified in television because the visual element can often substitute for the aural. If the writer can show the situation or present expository information through visual action instead of through dialogue, he should do so. Ordinarily time-consuming verbal descriptions sometimes can be presented through either long and close shots. Reaction as well as action can be concentrated upon. Television dialogue must be especially condensed and heightened from that of real life. It should avoid repetition, be character-delineating, condense the ideas being presented, succinctly carry forward each plot element, and present the necessary exposition and preparation even within the rising action of the conflict. The limitation of time requires a minimum of *exposition* in the television play. Exposition must be integrated into the action. The writer should be especially cognizant of the ways in which mechanical and electronic visual devices can help present needed exposition. *Preparation* also requires a special subtlety in television and can benefit, too, from the use of mechanical and electronic techniques. Although television *settings* serve the same basic purpose as do stage sets, they frequently must be modified in size, number, kind (exteriors) and use (large nature effects) by studio and screen space. On the other hand, the fluidity of the medium permits unlimited transitions among existing settings, and tape and film permit an unlimited broadening of the places of action.

Scenario and Manuscript

A good scenario should clearly show at which point the conflict is introduced, whether there is sufficient exposition accompanying it, where the complications occur, whether they lead inexorably to a climax, and so forth. When the writer has determined that the scenario is as complete and effective as he can get it, the next step is to write the play. If the scenario is well done, the play will virtually write itself. The good scenario is flexible and permits change, expansion and condensation. The final manuscript should have all the dialogue and stage directions complete. In addition, the author may indicate sound, music, camera and electronic effects which he considers vital to the action. Although producers and directors frown upon the writer entering what they consider their exclusive domain of "directions," when a writer devises a visual effect as part of the action or when it serves in place of dialogue, it is just as necessary a part of the script as is the dialogue. The form for the television manuscript varies. A frequently used approach utilizes a divided page: the right-hand column contains all the dialogue plus the characters' actions and the left-hand column contains the video — that is, the camera and control effects. The columns may be reversed or all directions may be placed in either column alone, with the opposite column free for the director's notations. The name of the character should be typed in capital letters in the center of the column, above the dialogue of the character. Dialogue should be double-spaced, with double-spacing between speeches.

The following scenario excerpt and script from a portion of the first act of a play entitled "With Wings As Eagles" indicates one type of scenario, the structure of a drama, and a format for the "live" television script.

Action Summary	Functional Analysis
	(1)
The scene is a Jewish ghetto in an unnamed Near East country. The camera opens on a muddy village street and pans one wood and mud-baked hut to another. A Narrator sets the time and place, describing the poverty of the inhabitants, and how their history shows that though they live in hunger, sickness and oppression, they will find the promised land.[1] The Narrator mentions that few have ever seen an automobile and few would believe that such a thing as an airplane exists.[2] He stresses that in all their ignorance and poverty the people have hope of going to the promised land.[3]	Exposition: the place, time, situation, the background and needs of the people. (Is this exposition too obvious, coming through a narrator in addition to the visual?)
	(2)
	Preparation: for their eventual departure for Israel and for the climax involving the airplane flight.
	(3)
	Preparation for the conflict: the stress on the hope of going to a promised land subtly suggests the conflict: will they or will they not be able to go?
	(4)
Reb Simcha goes from house to house, calling the people to a meeting. He does so stealthily, undercover.[4]	Exposition: shows the kind of existence of the people: fear, oppression.
	(5)
At one house, that of Simon and his son, Aaron, Reb Simcha encounters opposition to the meeting. At Aaron's insistence Simon finally agrees to go. We see that Simon's house is well-furnished, unlike the others.[5]	Preparation: for Simon's opposition, and for Aaron's opposition to his father.
	(5)
	Exposition: shows another aspect of the village life; someone in comparatively good circumstances.
	(6)
We follow Simcha to his own house. The house is fixed up as a small synogogue. He prays: "Please, God. This time, make men's words truth."[6]	Conflict: Without a clear statement yet, we learn something may be in opposition with something else. This is preparation for the revelation of the conflict.
	(6)
	Exposition: Reb Simcha's environment and profession.
	(7)
His daughter, Leah, enters. Reb Simcha complains about his tired feet.[7]	Preparation: The tired feet play a humorous part throughout and are particularly important for comic pathos at the end of the play.
	(8)
Leah says she saw some of the people, and that Aaron saw the rest, and that all are coming.[8]	Preparation and complication: We are prepared for Aaron's break with his father through the revelation that he is working on Reb Simcha's side. We are prepared for the relationship between Leah and Aaron in that they are working together. This preparation ties in with the later complications: Aaron vs. his father; Aaron and Leah's love.

WITH WINGS AS EAGLES

ACT I

Open FS Map of Middle East   NARRATOR (VOICE OVER)

This is a map of the Middle East: Egypt,
Syria, Iraq, Jordan, Israel. Of Arabs and
Jews. Of cities and deserts, of camels
and motor cars, of hopes and fears, but
Pan across map, picking no special spot,   mostly of people. This is the city of
dolly in, dissolve to a miniature of a   Mabbam. In what country? It doesn't
small city, several new white buildings   matter. Like in many other of these towns
and off, at one side, a dingy, dirty-   outside of Israel there are small Jewish
looking section, with mud huts and shacks. populations. Hebrew might be a better
                                            term, for these people are the direct
                                            descendents of Isaiah and Abraham, those
                                            who were led by Moses through the wilder-
                                            ness to the promised land, who fell by the
                                            waysides. The waysides grew into
                                            sections and streets . . .

Dolly in closer to the miniature of the   . . . like that one. Aviv Street, it's called.
town, showing the street of the mud huts   Aviv means hope. That is about all they
and shacks.   have, these Hebrews—hope. There is no
                                            special industry, no principal occupation—
                                            unless one can call hunger, fear, sickness
                                            and poverty occupations.

Pan down street, show dirt streets, wood   It is not easy for the Hebrew these days.
and mud-baked huts.   The new state of Israel has been steadily
                                            growing and the other countries hold no
                                            love for these people whose kinsmen they
                                            have fought and continue to fight. The
                                            Hebrews are beaten, jailed and starved.
                                            Everything the centuries have visited upon
                                            their brethren has not stopped because they
                                            are suddenly thrust into the middle of the
                                            20th century. And that is an odd thing, too,
                                            for although the calendar of the western
                                            world reads in the 1960's, the environment
                                            of these people is that of centuries before.
                                            No newspapers, no movies, no automobiles.
                                            Few have ever even seen an automobile.
                                            And as for airplanes, why none in this out-
                                            village of Mabbam would believe you if you
                                            told them that such a thing exists. But
                                            whatever else may be lacking, they have a
                                            rich heritage of spiritual inspiration. They
                                            have a Rabbi. They have hope—the hope
                                            of the promised land. Poverty . . . hope . . .
                                            . . . fear . . .

Dissolve to live set. CU of a fist knocking
on a door. The door opens revealing a
small, cluttered room. Several small
children cower in the back. Hannah, a
woman of about 40, but looking tired and
worn and much older, in tattered clothing,
is at the door.

                                         VOICE (OF KNOCKER, REB SIMCHA)

                                         (Reb Simcha is not yet on camera.) Half-
                                         an-hour after sundown. Tonight. At my
                                         house. (THE DOOR CLOSES).

CU feet moving along the dirt street. CU
fist knocking again. Door opens. A man,
Schloem, the street-washer, old and
wizened, stands in back of the door.
Esther, his wife, stands in back of him.
They are both in their late sixties.

                                         VOICE (REB SIMCHA; OFF-CAMERA)

                                         Half-an-hour after sundown. At my house.
                                         Tonight. (SCHLOEM CLOSES THE DOOR
                                         FURTIVELY.)

CU feet moving again. This time they
reach a small concrete patch in the street.
The fist knocks on a door, ignoring the
knocker there. The door is opened by a
good looking young man of about 25. This
is Aaron.

                                         VOICE (REB SIMCHA; OFF-CAMERA)

                                         Your father? You haven't told him?

                                         AARON

                                         No. A moment, please.

                                         (AARON RETURNS A MOMENT LATER
                                         WITH A LARGE, PORTLY MAN OF
                                         ABOUT FIFTY. THIS IS SIMON, HIS
                                         FATHER, THE MERCHANT OF THE
                                         GHETTO. THE INSIDE OF THE HOUSE
                                         CAN BE SEEN. THERE IS SOME FURNI-
                                         TURE, INCLUDING A BED WITH A BED-
                                         SPREAD, TWO COMFORTABLE CHAIRS,
                                         A TABLE WITH A CANDELABRA. IT IS
                                         POOR, BUT WEALTHY IN COMPARISON
                                         WITH THE HOMES OF HANNAH, THE
                                         WIDOW, AND SCHLOEM, THE STREET-
                                         WASHER. SIMON IS DRESSED IN A SUIT,
                                         NOT IN RAGS LIKE THE OTHERS.)

                                         SIMON

                                         What? What do you want?

                                         VOICE (REB SIMCHA; OFF-CAMERA)

                                         Tonight. At my house. At a half . . .

                                         SIMON (INTERRUPTING)

                                         Again? More trouble-making?

                                         VOICE

                                         It is important.

SIMON

Always it is important. And always it causes
trouble. I've no time. I have to see about
some goods.

AARON

We should go, father.

VOICE

(INSISTENT.) It is most important.

SIMON

Well . . . all right.

VOICE

Half-an-hour after sundown.

SIMON

(ANGRILY) All right! (HE SLAMS THE
DOOR.)

CU feet again, walking down the street.
They stop in front of a door. This time the
fist doesn't knock, but the hand opens the
door, instead. The feet go in, past two
humble cots, an old table and two rickety
chairs, to a corner of the room where a
shelf is seen, with several old and tattered
books, two brass candlesticks. In the
wall there is a recession, the "Ark," in
which is seen a rolled up scroll. This is
the "Torah." CU of the Torah as a face
bends toward it and kisses it. Dolly out
and see, finally, the person of the feet and
the voice. It is Rabbi Simcha, a man of
about 50, dressed in a black gown, wearing
a "yarmulka," the black skullcap. He is
bearded, a gentle face, worn, but with
eyes bright with hope.

REB SIMCHA

Please, God. This time, make men's words
truth. (HE BEGINS TO PACE BACK AND
FORTH ACROSS THE SMALL ROOM. THE
FRONT DOOR SLOWLY OPENS. A
PRETTY YOUNG GIRL, ABOUT 23, A
SOFT FACE AND LARGE EYES, HER HAIR
LONG BEHIND HER BACK, COMES IN.
SHE IS UNHEARD BY THE RABBI. SHE
WATCHES HIM A MOMENT. THIS IS HIS
DAUGHTER, LEAH.)

LEAH

Father, your feet will wear off before the
floor will.

REB SIMCHA

(COMING OUT OF DEEP THOUGHT) Oh,
Leah! (HE LAUGHS, LOOKS AT HIS
FEET.) Oh, of course. The head some-
times pays not enough attention to the feet.
(SITS DOWN ON ONE OF THE COTS,
RUBS HIS FEET.) They hurt. These feet
will be the death of me yet. (AFTER A
MOMENT) Did you tell them, Leah? About
tonight?

LEAH

Those I was supposed to. Aaron saw the
rest.

REB SIMCHA

They're coming?

LEAH

Yes.

REB SIMCHA

Good. (HOLDS HIS HEAD IN HIS HANDS,
AGAIN IN WORRIED THOUGHT.)

LEAH

(SITS DOWN NEXT TO HIM.) You can tell
me, father.

REB SIMCHA

(SMILING) Tell? There is nothing to tell.

LEAH

Mother used to say—may she rest in
peace—"When your father says he has
nothing to tell, it is a sure sign he is
bursting to talk."

REB SIMCHA

(FONDLES HER FACE, WISTFULLY) You
are like your mother. (AFTER A MOMENT)
I am worried.

LEAH
About the meeting?

REB SIMCHA

About the meeting, about the authorities,
about our people, about whether what my
ears heard today was really true or just
another one of their stories.

The Television Play on Film and Tape

The basic approaches applicable to writing the play for live television are valid for the television play that is filmed or taped. The play is being produced for viewing on the small screen, with the same time restrictions, for the same audience and under the same limitations of subject matter. The differences relate primarily to the mechanical and electronic techniques involved. Whereas live television is continuous, filmed and taped television permits editing, even after the script is shot, and the director and editor can virtually rewrite the entire play in the editing room. The filmed play permits greater fluidity of time and place and results in sequences which are shorter than in live or live-type taped television; the film sequences are shot separately. It is more difficult to achieve a clear and concrete unity of impression in the filmed play. The filmed play permits outdoor sequences, on-location scenes, chase sequences not possible in the studio and a greater variety of settings. Exposition and background are much easier to bring in. Sequences lasting only a few seconds each can be integrated in such a manner as to provide information and effects for which live television would need much longer time. Greater technical proficiency results in the filmed play, in which sequences may be reshot until they are perfect. Scenes which would not otherwise be possible for the actors can be effected, and editing can create a polished, finished product. A major disadvantage of the filmed play is that the lack of live, continuous performance often results in mechanical and contrived writing and production.

The filmed play requires a different form in the actual writing. Instead of writing scenes, the writer writes shots. Each shot is set in terms of a picture rather than in terms of character action, although the latter should still be the motivating factor. The writer states the place, such as INTERIOR or EXTERIOR, and the shot, such as FULL SHOT or CLOSE-UP. He also describes the setting, states the characters' physical relationships to the set and to each other, and then presents the dialogue for the shot. The dialogue may be only one speech or there may not even be any. The individual shots are numbered in consecutive order so the director easily may pick out any sequence he desires for initial shooting (the filmed play is not shot in chronological order), retakes and editing. The following excerpt from the "Have Gun, Will Travel" series illustrates the filmed or, as it is sometimes called, the "Hollywood" format for the television play.

HAVE GUN, WILL TRAVEL

FADE IN:

1.   EXT. SAN FRANCISCO - ESTABLISHING STOCK - NIGHT   1.

DISSOLVE TO:

2.   INT. FULL SHOT - CARLTON LOBBY - NIGHT   2.

      The usual lobby crowd. Paladin appears as from outside, his hat in his hand,
      a newspaper under his arm. HEY BOY, carrying a tray appears at right from
      the dining room and they cross toward the stairs.

3.   MED. SHOT - THE STAIRS   3.

      As they meet. Hey Boy does a take that almost slips the tray from his
      grasp. Paladin takes in his dismay.

                               PALADIN
            Hey Boy.

                               HEY BOY
            He ordered black-eyed peas, brussel
            sprouts, hominy grits and chili!

      Paladin peeks under the silver covers and is appalled.

                               PALADIN
            He must have a copper stomach . . .

                               HEY BOY
            You know soon enough; he is in your room.

                               PALADIN
            He? Who?

                               HEY BOY
            Little man say you expect him . . .

      Paladin gives a start and peeks under the silver covers again as
      though the secret guest's identity were to be discovered under them.

                          HEY BOY (CONT'D)
            . . . he had your card . . .

      Paladin turns in horror and sprints up the stairs.
      Hey Boy begins to follow and we . . .

                                                      DISSOLVE TO:

4.   OMITTED.   4.

5.   INT. PALADIN'S BEDROOM   5.

      Featuring his ornate bed. MONK, in Sybaritic if rancid splendor, sprawls in
      the middle of Paladin's satin bed spread. He is surrounded by food and
      nibbles daintily from a kumquat and a whole apple pie. CAMERA MOVES IN
      to show a plate of oysters precariously askew at his elbow. He is as happily
      oblivious as ever and is clad as when he was last seen. Putting aside his
      other food, he plucks up an oyster and pokes and studies it at length. He
      doesn't quite trust the thing but finally plops it into his mouth. He stiffens,
      his eyes widen, he half rises and looks as if he might become sick.

6.   MED. SHOT - THE ROOM DOOR - MONK POV   6.

      As it opens and Paladin steps inside, followed by Hey Boy. He gives an
      anguished, outraged, indignant roar and stops short.

      Script written by Jay Simms for the CBS Television Network program HAVE GUN,
      WILL TRAVEL.

The successful writer, in terms of the social and economic mores of our society, is the one who gets paid for writing. Artistic success, unfortunately, has not yet achieved the status of commanding concomitant physical subsistence. The writer of non-dramatic material has an opportunity for a staff position with networks, stations and agencies. The playwright may write under contract — that is, he is part of a regular staff writing plays for a particular series or he is asked to write one or more plays to order for that series. The person who attains such a position usually has a background of previous commercial success. It is extremely difficult to free-lance. If you wish to do so, determine first whether a given show will even consider unsolicited material. If it does, obtain an information sheet from the script editor of the program delineating the special writing requirements and taboos of that show. Then study very carefully the televised programs of the series so that you know the formula precisely and can tailor your script accordingly. Any writer, especially the free-lancer, would do well to obtain a recognized literary agent who can serve not only as a clearance and selling agency, but who can also advise on the needs of the market before the writer spends any time on a project. The writer may frequently create a series — that is, sell the idea for the complete series without having prepared all the scripts. Usually the writer will submit a pilot script and an outline of the remainder of the series, which is then considered by a producing or packaging organization. If accepted, a pilot film is made which, in turn, is considered by an advertising agency or network. Although new series are begun by networks each year and, depending on the success of those already begun, further new ones are presented during a season, the number of pilot films far, far exceeds the relatively few that are purchased. Timing is important. An idea that is unsaleable one year may be commercially valuable the next. For example, consider the following "series" submission:

FOLKSONG, AMERICA

by

Stanley N. Anton and Robert L. Hilliard

This series features a folksinging wayfaring traveler as the central character who travels through the era or event suggested by a different folksong chosen as the theme for each individual program. Through his travels and relationships to people and places we see the events, lives and surroundings of the particular time and the particular part of the country. Each program is a drama, oriented around the specific folksong and includes other folksongs sung by the Traveler as part of the dramatic action. The pilot script, *Low Bridge*, is based on the folksong, "E-RI-E." In the brawling, wild, western terminus of the Erie

Canal, Buffalo, a railroad agent argues with a Boatman and a Canawler (who led the mules which towed the boats) that the canal boats would soon be put out of business by the railroad. On the docks at Albany the Captain of the "Buffalo Traveler" must make Buffalo in four days to keep his freight business. He hires as a Canawler a young man who sees the end of an era, is taking his last trip, and will buy a farm in Ohio. Among the passengers are immigrants seeking a new life: a man, a woman and their child; an unrestrained traveling salesman; an elderly spinster going to visit her sister; a young "redemption" girl (two years of bonded labor to pay off her passage to America); and the Wayfaring Traveler. The action of the trip follows that of the song, the "E-RI-E," and includes a terrible storm which holds up the boat, and the eventual landing at Buffalo. The Traveler also sings other folksongs of the canal as the drama demands. Action, pathos, romance, comedy and suspense mark the script, as well as an historical showing of the life in the ports and of the inevitable decline of the canal; for example, the Canawler falls in love with the redemption girl and sacrifices his farm to buy her bond.

The same kind of bases, providing a play with dramatic action and suspense in the vein of most action series, a continuing character, historic backgrounds, and folksongs, were developed for the remainder of the scripts. A good series? It seemed to have possibilities. The authors' agent submitted it to all the networks. It was turned down. That was in the early 1950's. Yet, ten years later, in the early 1960's, the folksong became popular entertainment and it may be that the networks would very well search out this script and idea from their files. One problem the writer faces in this kind of situation is that the sudden popularity of a previously rejected subject may result in seeming plagiarism — usually quite unintentional or unknown by the network or agency. Excepting the standard types of series which retain popularity for a relatively long period of time, guessing the television writing market is sometimes like playing the stock market!

Television, for the most part, has not lived up to its potential. As far back as 1931 Gilbert Seldes anticipated what would happen. The commercialization of television is a great fault, he warned, for although it is a magic miracle, it will be used as "a miracle made for money." That this need not be so is especially disconcerting. Television can be a most effective art form and contribute in much greater fashion than it does now to entertainment and culture. Only through individual interest and responsibility — through letters, phone calls and other communications from viewers and listeners to broadcasters and civic and governmental agencies — can a change be achieved in the programming practices of this mass-oriented and product-controlled medium. Despite all the restrictions put upon him, however, by the many areas of sponsorship and production, the writer is still the prime mover, the one element upon which all the other elements stand or fall.

With a script of high quality, with writing of ethical and artistic merit, the writer may at least take pride in knowing he has made an effort to fulfill some of television's infinite potentials.

BIBLIOGRAPHY

Barnouw, Erik, *The Television Writer*. New York: Hill and Wang, 1962. The ethical and artistic problems and duties facing the writer, as well as a technical analysis of actual practice.

Curran, Charles W., *Screen Writing and Production Techniques*. New York: Hastings House, Publishers, Inc., 1958. Analysis of filmed and taped TV techniques, including section on writing the original film play.

Greene, Robert S., *Television Writing*. New York: Harper and Brothers, 1956. Rev. Ed. Basic, clear analysis of television dramatic writing. Explicit examples.

Hilliard, Robert L., *Writing for Television and Radio*. New York: Hastings House, Publishers, Inc., 1962. Comprehensive analyses and examples of nondramatic forms of mass media writing. Section on the play based on new, modern concepts of dramaturgy.

Lawson, John Howard, *Theory and Technique of Playwriting and Screenwriting*. New York: G. P. Putnam's Sons, 1949. Analysis of playwriting is directly related to special requirements and techniques of the film. Includes social and historical background.

McMahan, Harry W., *The Television Commercial*. New York: Hastings Publishers, Inc., 1957. Rev. Ed. Techniques of creating live and filmed TV spots. Analyses of various formats and types of commercials.

Seldes, Gilbert, *Writing for Television*. New York: Doubleday and Co., 1952. Writing as an artistic function within the medium. Delineation of significant principles and practices.

Siller, Bob, Ted White and Hal Terkel, *Television and Radio News*. New York: The Macmillan Company, 1960. Basic techniques of network and station operations with various news forms.

TOM C. BATTIN

Professor of Communication Arts,
University of Houston

●Dr. Battin has produced and directed more than 2,000 programs in educational television experience that spans more than a dozen years. He has been at the University of Houston since 1954, where he is a member of the staff of KUHT, the nation's first ETV station, and holds the rank of full Professor of Communication Arts. His 20 years of university teaching includes the University of Michigan, and the University of Florida — where he initiated television production and wrote, produced and directed numerous educational television series through the facilities of two commercial stations in Jacksonville. His work in the mass media has not been restricted to educational applications only; for a time he was associated with the production staff of General Electric television in Schenectady, New York.

Dr. Battin received the B.A. degree from the University of Ohio, and the M.A. and Ph. D. degrees from the University of Michigan. His dissertation was the first doctoral level research in the nation in the field of television. Dr. Battin has published 15 articles on television in educational and trade journals. He has been active in professional associations and among the offices he has held are those of Chairman of the Radio-TV-Film Interest Group of the Speech Association of America, Chairman of the Radio-TV-Film Interest Group of the Southern Speech Association, and Chairman of the Radio-TV-Film Interest Group and Director of Public Relations of the Texas Speech Association. He has presented numerous scholarly papers at national, regional and state conventions over the past 15 years. In addition to television, Dr. Battin has had many years' experience in university and semi-professional theatre. He has also worked in motion picture production and has played character roles in several major motion pictures.

5

DIRECTING

BY TOM C. BATTIN

TELEVISION DIRECTING is one of the most exciting, most challenging, most demanding and, frequently, most frustrating activity in which any individual can participate.

The medium of television is a combination of three means or methods of communication — sight, sound, and motion, in that order of importance. Since sight in television is "sight in motion," this adds to the impact of the already powerful combination of sight and sound. Therefore, television is essentially photographic, which demands that the director be visual-minded. However, the director must be cognizant also of the great importance of sound relative to the picture. He should be sensitive to sound and its properties. The beginning director must understand that he is working in a medium of intimacy and immediacy which demands constant alertness and good common sense intelligence from him during every moment he is rehearsing and/or directing a program.

The Chinese proverb, "One picture is worth ten thousands words," does not readily apply to television. Sound must balance the picture — sight and sound must work together — this must be a congenial, compatible marriage. Sometimes the picture dominates the sound, other times the sound dominates the picture, but most of the time there is a very definite balance between the two, for one cannot endure long on the TV screen without the other.

161

Television is a medium of action which requires that both sight and sound have motion and movement; otherwise TV becomes static. The director must be capable of blending well the three ingredients of sight, sound and motion, if he is to achieve the utmost in quality production. Therefore, the director must be able to tele-visualize a script or sequence as he reads it. He must train himself to think in terms of pictures, action and movement. The director must be sensitive to the selectivity of the human ear and must have a workable knowledge of sound perspective if he is to successfully balance picture, sound and motion.

THE DIRECTOR AND HIS RESPONSIBILITIES

In the majority of local TV stations a director generally assumes also the responsibilities of a producer. In the local station, many of the responsibilities in producing and directing overlap and become a combined task for one person, who then becomes a producer-director. His job, then, becomes a dual activity which requires a broad working knowledge of all studio and control room equipment, coupled with an equally broad knowledge of the programming and production side of television. In short, a producer-director must be a person of many talents and qualifications. The producer's role is discussed in Chapter 3 of this book.

The producer-director in the role of director has the sole responsibility for putting the television program on the air. All the efforts of the production staff and talent reach a climax in his performance as a director. Since all programs are telecast for a viewing audience, a most important directorial responsibility is to the audience. He must understand its needs and wants and be capable of fulfilling them. The director is a conductor and his symphony is one of picture, language, music and motion. All these things the director molds into moving patterns which are readily understood and enjoyed by his audience. It is the director's task to present visually, as closely as possible, the work of the writer as the latter visualized it while writing.

Personal Qualities

The director must be able to communicate his instructions rapidly and clearly. He must be definite, decisive. Due to the pressure of time, there must be no hesitation in his decisions. He must be capable of putting his thoughts into as few words as possible for easy and quick comprehension.

The director must be a showman in every sense of the word. He must be adept at exhibiting things effectively and without "gimmicks" or through "unorthodox" methods. He must have an instinctive sense of good taste and must never intentionally offend in what he visually presents. The director should have the ability to recognize a good script and its potential for the TV medium. He should make every effort possible to present his script content in a manner in which it will be accepted by everyone.

The director must be stern, but his sternness must be seasoned generously with understanding and tact. He must remember he is working with human beings and recognize when his performers and staff are tired and need a rest period. However, he must adhere to rigid deadlines and rehearsal schedules if he is to make a success of his on-the-air presentation. The director commands the respect of his technical staff and talent by the way he handles his rehearsals and accomplishes what must be done without waste of time.

The director must have a keen sense of observation to enable him to recognize those things which add to the quality of a show as well as increase viewer interest. He must be able to recognize the need for any necessary last minute changes.

The director must be a person of foresight, one who projects his thinking and anticipates problems before they occur, thus avoiding what otherwise could develop into major difficulties.

The director must be alert to the pressures and strictures of time, for time in television is evanescent. He must be alert to the many and varied details inherent in any TV production, and be capable of making fast and correct decisions.

The television director is working with a great many different persons involved in many different individual tasks. He is participating in what appears to be "organized chaos," working under tremendous pressure and nervous tension, but he must remain calm and not expose his tension, for tension is contagious.

The director must be able to work under extreme pressure — the pressure of numerous responsibilities being carried out simultaneously. He lives by the sweep hand of the clock. To the director, speed is of the utmost importance.

The director must be able to set in his mind the many details of his directing assignment. He must be capable of quickly recalling any or all details at a moment's need. He must be able to memorize rapidly an entire script, all movements, camera shots, business, cues and other details. During the on-the-air telecast the director cannot afford to be imprisoned by his script. He must know it — forward and backward.

The director must be a strong self-disciplinarian. While he is directing he must depend entirely upon himself in the directing of the production. No one tells the director what to do. He is constantly telling others what to do, and while doing this he himself must adhere religiously to the standards and demands he is making of others. He must demand more of himself than he does of others.

The director must consider the great responsibility he has to the station for which he is producing and directing programs. He must do the very best job humanly possible for the station. His goal should be for quality, perfection, and he should never settle for mediocrity.

The director must be able to evaluate a script well enough to determine the good from the bad. As he reads the script he must tele-visualize it, be capable of mentally telecasting the content. This visualization of script content is extremely helpful in determining the value of the material relative to its production.

The director is the pivotal figure around which the production revolves. It is his task to coordinate the many elements of production while he is functioning as an on-the-air director. He is working in a highly technical medium and he must be skilled enough to use it artistically.

Control Room Activities

Most of the time the director will be in communication with many members of his technical staff involved in the on-the-air telecast. This he does through his inter-com system consisting of head phones and a small microphone. He is involved in many activities, most of which are going on simultaneously. Some of these activities are:

1) Talking with members of his technical staff such as those in the control room and master control room, the audio engineer, technical director (if he has one), VTR operator, film and slide projectionists.
2) Conversing with the light director relative to any special lighting effects during the show.
3) Talking with the production crew in the studio: floor manager, cameramen, microphone boom operators. (The inter-com is vital here.)
4) He must watch, depending upon how many cameras he is using, at least three monitors almost simultaneously: two camera monitors and the program line monitor. Frequently he must also keep an eye on the film and/or VTR preview monitors.
5) He must listen to all sound: speech, music and sound effects.
6) He must have contact with announcers, narrators and any other persons involved in any off-camera speaking.
7) He must follow the script, routine sheet or whatever type format is used. An alert director will memorize basic elements in script material.
8) Finally, he must keep an eye on the control room clock for the overall timing of the show. Some directors use a stop watch for keeping check on certain portions or segments of the show such as commercials, opening and closing announcements, and so forth.

If the director is going to do his own switching, and in most local stations he will, then he must be a very alert individual who can set up camera shots, call them, switch them and, at the same time, maintain all communications necessary with the various members of his technical staff.

The director must check the availability of all equipment to be used before he goes into any rehearsals. He probably will have to set up rehearsal dates according to when equipment is available. He must make a check on all equipment he will be using during rehearsals and for the on-the-air telecast, including cameras, lens complements, special lenses such as Zoomar, special effects equipment, all audio equipment such as microphones, live sound such as music and sound effects, films and slides and film and slide projection equipment. He must make a request for all such equipment well in advance of the dates of rehearsals and telecast.

The director should be familiar with the NAB TV Code. He must determine whether or not his program is in good taste. Is the material suited for the mass audience of TV viewers? He must make certain there is no material in the script which might offend; this means checking for any objectionable material before going into rehearsals.

TELE-VISUALIZATION

The director must learn to think in terms of pictures, images or shots. The camera is a relatively flexible and mobile piece of equipment which, when handled by an imaginative and skillfully adept person, can make a viewer feel that he is actually present at the scene of action. Carroll O'Meara, former producer-director for NBC, writes in his book, *Television Program Production:*

"A person attending a three-ring circus has an over-all view of a vast panorama of assorted action and sights. But he does not watch the over-all performance at all times. Instead, he alternately concentrates on one ring at a time, focusing his attention on a nearby clown, looks at the trapeze performers on their lofty swings, then turns to see the face of the friend seated next to him. With nature's magnificent optical system and perception senses, he is in effect constantly cutting from one shot to another, instantly and automatically focusing at will. He sees what he wants to enjoy, what he accidentally discovers, or what attracts his attention."

The director must select shots according to their interest value, their significance, their dramatic impact. He should look for unusual composition which will attract attention to the subject and not away from it. He must select shots which visually tell the story and which enhance the action and the speech or sound. He must add variety by introducing varied camera angles and levels in his shots, but he must not cut for the sake of cutting. Each shot should be selected for its importance in adding to the viewer's pleasure and interest in watching the program.

The director must use the cameras as he would use his own eyes when viewing a scene. He must be cognizant of the fact that the viewer actually sees everything through the eyes of the director; therefore, the director must think of the camera as the eyes of the viewer when he is shooting a program. He alone must judge what the viewer wants to see, how he wants to see it and when he wants to see it, so his judgment must be good. He must select the best camera angles as motivated by the action and/or dialogue of the performers. He must vary those angles and movements, creating dramatic emphasis and emotional impact which will arrest and sustain viewer interest.

No two directors will "shoot" a program alike. The shooting of any show is determined by the individual director's ability, imagination, judgment and good taste, coupled with his understanding and knowledge of the medium. He is dependent upon his knowledge of the equipment and his ability to use such equipment in producing the very best possible results. His creativity and imaginative skill, united with his ingenuity, will enable him to present program content significantly and effectively.

The director must know when and how to use wide shots, close shots, close-up shots, and understand the importance of the necessity to modify and to use the many variations of such basic shots for purposes of visual continuity. There must be a reason for showing a certain view (shot) of a subject or object in a certain way at a given time or moment. There must be a premise, a motivation, a purpose behind such a shot. For example, suppose the director has a waist shot of a man. As viewers watch this man he looks off camera or out of the frame of the picture toward the left, and suddenly he reacts to something he sees. The viewers now are curious about what it is off camera which causes the man's strange reaction. The director immediately cuts to another camera which reveals the picture of what had caused the man's reaction. The cut to the other camera was motivated by the man's reaction, which in turn aroused the viewers' curiosity and desire to see what he had seen. In other words, the director had a motivation or purpose for cutting to the other camera.

Points of View and Impact

The director has several points of view at his disposal as he uses his cameras. He is viewing the scene from as many angles as he has cameras working his show. Two cameras are used on most programs in most local stations. The director must establish the setting or locale of the show to orient the viewer as to where the action is taking place. This should be followed by a closer view of certain parts of the setting as motivated by the action. At times it is necessary to go to close-up or tight close-up views, depending upon how minute the detail, how intimate and dramatic the scene, or how important the specific information may be.

When setting up or plotting shots, the director should keep in mind the impact or effectiveness of each individual picture or shot. Each shot must be meaningful. Each shot must have a relationship to the visual continuity, and relate to or affect the shot which precedes it and the one which follows it. Dollying to change angles of view may take place while the camera is on-the-air or when repositioning for a new shot. Camera movement is based on the psychological effect it will have on the viewer. Regardless of the type of program being telecast, there should be dramatic value in any and all camera movement — movement based on motivation or purpose relative to the continuity of the program. Movement should never be done or used just for its own sake — unless, as a last resort, to give life to an otherwise dead show. However, proper directorial preparation, analysis and diagnosis can avoid what could be a dead show.

Pictures — Images — Shots

Before he can know the basic shots in TV, the director must first understand what is meant by the term "shot." A shot is a picture which appears on the TV screen and which may last for a few seconds or for an indefinite period. It is the picture or image created by a camera and it is usually held as long as the director feels it is effective or motivated.

The television program is usually made up of a series of different shots which result from combining a long shot, a medium shot and a close-up shot. There must be a progression of shots — related pictures — if the program is to have visual continuity. As the director makes use of these basic shots he begins to understand shot or picture relationship and so learns the importance of progression. Progression simply means he is using his camera cuts or changes according to lenses. He is cutting from a camera on the air with a 50mm lens to a camera using a 90mm lens to a camera using a 135mm lens, or vice versa. This type of cutting or switching gives the viewer a feeling of smooth movement from one picture to another and imparts a close relationship among the various shots being used. Of course, there are times when the director wishes to alert or shock the viewer. This he does by cutting from a long or wide shot to a close or close-up shot, which achieves the desired dramatic effect. Or he may cut from a medium shot to a close-up. However, he should never cut from a long shot to a close-up unless there is a very special reason. He may be on a wide shot, then dolly in to a close or medium view and then cut to a close-up. This gives the same relative effect as progression of lenses.

The most frequently used shots in television are the close and close-up shots, reflecting not only a consideration of the size of the TV screen, but the fact that television is an intimate medium requiring the intimacy of the close and close-up shot. This is not to indicate that the long shot is not valuable; on the contrary, the long shot is the only means by which the setting, locale or environment of the drama or show can be established for the viewer. The wise director, the thinking director, will never repeat the same shot set-up from the same angle — except on occasions when he may have a very special reason to do this for dramatic emphasis. The thinking director will hold a shot only as long as he feels the viewers need it to quickly and clearly grasp the visual significance of the shot. The director must remember that varying the angles of his three basic shots is actually the only way he can add visual interest; the various changes of angles change the viewpoint and accentuate important detail.

Identification of Shots

Let us visualize the human body as the subject relative to the identification of shots:

Long shot — a wide, full length shot of the person.

Medium shot — a close shot, usually from the waist up.

Close-up shot — usually a shot of the head and shoulders.

Many directors use terminology relative to portions of the body, as follows:

Knee shot — from the knees up.

Thigh shot — from the thighs up.

Hip shot — from the hips up.

Waist shot — from the waist up.

Chest or bust shot — from the chest up.

Shoulder shot — from the shoulders up.

Head shot — a close-up of the head, often referred to as a Big CU or Tight CU.

Face shot — extreme close-up, shows only a certain portion of the face as indicated by director. Some directors call this the "slice" shot.

It is important to indicate the difference between a close shot and a close-up shot. The close shot is usually a shot from the waist up, while the close-up is from the shoulders up. If the director is on a waist shot of a person he can create a closer shot by moving the camera unobtrusively until the closer shot is accomplished. The director has at his disposal the full gamut of shots ranging from the long shot to the close-up, and he has the extremes of both. The close-up shot and the long shot offer the director a wonderful means for dramatic effect when the two shots are combined into what is termed the close-up-long shot. This is a shot set up on one camera combining a close-up of a subject in the foreground and a long shot of another subject or object in the background. This combination shot has many variations, particularly for dramatic programs; however, it can be used on other types of programs when wisely handled. The variations of this combined shot depend entirely upon the imagination, good judgment and common sense of the director.

The Studio Zoomar lens is quite easily operated. It gives the effect of a "zoom" toward or away from a relatively distant object or subject with considerable speed and smoothness. It permits a rapid, dramatic movement, one which literally sweeps the viewer's eyes from a wide view to a tight view of a subject or object, or vice versa. The Zoomar can be used with some excellent results for dramatic effects. At times it is an effective substitute for the dolly shot. It is particularly effective on commercials when the director wishes to emphasize detail or arrest attention quickly.

Be aware, however, of the aesthetic artificiality of Zoomar which is a limitation. Because of the Zoomar's adeptness, unless the director fully understands its use he may be "carried away" by the effect created by this lens — and over-use it. The beginning director is tempted to zoom instead of utilizing the dolly movement which provides a much more realistic picture for the viewer. He should practice using the Zoomar lens until he recognizes the difference between the perspective of objects on the Zoomar and that during a dolly shot.

Motivation and Editing

The director may do his own switching or he may use a technical director. Regardless of method, the director is his own editor — he decides what shots to set up and which to select to maintain good visual continuity. When the director plots his shots in the camera rehearsal, he will discover as he progresses that he becomes highly selective relative to the shots he will call during the on-the-air telecast. He may also plan his shots before rehearsals begin, in the very early stages of rehearsal or, as in the "winged" show, on the air. Whatever the method of planning, his selection and use of planned shots is termed "editing."

The director has the opportunity to select from a variety of images or shots and to determine which shot will be the most effective when sent out over the air. In this act of selection the director becomes his own "editor." His selectivity determines the strength of the visual continuity which must sustain the interest of the viewer. The director guides the attention of the viewer by varying angles and sizes of a scene or subject action during the show. His ingenuity in editing will determine the effectiveness and quality of the visual aspect of his show. There must be a succession of closely related shots which create a progression of closely related pictures telling a moving visual story. The manner in which the director edits his shots will determine the relative progression of pictures.

There must be a premise, a reason or purpose for setting up a shot in a certain way. There must be a motivation for every shot set up and sent out over the air. The director's premise indicates the what, how, and why of the shot. Let us assume it is a shot of a person, a certain portion of that person. The shot is set up at a certain direction from the camera forming a particular angle from which the viewer will see the person. The shot of the subject is well framed, sharply focused, and clearly visible to the viewer. The shot is well composed with good balance to intensify interest and pleasure. The shot is determined by motivation. What is motivation? It is the reason why the particular shot was set up by the director. For example, let us assume it to be a close-up shot, a shot of a name-plate on an apartment door. Prior to this close-up shot, the director has a shot of a young man moving down the hallway of the apartment house searching for this particular name-plate. He stops and looks at the plate. As viewers, we wish to see the name-plate too, so the motivation for the cut to the close-up is quite obvious.

Movement

Regardless of the type of program, the director must achieve some kind of dramatic effect. At his disposal are many things which he may use to help create the desired effect: camera angles, composition, lighting, setting, sound, music, and movement involving talent and/or camera or both. The director has three basic movements with which he can control visually the continuity of the program: 1) the subject moves as he performs on-camera, the camera and dolly remaining stationary except when necessary to pan or tilt; 2) the camera moves in or out, pedestals up or down, or perhaps moves in an arc around the subject, who remains relatively stationary; 3) both the subject and camera participate in the movement. For example, the subject walks toward a window and the camera dollies in or tightens up on him as he moves. The director draws upon his imagination and technical skill when using any or all of the basic movements.

It is quite possible for a TV program to become static because of a lack of movement or too little movement. Since TV is such an intimate medium, the performers are working in what we think of as the natural environment or setting. The space is usually comparable in dimensions to those of the actual living room or office. The actors' movements, then, are extremely natural and permit the director a lot of freedom in setting up shots. For example, two actors are talking in the family room of the house, one of them gets up from his chair and goes over to the fireplace to get a golf trophy. The other actor watches his every action and makes some move or does some bit of business, all of which help to keep the scene moving and interesting. At the same time, such movement and business give the camera new angles and a new point of view, enabling the director to achieve visual continuity. However, a director must sense when a movement is good or bad and must know why it is good or bad. If he will remember that TV is an action medium, as well as photographic, then he will always be able to visualize movement in a relative manner.

A good television show has movement because that movement is paced by the tempo of the story or other program content. The movement is paced by dialogue or by just plain conversation. The director must use movement with discretion and taste. He must not become so interested in movement that he will cause his viewers to lose contact with the story or basic content of the show. Beware of becoming involved in the "technique" of movement. Frequently the director wishes to make his transitions by other means than the cut, the dissolve or the fade. He will find, by experimenting, that camera movement often offers wonderfully effective ways of making transitions. For example, suppose he is doing a two-man interview and has a close or close-up shot of the interviewee. It is time for a commercial or a promo, so he cuts to a waist shot of the "host" and as the host orally cues the announcer, who is doing a live studio presentation, the director has the cameraman move in slowly and tilt up as he goes. The camera loses the host as it tilts up to the light background of the setting. A cut is then made to the camera positioned in the area where the announcer is located; this camera is already tilted up. As it tilts down the announcer comes into view in the same manner as the host was taken out of view. Experimenting with camera movement is fun, but do not overwork it.

COMPOSITION

The viewer's acceptance of any picture is dependent upon the composition of that picture.

Composition is the result of the combined efforts of the director, cameraman, set designer and lighting director. Let us assume the scene is a modern living room which is lighted to create the illusion of late evening. The director tells the cameraman that he wants a full length shot of the subject standing by the fireplace in the room. The cameraman sets up the shot as he visualizes it relative to his idea of composition. However, the director may wish to modify the shot a little, or he may wish to change the angle of the shot. He makes his suggestions to the cameraman who adjusts the shot according to the director's instructions, the result being a picture composed through the combined efforts of the director and cameraman. The director may have some suggestions for certain changes in arrangement of furniture and props, and possibly in lighting. All such combined efforts result in good composition.

The general layout, positioning of talent, scenery, props, mike booms and lights have all been carefully planned and set up relative to composition. The director and cameraman must think of the position and movement of the subject in relation to the camera, lights and scenery. The composition of any TV picture is never constant, but is always changing. Talent moves, scenes change, lights change, cameras move, all effecting a change in composition. It is easy to see how a static picture can be made to come alive, be given movement by simply changing the angles from which the camera shoots or views the subject.

If you study any picture carefully you will note there is an arrangement of shapes made up of line, mass and form. Instinctively, the human being has a marked emotional reaction to shape — for example, one's reaction when first viewing the Grand Canyon or the Washington Monument. Pictures must be composed to motivate a definite emotional response from the viewer. Any well composed picture has, or should have, a center of interest — a focal point — which is determined by the arrangement of the subjects in the picture. The director should concentrate on that center or focal point of interest when setting up his shots. Since every television picture or shot should be motivated, then the picture should be composed to accomplish a specific purpose. Composition must contribute to the telling of the story.

When a director thinks about composition he must think of depth. Without depth there is no composition; the picture becomes flat. Television is a two-dimensional medium and the director must give it depth by creating the illusion of a three-dimensional medium. If depth is to be achieved, there must be a balance between the foreground and the background. To create a feeling of great depth, of three-dimensions, there must be a foreground, a middle-ground and a background. It is very important to pay particular attention to the distance between each of the three things used to create foreground, middle-ground and background.

For example, the background could be rear-screen projection of a scene of the ocean with the surf rolling in, while the middle ground could be sand on the floor of the studio with a blanket spread out with one or two persons sprawled on it, and the foreground could be a prop rock with some pieces of driftwood to add the final bit in creating the three-dimensional aspect.

Composition should never distract. It must arrest attention and be pleasing to the eye. Try to avoid using the straight line arrangement, for example, in setting up products for commercials. Experiment with the triangular, the semi-circular, the circular, and even the square arrangement of objects being displayed. The broken-up arrangement of objects or subjects is always most appealing to the eye.

The director who is creative and artistic, who is imaginative and observant, generally is aware of good composition when he sees it. Although he may not know all the artistic rules and theories of good composition, the manner in which visual aspects are related provide him with enough sound principles to create good composition. The arrangement of shapes in any picture — the line, mass and form — directs our attention to a specific object or subject which influences our emotions. In the final analysis, composition is the placement of subjects or objects within the picture frame in a way which will affect us emotionally.

TRANSITIONAL DEVICES

The Cut

The quickest, simplest and most frequently used method of transition from one camera to another is the straight or direct cut. It is instantaneous and definite. It is the fastest means by which two scenes can be joined or related and which can show the viewer what he wants to see when he wants to see it. When a change is made from one camera to another it is usually done for the purpose of giving the viewer another look at the action from a different angle or view. This is what we think of as an immediate substitution of one picture for another.

The impact of the cut should not be underestimated. The direct cut can be used effectively in several ways: 1) As an excellent device for creating sudden shock by cutting from a long shot to a close-up, or from a medium shot to a tight close-up. The sudden cut creates a dynamic impact upon the viewer. However, this must be used wisely and sparingly and for a very definitely motivated purpose — otherwise, the visual continuity will be interrupted. 2) By fast cutting the director can create the illusion of increasing the tempo of an otherwise slow pace. 3) Cuts can be done to the rhythm of a dance or musical number. Short, quick cuts, when used wisely, can be exciting. 4) Cutting on action must be done so the visual shock of the cut will be unobtrusive. Generally, the shot is either held for the duration of the action or it may be completed in following cuts. Unless there is a very definite motivation for cutting away from the action, it is much wiser to remain on the first shot. 5) A direct cut from black to a picture of full intensity is frequently used to open a scene. It is dynamic and can be a very strong attention getting device. A direct cut from a picture to black has a very definite feeling of finality.

When to cut:

When action calls for a cut — when there is obvious motivation.

For variety. Keep continuity interesting. Cut to different angles.

For dramatic emphasis.

At the end of a sentence or phrase, not in the middle.

At the end of a musical phrase. Pace cuts according to pace of music.

On action or movement, within the action or movement.

For reaction, cut should be made a split second ahead of reaction of person.

When not to cut:

Don't overcut. A series of fast cuts are meaningless. However, if paced properly, cuts sometimes can be used to create the illusion of stepping up a slow pace.

Don't cut blindly. Always be aware of the need to cut.

Don't cut to identical shots. If you get "trapped" go to black and work out fast.

Don't cut to extreme angles (e.g. from a profile to a front view or long shot).

Don't cut from a pan to a stationary shot. This is disturbing to the eye.

Don't cut on a pan shot unless the cut is to another pan shot moving in the same direction as the one from which the cut was made.

Don't cut to extremely different angles. Subject must always be recognized immediately in any shot.

Don't be afraid to stay on one camera, even for a long period of time, unless there is a very definite reason for cutting to another camera.

If the director is well aware of the fact that the cut is an abrupt transition from one picture to another, he will recognize that the sudden change created by the cut produces a subconscious shock in the mind of the viewer. If the director selects the two pictures involved in the cut with great care, then there will be an immediate association of ideas which takes place in the mind of the viewer and the resultant emotional effect is that which the director wishes to achieve when shooting his program. Used wisely, the cut is exciting and stimulating.

There are times when a director wants to build suspense by holding a shot on the air when viewers would like to see what is going on off-camera. This is particularly useful in drama. For example, the director will use this "delayed cut" method to achieve greater suspense when he holds a shot just a second longer than usual before he cuts to another camera. By the time he makes the cut to the other camera, viewer empathy is usually much greater. Generally, viewers anticipate the director's cutting to new shots. When the director intentionally withholds cutting to another shot he increases interest and suspense.

The director should tell the floor manager to cue talent first before the switch is made to another camera, in order to insure a smooth transition by talent from one camera to another. To ready talent to "look" from one camera to another, the floor manager usually gives a "standby" cue first. As soon as the talent has reached the end of a sentence or phrase, the floor manager cues talent to the other camera. The cut from one camera to the other must instantly follow the cue to talent.

A director selects and changes shots when the new shot gives welcome relief, stimulates and increases interest. Action of any kind generally motivates a change of picture and new angles of view. To prevent a picture of the same subject or object from becoming monotonous, it is necessary to vary the angle and composition of shots of the subject. However, use these changes sparingly, and primarily to prevent the program from becoming static. Remember, too much cutting results in confusion, annoyance, and a jumpy effect on the screen.

The Fade

Fade is a term which means a major change is being made in the visual continuity of the show. If a "fade-in" is used, it means the picture is being brought in from a black screen to the picture's fullest intensity. The fade-in means "curtain going up" — beginning of action — opening of a scene or act. The fade-in should be done at a normal speed to insure the feeling of introducing the action without shock. However, sometimes a fast fade-in does a relatively good job of shocking if that is the effect desired by the director.

The "fade-out" is the reverse of the fade-in — it fades out the picture from full intensity to black. This indicates "curtain coming down" — end of scene or act or show. Here again the important factor is the control of the speed of the fade-out. A restful reaction can be created by the slow fade-out, while the fast fade-out has a tendency to destroy some of the feeling of whatever suspense may have been built up during the scene. Sometimes the fast fade-out can help strengthen suspense.

The Dissolve or Mix

The dissolve is blended transition, somewhat like the cross-fade used in radio. Two cameras are in action at the same time, each with a picture framed and focused for on-the-air. One camera is on the air while the other is ready and standing by. The two cameras are, in a sense, cross-faded. The camera on the air is faded-out as the other camera is faded-in simultaneously. The two pictures must pass on the way out and in. For a brief, split second the two cameras' pictures are on the air at the same time, thus assuming the role of a momentary superimposition.

The dissolve can be used to indicate a short lapse of time, a minor change of locale. It can mean a very smooth transition from one angle to another if proper attention is then given to such things as changes in angles, changes in movement, and changes in size of shot. Otherwise, at the moment of the dissolve when the two pictures are mixed there will be an unrelated conglomerate of images appearing on the screen. The dissolve can create a very nice, easy, smooth transition, one which is restful to the eye. The viewer does what we might think of as a mental dissolve as he witnesses the visual dissolve done by the director. The beginning director, as he practices with the dissolve, will note it has rhythm, a rhythm which is easy and smooth and has great harmony. The dissolve should blend one train of thought into another. The speed of the dissolve is pertinent to how well it fulfills its purpose. It must be done wisely and carefully; otherwise, it distracts.

The Matched Dissolve

This transitional device involves two cameras with shots of closely related subjects or objects. It is excellent for transitions in drama. Of course, it can be used effectively in other types of programs, too. For example, the director may dissolve from a shot of a professional baseball player in the batter's box to a shot of a small boy in baseball uniform standing in the batter's box on the local sand lot; or from a close-up of a model jet airliner to a shot of a real jet in flight.

Defocus to Refocus

This technique can be used in a number of ways (e.g. dream sequences, suggesting a person losing consciousness, creating a misty or hazy effect). It is an excellent device with which to change or move from a present day scene to one in the past — the flashback. This is done by defocusing the camera on the pivotal character at the end of a scene. During this action another camera, defocused, has been framed upon the character or on the area in which the flashback action in the next scene is to take place. The first scene ends as the camera is taken completely out of focus, the director dissolves to the second camera, also out of focus. Since both cameras are out of focus during the dissolve the viewer is never aware of the dissolve technique. As soon as the dissolve is executed, the second camera is refocused and the viewer is transported to the scene of the flashback. The return to the present or first scene is done with the same technique. There are a number of ways this technique can be used in the production of commercials.

The Super

This term is derived from "superimposition." The effect is comparable to the double exposure in photography. In television the picture from one camera is superimposed over the picture from another camera, blending the two pictures into one meaningful visual. The use of the "super" is left up to the discretion of the director. Great care must be taken in selecting the correct background for the supered material. In using a super all subject material must be easily identifiable and meaningful to the viewer.

Whatever method of transition is used, the director must remember its use is governed by motivation and not to use it as a "gimmick."

DIRECTING APPROACHES

Pattern Shooting

When shooting newscasts, interviews, panel shows and other programs which are usually unrehearsed, many directors set up a "pattern." Most of these types of programs are on the daily schedule and generally follow the routine sheet script format (see Chapter 4). Camera shots seldom deviate from the three basic shots — the long, medium and close-up. The director sets up his "editorial pattern" for a given program and then "wings" it with a variation of the basic pattern.

Winging, Ad-Libbing, Free-Shooting

These terms are synonomous and refer to a method of directing in which the director sets up and edits his shots while his program is on the

This method is used when there is no time available for rehearsing. When a show such as an interview is to be aired, the director usually does a short run-through rehearsal of the beginning and ending of the program to assure him of a smooth opening and closing as well as a means of setting up back-timing for controlling the close.

Instructions and Conduct

It is important that the director instruct his staff relative to his method of setting up and calling shots. For example, let us assume the director is to execute a dissolve between camera 1 and camera 2. He must indicate his intentions to his cameramen. He might instruct them to "hold" both cameras for dissolve, or he might say "Standby for dissolve" or "Hold for dissolve" and follow with "Dissolve two." As soon as the dissolve is completed he usually indicates that the other camera (number 1) is free to break set and reposition for the next shot. The director sets his shots during the camera rehearsal so that each cameraman clearly understands the type of shot, lens to be used, composition, movement and position. He should see that each cameraman has a list of his own individual shots. Often this list is attached to the back of the camera, on the left or right side, where it is clearly visible to the cameraman.

The director is entirely responsible for the interpretation of any dialogue, announce copy, or narration, and must express good judgment and taste in the selection of shots which best interpret visually the author's thinking and visualization. The director should protect himself when shooting a show by always keeping a "cover-shot," which is simply a wide shot covering everything of importance relative to the subject on camera. This will prevent getting caught with close or close-up shots on both cameras. Don't be afraid to move cameras on the air as long as the movement is meaningful.

The director must be able to listen simultaneously to all sounds such as dialogue, music, sound effects, keep his eye and mind on various monitors, carry on conversations with cameramen, floor manager, audio engineers, boom operators, and possibly roll film and/or video tape when needed. He should be able to anticipate any difficulties which might arise while on the air and be prepared to meet such situations without "falling apart." He should think of every program as a challenge to his ability. Regardless of pressures, the director must think about his staff, his co-workers. Be polite. Learn to say "please" and "thank you." Always compliment a cameraman when a shot is well composed or a movement is well executed. Compliment other deserving members of the staff and crew, particularly at the end of a program. This all helps on the next show to be done.

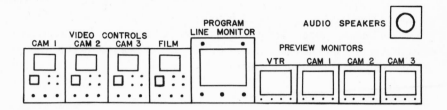

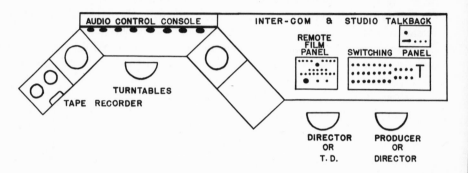

Fig. 1

THE VIDEO SWITCHER

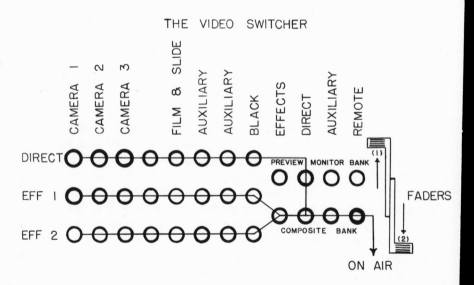

Fig. 2

THE CONTROL ROOM

The control room is the nerve center of television production. In Chapter 2 of this book is an analysis of control room equipment. The director is the pivotal figure in this nerve center, where he is in touch with the studio floor, announce booth, film and/or slide projection room, master control, video engineers, audio engineer and video tape recording room. The director's video switcher is located in the control room. During rehearsals and the on-the-air telecast the director sits in the control room facing a line of TV monitors, each with a picture from some video source (Fig. 1). In most control rooms there is, at least, one monitor for each camera, for preview, one for each camera for video control, one for film, one for the program line, and also one for general previewing. The director communicates via the inter-com with his cameramen to set up the shots he wishes to put on the air. On the program line monitor is seen the picture (shot) which is being telecast and which also appears on one of the camera monitors, depending upon which camera shot is being sent out on the air. On another camera monitor is the shot or picture being set up, checked and readied to be taken next by the director. When the director feels it is the moment to "take" this next shot, he punches the button on the switcher which controls that camera and the shot or picture is switched to on-the-air position on the program line monitor. He then sets up the next shot and gets ready to take it. The director must see his shots from several different angles. This gives him an opportunity to better select the shot which will present the subject most effectively. This activity continues throughout the show as the director interprets the script and transforms it into series of related visual images.

Video Switcher

In the control room is a special panel of buttons and levers with which the director or TD (technical director) controls all picture aspects of the program. This video switching panel may be relatively simple or it may be extremely complicated, depending upon the system used by the individual station. Regardless of the system, every video switcher must provide three possibilities: 1) switching between studio cameras; 2) special effects such as fading, dissolving and superimposing; 3) program monitoring and previewing. (See Chapter 2, Figs. 3, 4, 5.)

The buttons used for switching are the "push-button" type and are set up in parallel rows called "banks" or "buses." The simplest of switching systems usually has three banks or buses. One bank is for direct or instantaneous switching while the other two banks are used to create such effects as fading, dissolving and superimposing. The buttons are used for "punching up" shots during camera rehearsals or the on-the-air telecast.

The video switcher illustrated in Fig. 2 represents one of the simplest, yet most versatile video switchers on the market. Note the three rows of buttons in parallel arrangement.

Direct switching. The first, or top bank, is called the direct bank and is used only for direct or instantaneous switching, referred to as "direct" switching. This bank is activated by punching up the "direct" button on the "composite" bank, which puts on-the-air whatever is "pre-set" on the direct bank.

Effects bank. The second, or middle bank, is called "effects bank #1." The third, or bottom bank, is called "effects bank #2." Both effects banks are activated by the effects button on the composite bank.

Preview bank. At the right of the three banks you will note two rows of four buttons each. The top row is used for punching up pictures on the preview monitor, such as film, slides, VTR, and any special video effects that might be used in a program. It must be understood that anything punched up on the preview monitor row is not going out on the air at that moment.

Composite bank. The bottom row is the "composite" bank. This bank can be arranged so the first button at the left is set up to activate the two effects banks for on-the-air pictures. The second button activates the direct bank for on-the-air. The other two buttons can be set up to activate other video sources such as VTR, which gives the director or TD complete control of everything going out over the air.

If a picture from a camera punched up on the direct bank is to be put on the program line, the direct button on the composite bank must be punched up first. If a picture from a camera on either one of the effects banks is to be put on the air, the effects button on the composite bank must be punched up first.

During any program in most any station, direct or straight switching usually is done on either one of the effects banks. The direct bank is used frequently for previewing, however, and makes it possible for the director to set up and preview effects such as a "super" which he intends to use later on in the program. This is done by transferring his on-the-air camera to the direct bank. Then he pre-sets his super on effects banks #1 and #2. For example, assume that he is going to super credits over the shot of the setting on camera 2. He first transfers camera 2 to direct bank by punching up camera 2 on direct bank, then by punching direct button on composite bank he now has camera 2 on-the-air on direct bank. Then he pre-sets camera 2 on the shot of the set, on effects bank #1. He pre-sets camera 1 on a shot of the credits information, on effects bank #2. Then he moves the faders to mid-position and punches up the effects button on the monitoring (preview) bank. The super will appear on the preview monitor.

The faders. The two levers on the right side of the composite bank are for special effects such as fading, dissolving and superimposing. These levers are called "faders" — the left handle is used to activate the effects bank #1, while the right handle activates the effects bank #2. To activate these effects banks the faders must be moved together in the same direction, e.g.

both to the forward position to activate effects bank #1. Both faders must be pulled backward to put on the air anything punched up on effects bank #2. In either case, the effects button must be punched up on the composite bank before the picture on either effects bank will appear on the program line. These effects banks are used for fading, dissolving and superimposing. The faders are used to create these effects on the two banks. If the director wishes to do direct switching on either one of the effects banks, he may do so; however, he must remember to have the faders in position to activate the effects bank on which he will do the switching and also have the effects button punched up on the composite bank.

There are several variations of video switchers being used in the numerous TV stations on the air and a director starting in at a new station will be able to adapt quite easily to any or all of them after a brief "once over lightly" check out.

The dissolve or mix. Looking at the drawing of the switcher, let us assume camera 1 is punched up on effects bank #1 and both faders are in the forward position to activate that bank. The effects button is punched up on the composite bank, too. The director wishes to execute a dissolve from camera 1 to camera 2. He punches up camera 2 on effects bank #2. He is now ready to dissolve and does so by moving both faders from effects bank #1 back to effects bank #2. The speed of the dissolve is governed by the speed at which the director moves the faders.

Fade to black. Camera 1 is punched up on effects bank #1, with faders forward. The director wishes to fade this camera to black. First he punches up the button for black on effects bank #2 (this is the last button on the right of this bank). Then he moves the faders from effects bank #1 back to effects bank #2. The fade to black has been carried out. To fade back into camera 1, he now moves the faders forward from black on effects bank #2 to effects bank #1.

The superimposition. Camera 1 is punched up on effects bank #1, with faders in forward position. The director wishes to superimpose over the picture on camera 1 information in the picture on camera 2. He punches up camera 2 on effects bank #2; both cameras are now ready for the super. He moves the faders to the halfway position, midway between the two effects banks. Now each camera is on the air. Although each has only half the normal picture strength, a relatively decent super is seen. To improve this super, the director may "split" the faders. Assuming camera 1 is on effects bank #1 and both faders are in forward position, the director now moves only the right handle of the faders toward the effects bank #2. This fader is never taken all the way to #2 position. This method permits the director better control over the intensity of the super.

If you do not have any equipment available for practice in switching, you can "dry-run" an exercise by turning to the drawing of the switcher and practice punching up cameras, slides and film either by the direct method of switching or by going through the motions of handling the faders.

PRE-PLANNING

The director must have some type of format which will give him direction. This format is his road map, his guide, his blueprint which enables him to move from one point to another, namely, from the beginning to the end of his program. He must have a guide by which to develop smoothly the visual and aural continuity of his program. The format may take several different forms. It may be elaborate and very meticulously planned and set up, such as a complete script in "story board" form; it may be partially scripted; or it may be only a routine sheet. Regardless of which approach or method the director uses, it is necessary for him to pre-plan in one way or another. He must have something tangible from which to work as a director; otherwise, he will waste valuable time and the end result, generally, will be a somewhat "sloppy" production. Examples of each of the above types of formats are indicated later on in this chapter.

Any television program is an expensive and complex operation. Meticulous, thorough pre-planning is necessary before any rehearsals begin. The director must be aware of any visual and/or aural problems during the pre-planning stage and resolve them before rehearsals get under way. There are several reasons why pre-planning is of such great importance: 1) to meet rigid time schedules; 2) to reduce production costs; 3) to create a sense of direction and security for the director when he goes into the rehearsal stage; 4) to enable the director to gain the respect of his staff and talent by showing them he knows where he is going and how he is going to get there.

The director is called upon to do a variety of types of programs, such as interviews, commercials, public service, children's, audience participation and drama. Regardless of the type, he must do some pre-planning. Some directors go into what others might consider elaborate planning, that of setting up a story board layout of their script: a script with sketches using stick figures, or with very carefully done drawings of each shot to be sent out over the air. The degree of planning is up to the individual.

The director must pre-plan his set-up for rehearsals. He must know how much space he will need for housing his set and talent. He must know where he can place boom microphones, how much space he will need for cameras and movement. If he is to use easels he must know how many and where he will place them so cameras can be positioned on them quickly and easily. He must know what props are to be used, where, when, how, and by whom. He must know the lighting set-up and whether or not any special lighting effects are to be used. To have everything arranged and in proper order, the director actually should have a floor plan on which to sketch such arrangements. He should have a light plot worked out so lights will be placed exactly as he wants them. This pre-planning assures the director that things will be done correctly and in time for rehearsals. Such pre-planning is a time saving device, which he will find invaluable when he begins rehearsals, particularly in the studio. He will find that he needs every second of time available.

WORKING WITH THE SCRIPT

As indicated in Chapter 4 in this book, script formats differ, depending on the kind of show, whether the Hollywood or New York dramatic form is used, the requirements of the individual program, and the techniques of the author. Usually the director prefers to get a script with two distinct columns: audio and video. When the director gets the basic script duplicated for distribution to his cast and crew he frequently will transfer certain information into the appropriate columns, if it is not already there. For example, camera, set and stage directions, movements and "business" may be put on the video side; and characters' names, dialogue, music and sound effects, and interpretations may be put on the audio side. This varies with the individual director. Most directors prefer to have the timing indicated on the script, sometimes a timing for the whole, sometimes a timing of sections in minutes. Some directors number the dialogue lines to enable them more easily to indicate to a performer where a line or cue should be picked up during stops in a rehearsal. For similarly easy identification, directors prefer that all pages are numbered clearly at the top left or top right, such as 2/2/2/2..

Marking the Script

It is said that "the stamp of an amateur director is a script free of notes or marks." Of course, individual directors differ in the manner in which they mark their scripts or sequence sheets. However, they do mark them in order to have a means by which they can memorize the pattern of the show, a blueprint from which to maintain visual and/or aural continuity. A director should be thoroughly acquainted with his script or sequence sheet. He should use it as an aid and not be imprisoned by it.

How elaborately marked a script may be is the result of the individual director's own approach to marking. Most directors use a shorthand or abbreviated method of marking. That is, instead of noting on the script, "dissolve to camera #2 — long shot of patio," the director might mark it "DISS 2 — WIDE PATIO." Mark the script and standardize symbols, but because elaborate marking often is confusing and time consuming, use markings wisely and do not overmark. The director should indicate information for all shots, movements of actors and cameras. Some directors go so far as to include the lens to be used on each shot. Cues for talent, music and/or cues for sound must be noted. Many directors like to set up both front- and back-timing indications. This makes it much easier to follow the control room clock. Everyone involved in the on-the-air telecast should have a copy of the final script, marked exactly as the director will use it. One example of a director-marked script is shown on page 185.

Symbols

As previously stated, the director must tele-visualize his script as he reads it. He must think in terms of shots he would like to have relative to the action, dialogue and movements, and must write these in the video column of the script. He must either circle or underscore audio cues such as those for music and sound. He must mark where the talent is to be cued. Generally, the audio aspect is marked in red or blue pencil or in ink. All marks must be clearly visible. Some writers indicate camera shots or directions in their scripts, but usually this is only when it is something very specific or critical which they wish to make certain the director will get. If such shots or directions appear, the director usually circles or underscores them.

It is not possible to list all symbols and cues being used today in all TV stations, but the following are examples of some that are most commonly used in the industry.

T-1	Take 1	Switch to camera 1.
DISS-1	Dissolve 1	Dissolve to camera 1.
DI	Dolly in	Move in close to subject.
DB	Dolly back	Dolly out to a wider shot.
Tight CU	Tight close-up	Very tight shot of subject or object. Usually a head shot.
Loosen up	Wider shot	Usually given when camera is off air. A change of lens is in order.
CU-LS	Combination close-up and long shot	Shot of two persons, one seen in close, other seen in distant background.
OS	Over shoulder shot	Shot taken from over the shoulder of a subject and including another subject in background, or over shoulder as subject is looking in close at some object such as newspaper.
SUP	Superimposition	A super is to be done at this point in the program.
F-I	Fade in	Means to fade from black to a live scene. Fade in the film, the VTR, etc.

F-O	Fade out	The opposite of fade-in.
Pan-L Pan-R	Pan left or right	Pan the camera to left or right.
Tr R Tr L	Truck right or left	Camera and dolly moved in a horizontal direction to the right or left.
Tilt up Tilt down	Tilting action	Camera is moved vertically on axis up or down.
FL	Flip card	Cue floor manager to flip card.
SL	Slide	A slide is to be used at a given time in the program.
CUE or Q	Signal to talent	The word cue or letter Q is usually written in video column right next to line of copy or dialogue to indicate when to cue performer.
THEME	Music	The word theme is usually written above the word music, which is circled in ink.

The Dramatic Script

Some directors set up a dramatic script in the following manner, while others use the film or Hollywood format. This is one example of a dramatic script with the director's prepared shots, movements, cues and symbols. Examples of symbols are in parenthesis. Note that a filmed opening is used on this live production.

THE TIN STAR

By Lou Brown

VIDEO	AUDIO
FADE IN: FILM EXT: DAY LONG SHOT THREE COWBOYS ON HORSES RIDING INTO TOWN. MARTY IS DRESSED IN BLACK HAT. NICK IS TALL, THIN, DIRTY, MEAN LOOKING. RIO, OBVIOUSLY MEXICAN, DIRTY AND TOUGH, BUT HIS TEETH SET IN A PERPETUAL SMILE. THEY RIDE DOWN THE CENTER OF THE STREET, THREE ABREAST, TOWARD THE CAMERA . . . PASS IT AS IT PANS AND FOLLOWS THEM TO THE FRONT OF THE SALOON. THEY DISMOUNT, TIE UP HORSES AND LOOK AROUND. CLOSE THREE SHOT . . . . WAIST SHOT – MARTY	

VIDEO	AUDIO

WAIST SHOT — MARTY

MARTY

Just like I told ya . . . this town's gonna be easy . . . take a look around . . . no one out . . . the bank over there just waiting to be knocked of . . . . Come on . . . let's get a drink . . . I'm dry . . .

THREE SHOT   3 - SHOT

THEY MOVE AROUND HORSES UP STEPS AND THROUGH SALOON DOORS. CAMERA PANS ACROSS STREET TO DOORWAY OF STORE NEXT TO BANK. DEPUTY NED STEPS OUT OF THE SHADOW OF THE STORE DOORWAY. HE STEPS OUT INTO STREET TOWARD SALOON . . . STOPS CLOSE SHOT.   CU

NED

Q

(MUMBLING TO HIMSELF) Those three . . . the ones on the wanted posters Sheriff Marsden was showing me yesterday.

NED TURNS AND HURRIES TOWARD SHERIFF'S OFFICE . . . .
LIVE STUDIO:
CUT TO INTERIOR OF OFFICE AND SHOT OF SHERIFF JOEL MARSDEN AT HIS DESK LOOKING OVER WANTED POSTERS.

Q THEME

(MUSIC:) THEME IN FULL . . . ESTABLISH . . . HOLD

SUPER 1—TITLES   SUP 1—TITLES
AS TITLES END DISSOLVE 2 WIDE OF
JOEL   DIS - 2 WIDE JOEL
TIGHTEN OF SLOWLY TO DESK SHOT. TIGHTEN
TAKE 1 OF POSTER . . . SET UP IN T-1 POSTER
HANDS OF ONE OF CREW OFF SET.
2-WIDE INCLUDING JOEL AT DESK
AND DOOR OF OFFICE AT HIS RIGHT.
TAKE 2 AS NED BURSTS INTO OFFICE
AND UP TO DESK   T-2

Q

MUSIC: SNEAK OUT AS NED ENTERS.

Q

JOEL

Where are they?

TIGHTEN 2—   2 - SHOT

JOEL RISES . . . MOVES TO SIDE OF DESK ON NED'S LINES. TAKE 1—OVER SHOULDER   T-1 - OS
SHOT NED AND JOEL

NED

Over at the saloon . . . three of 'em, rode in about ten minutes ago.

JOEL

Well, it had to come to this some day. Guess I've been a sheriff too many years.

TAKE 2—CU NED   T-2 - CU

NED

(VERY CONFIDENT) What do ya mean? There's only three of 'em . . . you and me, we can . . . .

TAKE 1—OVER SHOULDER   T-1 - OS

JOEL

(STERNLY) We can do what? Walk across the street, put the cuffs on them . . . and that's it. Sure . . . things are not always that simple, Ned.

In the dramatic script some directors like to have every shot, action and movement indicated by some identification symbol or illustration which can be easily and quickly interpreted. However, there is seldom enough space on the original script for such elaborate markings. The director frequently uses a looseleaf binder or notebook in which he places each page of his script on the left, with a blank sheet of paper on the opposite side at the right on which he puts his "storyboard" layout of the shots, actions and movements. He sometimes draws small 3:4 aspect ratio boxes in which he makes sketches (often using stick figures) which represent the types of shots or movements he has blocked out. This is one method. Other directors have their own techniques of marking scripts, standardized to their individual directing assignments.

The Semi-script

Many non-dramatic scripts are fully written out, with complete dialogue and author's directions. The director's approach to marking follows that for the dramatic script above. In the semi-scripted or detailed routine-sheet kind of program, the director's markings may not be quite so detailed, although he should attempt in his pre-planning to make them, nevertheless, as complete as possible, as exemplified in the following.

TWO SHOT	2-SHOT	Dr. Jenkins, why was Andrew Jackson considered such a great soldier and statesman?
CU JENKINS		JENKINS
		EXPLAINS THAT JACKSON WAS A MAN OF THE COMMON PEOPLE, NOT A LEARNED MAN, BUT A MAN OF COURAGE, STRONG BELIEFS . . . .
TWO SHOT	2-SHOT	JONES
		Then he was not an educated man, that is, a man of formal education?
CU JENKINS		JENKINS
		EXPLAINS HOW LITTLE EDUCATION JACKSON ACTUALLY HAD, HOW AT TIMES HE WAS EVEN UNWISE . . . .
TWO SHOT	2-SHOT	JONES
		Is it true that he was a rough, often crude type of person?
CU JENKINS		JENKINS
CU PICS OF JACKSON		REPLIES THAT HE WAS A MAN OF PROFANITY WHO OFTEN LIKE TO DRINK . . . .

Routine or Rundown Sheet

These types of formats are usually used in programs having established patterns or routines, shows which are telecast five days a week. These shows are done by what might be termed "pattern shooting." A set pattern of camera coverage is set up and then a form of "free shooting" or "ad libbing" or "winging" is used in directing the program. In this type of script most directors will indicate the continuity of the show in segments, the set areas in which each segment takes place, and the over-all running time, time of each segment, and whatever back-timing they feel necessary, as exemplified in the following rundown sheet.

11:07:30	Jud Welcomes Sen Kefauver	(10:00)	(Center Area)
11:17:30	Jud Cues	(0:30)	
11:18:00 SOF	*Clorox* Com	(1:00)	(SOF)
11:19:00	Teddy Bart Sings	(3:00)	(Band Area)
11:36:30	Jud Intros Barbara	(1:00)	(Center Area)
11:37:30	Barbara Welcomes Playwright, George Hitchcock	(6:00)	(Corner Table)
11:43:30	Jud Reads Some Anncts and Goes Into News	(3:00)	(Center Area)
11:46:30	Jud Closes Out News and Intros	(3:00)	(Center Area)
11:49:30 SOF	*B.C. Remedy* Com	(1:00)	(SOF)
11:50:30	Jud Welcomes Red O'Connel and Guest	(6:00)	(Center Area)
11:56:30 SLIDE	Booth Does *Sunbeam Bread* Com	(1:00)	(Booth)
11:57:30	Jud Wraps Up Show	(0:30)	(Center Area)
11:59:00	Marvin and Band	(1:00)	(Dome Area)
11:59:00	Super Credits Over Band	(0:30)	

11:59:30 FADE PIC AND MUSIC

THE DIRECTOR IN ACTION

Most directors will be working in a local TV station where there is always the problem of inadequate rehearsal time. The director must make profitable use of every moment and, therefore, should be familiar with several methods of rehearsing. Assuming the director has the complete script and has cast the show, his first responsibility is to analyze the script. While reading, he must be able to visualize every infinitesimal part of it and know it from beginning to end. Once the director has thoroughly mastered the script, he will set up his first rehearsal.

Rehearsals

At the first full cast rehearsal, the script is read through and discussed in terms of theme, mood, atmosphere, characterization, plot and plot development, character relationship to plot movement, and relation of character to character, among other dramaturgical elements. Next, a dry-run rehearsal is conducted outside the studio, usually in a large room or a rehearsal hall where the director can work freely in working out business, movement and action. The rehearsal room may be set up in the following manner:

1) Mark off the floor using masking tape to outline walls, doors, windows, furniture, set pieces, and any other details which should be represented. The outside area should be taped to the dimensions of the studio space in which the show will take place.

2) Chairs may be used to represent davenports, tables, floor lamps, doorways, etc. This enables the director to work out details of action, business and movement.

During this rehearsal period the director begins to think in terms of pictures and makes an attempt, as he moves about, to set up tentative shots at various angles and positions where he will later place his cameras, relative to shots he will use on the air. He makes notes of possible shots, movement, business and action. Since there are no cameras at this stage, a director may make use of his hands in framing a picture by placing the two thumbs together, end to end, forming a horizontal base, and with the two index fingers in vertical position he has a rectangular frame through which he may view a scene or subject. He can move closer to the subject to simulate a closer shot, or he can move back from the subject to simulate a wider or longer shot. Most of the problems and details of action, business and movement can be worked out here. This makes camera rehearsals much easier and faster since there would be little need for the trial and error method.

Dry-run. When the cast has all lines memorized and can move through rehearsal without scripts in hand, the dry-run takes place. This is frequently done in the studio and is a walk-through of the entire show. No facilities are used, although cameramen, crew, engineers and other key technical personnel are present to get an idea of the complete show well in advance of air time. The director walks through all camera positions and shots as he has set them during the earlier rehearsal period. He is able to get a rough over-all timing. All cues are given aloud, and positions of the boom microphones in relation to action areas and camera placement are anticipated.

Camera blocking. Everyone concerned with the production telecast is present, including cameramen, technical director, audio engineer, lighting director, floor manager, boom microphone operators, script girl, and all crew members involved in handling props, set changes and other technical movement. Camera blocking — all shots, camera positions, angles and camera movement — must be established. Coordination of camera and actor movement must be set. Some directors move through the entire show, setting up shots as they go. Other directors use the stop-start method in which each shot is set before going to the next. Many directors take the show scene by scene, working out all shots in each scene or act and, after setting up each shot in a scene, run the scene again to assure a visual continuity in the mind of each person concerned with the telecast. Some directors like to plot shots in the studio, viewing each shot through the camera viewfinder. The choice of method is up to the individual director.

Critical shots and special shots must be carefully established in this rehearsal. Boom microphones are set in their relative positions. Use of props and scenery and any set or prop changes must be rehearsed at this point to clarify camera and mike positions and actor movements. Lighting and special effects must be checked out on camera monitors to assure any necessary changes before dress rehearsal.

Camera rehearsal. Quite different from the camera blocking rehearsal is a complete run-through of the show without stopping. This can be done several times. It gives the director, cameramen, talent and crew a chance to set all shots, cues and movement before the dress rehearsal. It also provides a relatively accurate over-all timing of the show. All props, business, movement and scene changes are carried out without stopping. However, the emphasis is on camera continuity.

Dress rehearsal. Usually there is time only for one dress rehearsal. All video and audio elements are included, such as music, sound effects, film, slides and video tape. All costumes, make-up, scene changes, props, lighting and special effects are utilized. This is the time for minor changes to be made; *never* make any major changes during this rehearsal. An accurate check on over-all timing must be made. This rehearsal should be conducted as if it were an on-the-air performance.

The director should be wise enough to finish "dress" early enough to allow time to permit a rest period before air time — and to permit himself to make last minute security checks.

Short-cut rehearsal plan. The preceding rehearsal method is ideal; in most stations, however, seldom is there time for this. The director must establish a "short-cut" method of rehearsals, such as the following:
1) Read through.
2) Stop-start, by scenes or acts. Re-run of scene to crystallize.
3) Complete run-through several times, checking for over-all timing, audio peaks, mike placements, coordination of camera and actor

movement. Make notes of mistakes which can be cleared up on the next run-through.

4) Dress rehearsal, complete with all video and audio elements, scenery and scene changes, props, make-up, costumes, lights, titles and credits. Make final security checks on everything involved in the production, then see that everything is set up again ready to go for on-the-air telecast.

Regardless of the type of rehearsal method used, the director must set deadlines for memorization of script material such as lines, movement and business. He must set up and rigidly enforce rules for promptness — there is no place in television for the "late-comer." He should have the visual and aural aspects of his production definitively planned on paper before he calls his first rehearsal.

Timing the Script

The timing of any program has to be accurate to the "split second." There are two methods. In "front-timing," programs are usually timed in segments: the opening, the program content up to the first commercial break, the commercial, the program content up to the next commercial break, etc., and the close. The director adds the time of all program segments and the result is an over-all timing from the top of the show to the close. For example, suppose you have a panel type program such as "Meet the Public" with an over-all timing of 29:30, including opening, program content, several commercials and the close. The program is to begin at 5:00:00 P.M., the first break for commercial comes at 5:13:00 and finishes at 5:15:00.

Running time	Segment	Time of segment
5:00:00	Opening	00:30
5:00:30	Panel	12:30
5:13:00	Commercial (LV)	2:00
5:15:00	Panel	13:00
5:28:00	Commercial (LV)	1:00
5:29:00	Close	00:30
5:29:30	(Station break)	

Of course, you would use a stop watch to determine an accurate timing of each segment.

As a director your responsibility is to close your show on time, and "back-timing" is a device many directors use to pace the last few minutes of the program. To back-time, the director first checks the station log to determine the time of the program segment which follows his program. He then counts back the number of minutes and seconds he feels necessary to pace the last few minutes of his show. Usually, most directors back-time three to five minutes, giving cues at five minutes, four minutes, two minutes, one minute, and the last 30 seconds.

For example, suppose your "Meet The Public" program is followed by a special announcement for the U.N. at 5:29:30. Your moderator wants a five-minute cue to be followed by one-minute cues. You, as director, must know at what time in the program to give him the desired cues. You would begin with 5:29:30 and count back in minutes to the place in the script where the front timing indicates there is only five minutes time remaining in the program.

Your back timing probably would be indicated on the left of the script and should look something like this:

5:24:30 5
5:25:30 4
5:26:30 3
5:27:30 2
5:28:30 1
5:29:00 ....30 seconds
5:29:30 (The U.N. announcement and station break)

Cueing

The director must have some means by which he can cue performers while the program is on-the-air so that the action and speech may begin at the exact moment needed to insure proper over-all timing and closing of the program. All cueing in the studio is done by the floor manager who, in turn, receives his cues from the director via inter-com and who "shoots" hand-signal cues to the performer to begin speaking, to make an entrance, to stop, speed up and so forth. The performer should know all hand-signal meanings. Many of the cues used in TV are a carryover from radio. Examples of hand-signals used by the floor manager to cue talent are shown in Fig. 3.

The Telecast

The beginning director will learn the "what about" and the "how to" in his course in beginning directing and/or production. Actually, however, he will "learn to" when he joins the staff of a station, either commercial or educational, and begins his real experience in directing.

Prior to air time. The director's final security check should include the following:

1) With floor manager, on studio: setting, props, lights, microphones, easels, graphics, charts and other visuals.
2) With floor manager, on talent: all present, make-up, costumes, ready for places.
3) With audio engineer: theme, other music, recorded sound effects.
4) With video engineer: film, slides, video-tape, use of supers for proper shading and focusing.

FLOOR MANAGER SIGNALS

 Stand by; go ahead.

 Cut it; stop; finish; omit rest of item.

 You are cleared. You are now off camera and can move, or stop action.

 Volume up; louder.

 Volume down; quieter (sometimes precede by "Quiet" signal).

 Quiet; stop applause.

 Tighten-up. Get closer together.

 Open-up. Move further apart.

 Come nearer; come downstage.

 Go further away; go upstage.

 You're on that camera, play to that camera. (Sometimes preceded by "Turning actor's head" gesture.)

 Play to the light indicated. (When actors are shadowing, point to light source and to area of face shadowed.)

 Turn around (in direction indicated).

 Speed up; faster pace; quicker tempo. (Movement's speed shows amount of increase.)

 Slow down; slower pace; stretch it out. (Indicated by slow "stretching" gesture.)

 O.K.; you're all right now; it's O.K. (Confirmation signal.)

OR

 We're/you're on time.

 Are we on time? How is time going?

 You have ... time left (Illustrated—2 mins and ½ min.)

2 MINS. OR ½ MIN.

 Wind-up now.

 To audience: you can applaud now. (May be followed by "Louder" signal.)

Stop. (For applause, widespread action, etc.)

5) With film projectionists: projectors and cues.

The floor manager must know how he is to receive and give opening cues, and he must relay this information to the talent. The talent must know their positions and which cameras are to be used for the opening shots. Cameramen are similarly alerted to their first few shots. The count-down varies with directors, but the general approach is the same. Some directors will indicate a five-minute period remaining before air time, announcing the passing time at one-minute intervals: "five minutes to air, places everyone, four minutes, three minutes, two minutes, one minute, 30 seconds, 10 seconds, stand by." Other directors give only a one-minute cue after the initial five-minute announcement. The following is a typical count-down and opening by a director:

"One minute. Pictures please. 30 seconds. 15 seconds, quiet in studio please. Stand by theme, stand by announce booth. 10 seconds. Ready theme. Ready slide. Hit theme. Up on slide. Theme under. Cue booth. Ready 1 on title card. Take 1. Ready 2 on host. Ready to cue host. Cue host, take 2. Trim head room. 1 on model car. Hold for dissolve. Dissolve 1. Ready 2 on host, take 2. Tighten up a hair, two." (And so on, until the close of the show.)

On the air. To apply this procedure to a specific instance, let us see what occurs when a director does his own switching, using the script, "The Tin Star," which begins on page 185. The five-minute cue is given either by the director through the "talk-back" system to the studio or via inter-com to the floor manager, who relays it to those in the studio. "Five minutes to air — everybody in places." At three minutes the cue is given, "Three minutes — stand by in studio, please." The director contacts his cameramen via inter-com, asking for "Pictures, please." The cameramen rack over into "take" positions the lenses to be used and "frame-up" the first two pictures for opening shots. As soon as the camera shots are set or lined up, the cameramen half-rack to prevent any possibility of "burn-in" before the show opens.

It is now two minutes to air time, the director calls it and the floor manager relays the signal, "Two minutes." Final security checks are made at this time. The control room clock shows one minute to air time and the director shoots the cue to the floor manager, who calls "One minute — stand by, and quiet in the studio, please." At the same time, the director asks for opening shots, calls the projectionist for a last-minute check on film and checks which projector is being used for the opening. As he watches the preview line monitor he sees the close of the preceding show, which indicates there is just 30 seconds before his show hits the air. He calls "Stand by and ready to go" to all those involved in the telecast. The ID slide is up and the audio man is ready to roll the theme as the director says "Stand by music and film." He then calls "Stand by to roll crawl with opening titles."

As the ID slide fades out, the sweep hand on the control room clock indicates it is air time and the director calls "Roll music — fade in film." The music is up, the film is up, and the opening of the program is established. The director says "Ready 1 for super" and "Ready to roll crawl." As the exterior scene at the opening of "The Tin Star" is established by film, the director says "Super in camera 1 over film," and the titles and other opening information appear on the program line monitor. The director cues the floor manager to "Stand by to cue performers" as he gets ready to dissolve to camera 2 for the first live studio shot. He calls "Dissolve to 2" as he executes his dissolve to camera 2 on a shot of Sheriff Joel Marsden seated at his desk. The director then tightens up on camera 2 by indicating "Tighten up 2." He instructs camera 1 to set up on the "wanted" poster being held off by a member of the crew. (Joel is looking at a wanted poster and to make it possible to see the poster, and create the illusion of looking over Joel's shoulder, this system is used rather than having to position a camera behind Joel.) As Joel is looking at the poster the director calls "Take 1" and a picture of the wanted poster appears on the program line monitor.

The director now sets up camera 2 on a wide shot showing Joel at the desk and including the door to the left of the desk. He "Takes 2" as Ned bursts into the office and moves to the edge of Joel's desk. As Joel speaks, the director tightens up camera 2 for a two-shot. The camera moves in, creating a loose two-shot. As Joel rises from behind the desk, the director instructs the cameraman to "Ease back" to hold the two-shot. He sets up his next shot, an over-the-shoulder shot on camera 1 which shoots over Ned's shoulder to pick up Joel, too, as he turns to speak to Ned. As Joel turns, the director "Takes 1." While Joel speaks his lines, the director sets up a shoulder shot of Ned on camera 2 and as Ned picks up his line, the director "Takes 2." He follows this shot with a cut to camera 1 again, which is the same over-the-shoulder shot he used before — and so on to the end of the drama.

There are several techniques of good operation to remember while on the air. Be prepared to give the cameraman a "ready" signal or cue on time, preferably a second or so before the take. Be fast. Ready and take cues must be close together time-wise, with no lag. If a director readies a camera and then decides not to take it, he must immediately tell the cameraman to ignore the cue. Know the numbers of the cameras and call cameras by number and not by the names of the cameramen. Keep the cameras on the move; do not let the show become static. Check the time and communicate with the floor manager relative to remaining time so that he will be ready to cue talent when they need time cues. Always cue talent before taking a shot. This avoids having on the air a picture of a performer obviously waiting for a cue. The cue to the performer and the take are almost simultaneous.

The close. The closing of a show follows a rather standard procedure, too. Let us return for a moment to the example given earlier using a host. Assuming the host has been given proper cues up to the last minute for winding up the program, the final director's instructions might go like this:

"One minute to close. 30 seconds. 10 seconds and wind up host. Ready theme. Ready 1 on crawl and credits. Ready floor to roll credits. Ready booth. Hit theme. Take 1. Roll crawl. Theme under. Cue booth. Theme up. Fade pic and music. All clear in studio. Thank you, everyone. Very nice show. Secure everything."

For best results, be courteous, be thoughtful, and be thankful!

APPENDIX A.

The Television Log

The director would have a difficult time knowing when he should start his program and end it, when to break the station, insert commercials, do public service announcements and promos, unless he had a television station log to direct him. The TV log is a schedule of the daily on-the-air programming of the station. Television logs differ in their arrangement of the various items listed. The basic content, however, is the same in any station.

The following is an example of the content portion of a typical log used at KUHT, the University of Houston Educational TV station.

KUHT DAILY PROGRAM SCHEDULE AND LOG

DAY: Thursday — P.M.   DATE: July 9, 1963

TIME	TYPE	ORIG.	PROGRAMS & ANNOUNCEMENTS	ON	OFF	ANNC.
4:44:00	SP-MU	SL-AT-RC	Sign On Announcement SL 201	60 sec.		
4:45:00	SP-ED	SOF-NET	The Friendly Giant		14:21	PROJ-
	CH		(8006-SOF)			
4:49:21	SP-PS	SOF	Keep Amer. Beautiful		20 sec.	PROJ-
4:49:41	SP-PR	SL-AT	Promo & ID	SL 177	19 sec.	
				SL 347		
5:00:00	SP-CH	VTR-NET	What's New		29:02	VTR-1
	ED					
5:29:02	SP-PR	SL-AT	TV Promo	SL N-369	00:22	
5:29:24	SP-PR	SL-AT	Red Cross	SL X-208	00:26	
5:29:50	SP	SL-AT	ID-Preview	SL 106	00:10	
5:30:00	SP-ED	SOF	KUHT Travel Club		27:45	PROJ-
5:57:45	SP-PR	SL-AB	The Museum of Fine Arts SL 207	00:60		
5:58:45	SP-PR	SOF	NASA		1:15	PROJ-1
6:00:00	SP-PS	VTR-NET	Industry On Parade		14:00	VTR-2

And So On Until End of Broadcast Day.

APPENDIX B.

Director's Vocabulary: Terminology, Language, Cues.

The terminology of the director varies from station to station; yet, there must be a basic language upon which the director can draw to communicate his needs to his technical staff during a telecast. Some directors coin new words, expressions or phrases derived from the existing language and terminology. The beginning director, as he acquires more experience, will no doubt find himself coining some of his own terms. To indicate the vocabulary used and/or coined by all directors would be an interminable task, so let us take a look at those words, expressions, phrases and cues most commonly used. Note the variations of some terms which have the same relative meaning.

Video Cues

Dolly in Move in Push in Go in	Camera moving in for a closer look at subject.
Dolly out Dolly back Pull out Pull back Come out	Camera moves away from subject, creating a wider angle shot. Often used because the field of interest is broadened by the movement.
Pan	A horizontal movement of the camera on the friction head without any dolly movement. Either to left or right.
Tilt	A vertical movement of camera on the friction head without any dolly movement. Either up or down. Some directors say "pan up" or "pan down" instead of using the word "tilt."
Truck Travel	Usually a lateral movement of the dolly and camera. A shot which is not toward or away from the moving subject. Camera movement which parallels the scene.
Arc	A truck or curved dolly which travels a curved path or arc. Either left or right.
Follow shot	May be defined in several ways. In the true sense of the term it means to follow by moving both dolly and camera with actor movement. It may be a shot in which the camera pulls back as the actor moves toward it, the distance between actor and camera remaining relatively constant in the movement. It may be the reverse of this, the actor walking ahead of the camera as it follows him from behind in whatever direction he is moving. The director must be cogni-

zant of the basic difference between a pan shot and a follow shot. In the pan shot the dolly and camera remain in a fixed position while the cameras pan either left or right. In the follow and/or truck shot the dolly and camera both move with the actor or subject.

	Zoom shot	The zoom shot most certainly can be related to the dolly shot. In the case of the zoom shot the difference is speed. Usually the zoom shot is created by moving the dolly and camera in or out fast.
1-Shot	One shot Single shot	A shot of an individual.
2-Shot	Two shot	A shot of two individuals.
3-Shot	Three shot	A shot of three individuals.
	Group shot	A shot of more than three individuals.
LS ES	Long shot	A shot of the full figure of the person or persons, in which much of the setting is seen behind and beside them. Often called an establishing shot (ES).
ELS XLS	Extreme long shot	A very wide shot of a large area or setting.
FS	Full length shot	Generally a shot of a person from head to feet.
MS	Medium shot Close shot	Generally a shot from the waist-up, unless otherwise specified.
CU	Close-up shot	Generally a shot of the head and shoulders, unless otherwise specified.
BCU TCU	Big close-up Tight close-up	A shot of only head and face.
ECU XCU	Extreme close-up	A shot of a portion of the face or head. A "slice" of the face or head.
CS	Cover shot	Usually a wide angle shot covering a relatively large area in which action is taking place.
CU-LS	Combination close-up and long shot	Usually a shot of two persons, one seen close to camera while other is seen in distant background.
OS	Over-the-shoulder shot	A shot of two persons taken over the shoulder of one of them. For example, in an interview situation involving two persons, we see one person over the shoulder of the other. Quite frequently this type of shot comes in pairs, in which case the over-the-shoulder shots are matched. For example,

we see Mary over the shoulder of Jane and when the cut is made to the other camera we see Jane over the shoulder of Mary. The over-the-shoulder technique is very effective when used in dramatic shows.

Imaginary line	In an interview situation, for example, the director may visualize an imaginary line joining two people conversing. He must be cognizant of this line so he will not make the mistake of positioning one of his cameras on the opposite side of the imaginary line. If he does position one camera on the opposite side, then the cut to that camera will reverse the direction in which the subject is looking.
Defocus	The camera is cranked all the way out of focus by rotating the optical focus control.
Soft focus	The camera is cranked slightly out of focus until the subject appears to be in a hazy atmosphere. This is excellent for drama.
Other ways to indicate shots	Knee shot. Thigh shot. Waist shot. Chest shot or bust shot. Shoulder shot. Head shot.

Audio Cues

Ready audio	Standby cue to audio engineer.
Standby music, theme	Cue to audio engineer to standby with turn-table going and ready to slip cue record of theme or music being used in program.
Hit theme, music Roll theme, music	Cue to audio engineer to bring in music at full peak or volume and hold until established.
Music in full	Music is brought up to normal peak set for the introduction of program or at any other specified spot in the program.
Music under Take music under	Volume of music is taken down under the dialogue or sound being used, usually for background purposes.
Sneak in music	Music is rolled with volume either all the way down or very low. Then the volume is gradually increased until desired peak is reached. Generally used to bring music into BG as a scene is progressing.
Music down and out Fade out music	Music is taken down and faded out completely, according to speed desired.

Music up Bring music up	Increase volume of music. For transitional purposes, at the end of a scene, and usually at the end of the program.
Sneak out music	Music is being used in BG and director wants it to fade out completely. He may want it faded out slowly or rapidly according to effect he desires to convey.
Fade music and pic	At the close of the program the music (audio) and the picture (video) are faded out simultaneously.
Open mike	Cue to audio engineer to throw switch which controls the particular mike to be used.
Mike check	Director or TD asks audio engineer to have all mikes checked to make certain they are functioning properly before program hits the air. Usually an assistant on the studio floor does this with a "count down" technique.
Mike level	The mike is opened and the talent speaks relative to placement of mike. He speaks lines exactly as he would were he on the air. Director often wishes to hear this level check.

Variations of Cues to Announcer

Cue booth Cue announcer Announce Read	Cue booth announcer in announce booth, either by inter-com system or hand cue. Method of cueing depends upon where booth is located relative to control room. It is possible the announcer may take his cues by watching TV monitor in booth. Such cues are arranged prior to on-the-air telecast.
AB (Announce booth)	In some stations this type of cue is used.
Take it from the top	During rehearsals such an instruction might be given the announcer and/or cast relative to the script or announce copy. Means to begin at the beginning of the copy or script material.

Film or VTR Cues

Ready film Ready A or B (projectors)	If film is being rolled from the control room it is wise to make certain the audio man knows which projector is being used so he can punch up the correct button on the audio console to put sound on film on the air.
Ready VTR Stand by VTR	Used when the video engineer rolls the VTR.
Roll tape Roll VTR	To video engineer to roll VTR.

Hit film Roll film	Cue to start film projector.
Fade in film	Film is faded in by using fader levers on video switcher. Done by director or TD.
Take film	Direct cut to film, may be from live studio to film, etc.
Dissolve film Dissolve to film	By using fader levers director dissolves from live studio to film, or from slide to film, etc.

Examples of How Some Directors Give Instructions

Frame up	Means to center subject or object.
Move in to lose him	Camera moves in closer until subject indicated is out of frame.
Follow him or subject	Usually means to pan with subject as he moves about. Cameraman should always lead the subject a little in executing the pan.
Ease in Move in slowly Go in slowly Tighten up slowly	Camera is dollied in slowly.
Dolly out fast Pull out fast Pull back fast	Camera is dollied out from subject as fast as indicated by director.
Trim head room Trim head	Cue to cameraman to decrease the space between the top of the subject's head and the top of frame.
Trim head a hair	Means to trim head room slightly.
Pedestal up Pedestal down Boom up Boom down	This applies to the pedestal type dolly or mount. This cueing means camera is raised or lowered by raising or lowering the pedestal itself. Director indicates how high or low he wishes it done.
Fade to black Black it Go to black	Cue to fade out picture to black screen.
Cut	In rehearsals the director will call "cut" to all involved in the rehearsal in order to stop everything.
Zoom in	Camera with Zoomar lens. Director indicates to the cameraman to zoom to the desired shot, e.g. zoom to waist.
Zoom out	Same as above, only the zoom is out to the desired shot indicated by director.

Check focus Focus up Sharpen focus	Obvious meaning. Sometimes director or TD must check cameramen on this.
Tighten up one lens (or two)	Camera is not on air. Cameraman racks over one lens longer than he has been using on previous shot.
Loosen up one lens (or two)	Just opposite of above.
Winging Ad-libbing Free shooting	Refers to director planning, setting up and editing shots while on the air. Show has not been rehearsed.
Widen out	Camera is dollied back to a wider shot while on the air. If off the air, the cameraman may rack to a shorter lens.
Ready for super Hold for super	Director must ready cameras before going into a super. This assures him that both cameramen know they are to hold their shots steady for super.
Going into super Supering	To let cameramen and engineers involved in the execution of the super know the super is being aired.
Coming out of super Supering out	To let cameramen and engineers know director is taking out super.
Supering out full into 1, or 2	To let cameramen and engineers know which will be on the air when super is out.
Standby for dissolve Ready for dissolve Ready to dissolve Hold for dissolve	The two cameras involved in the dissolve must hold (freeze) their shots while the dissolve is executed.
Dissolve to 1 (or 2) Dissolve 1 Dissolve 2	Directions for dissolving. Depends on the individual director's method of giving instructions.
Cheat to light	Floor manager cues talent to turn or angle head or body toward a particular light. The movement should not be discernible to viewers.
Cheat to camera 1 (or 2)	Same as above, only direction or cue is to a particular camera.
Open up Pictures, please	Cue to cameramen to open lens by removing lens cap and shooting a picture of subject or object so director may check out his cameras. These cues are frequently given just prior to air time so director may view the first shots he will be airing on the opening of the program.

Lens rack super	Sometimes referred to as "offset turret," it is simply racking the lens over until most of the picture is blocked out. This rack leaves only a small portion of the lens open, in either of the four corners of the frame of the picture on the viewfinder. It is then possible to pick up an object or a portion of a subject in open area of the lens or viewfinder. This image can now be superimposed over the picture from the other camera.
Check for burn	Instruction to cameramen to check their cameras to see whether or not there is a "burn-in" on the I.O. tube. This instruction is given at the end of a program when cameras are not going to be used immediately on another program.
Cap up and secure	Instruction to cameramen after program is off the air or at close of day's operation. Means to cap the lens in take position (usually need to cap only one if capped lens is racked to take position). Camera is then moved into a position in studio where it stands when not in use. Generally, it is wise to roll the camera cable into a "figure-eight" arrangement to prevent snarling of cable.

BIBLIOGRAPHY

Bretz, Rudy, *Techniques of Television Production*. New York: McGraw-Hill, 1962. Rev. Ed. A very thorough text which covers the many facets of television production. Well written and well organized. Excellent pictorial illustrations accompany the theory aspect of the text.

Livingston, Don, *Film and the Director*. New York: The Macmillan Company, 1953. A compact, extremely thorough book covering the production and direction of a motion picture. Invaluable to the beginning TV director.

McMahan, Harry, *The Television Commercial*. New York: Hastings House, Publishers, Inc., 1957. An excellent book for background and reference material for practical application.

McMahan, Harry, *TV Tape Commercials*. New York: Hastings House, Publishers, Inc., 1960. A small handbook (now out of print) which introduces the student to the procedures and problems encountered in the writing, producing, directing and taping of TV commercials.

Millerson, Gerald, *The Technique of Television Production*. New York: Hastings House, Publishers, Inc., 1961. A thorough, very exacting text with excellent sketches done in great detail to illustrate theory. Excellent book for reference and background material. The hand-signals illustrated on page 193 were sketched by Mr. Millerson and are reproduced from this book.

O'Meara, Carroll, *Television Program Production*. New York: Ronald Press, 1955. Written by a former NBC producer-director, this book contains elements which will always remain basic, regardless of how many new gadgets or equipment modifications and changes may take place in the future.

Zettl, Herbert, *The Television Production Handbook*. Belmont, California: Wadsworth Publishing Company, Inc., 1961. An excellently written and well organized text for the school in which there is a limited number of courses offered in the field of television.

Rehearsal for "Target: Delinquency," a series of nine videotaped programs on juvenile delinquency, written and produced by Tom C. Battin for the University of Houston under a joint grant from the Health, Education and

Welfare Department, Washington, D.C., and the Citizens Committee of the City of Houston. These programs were telecast over the University's station, KUHT-TV, and the three commercial television stations in Houston.

VERNE W. WEBER

Assistant Professor of Speech and Dramatic Arts
Coordinator of University Instructional Broadcasting,
Eastern Michigan University

● Professor Weber received the B.A. and M.A. degrees from the University of Michigan. Prior to his appointment at Eastern Michigan University he was staging supervisor at the University of Michigan Television Center with responsibility for settings, lighting, properties, makeup and costuming for all television productions. He is featured as the teacher and principal performer in the 30-minute, nationally distributed television production made by the National Educational Television and Radio Center, *Staging for Television*. He has been consultant to NETRC member stations, to the National Association of Educational Broadcasters Conference on Staging and Lighting, and to the Ford Foundation Television Workshop. Among his positions with national and regional organizations are those of Chairman of the Television Project of the American Educational Theatre Association, and of representative to that organization of the National Association of Educational Broadcasters. Professor Weber is a contributor to the *Production Handbook* issued by NETRC and has published articles on television in professional journals. In addition to the University of Michigan, he has taught at New Mexico State University and is at present Assistant Professor in the Department of Speech and Dramatic Arts and coordinator of Eastern Michigan University's closed-circuit television system.

6

STAGING

BY VERNE W. WEBER

TV IS A MEDIUM of communication — an aural-visual medium. Radio is only an aural medium — the pictures of radio are built on the imagination of the listener. Television must provide the picture with the sound. The question, "What is the viewer looking at now?" must be ever-present in the mind of the TV scene designer.

DESIGNING THE SETTING

The purpose of the television setting is to provide the physical space and the decor (furniture and setting) required by the television presentation. But the TV setting is more than physical space. It is the space (area, locale) to which the performer can relate as an actor, as a human being, as a performer. For the actor, the setting provides a scene for the action. It becomes for him a location within which his characterization can find expression. It must have doors and windows, and be scaled to permit the actor and the audience to associate the setting with a human scale. For the performer the setting must be usable. It must be possible to move about in, to enter into and exit from, to manipulate the television paraphernalia around in. Not only is a TV setting physical space, it is a visual representation of the thoughts, ideas and purposes of the television script.

The Designer and the Setting

The scenic designer for television, as for films and the stage, must be a skillful blend of artist, craftsman, home decorator, architect, and art historian. He must insure that there is a picture suitable to the script, idea, content or intent of the presentation at all times on the TV screen. As he visualizes the entire presentation he must think in much broader terms than the stage designer. He must think not only of wide shots, including entire settings, but of extreme close-up shots of fine detail.

The television designer uses the same elements as does the stage or film designer: line, space, mass and color. In addition, light and lighting effects are an important part of TV scenic design.

Line is the delineating device used to indicate the contour or shape of an object. Lines may be used in combination to provide a realistic form (one taken from nature or realia), a stylized form (one having a basis in realism but altered through stylization), or an abstract form (one whose basis is solely in design). Space is the area encompassed within the setting. The need for space is compensated for or eliminated in many instances by the use of the wide angle lens. The technique of utilizing a lens with a short depth of field, thus throwing the background out of focus, may provide in individual shots a feeling of space not achievable with realistic space delineating devices. Whereas space is area in a setting, mass is the bulk. Because all objects occupy space, size determines the mass. The limitation of the TV optical system often precludes the need for three-dimensional mass, permitting two-dimensional or even painted mass to be used. Color use in TV scene design, because of the 10-step gray-scale reproduction limitations of the monochrome system, is based largely on the psychological effects of color on the performer. The all-gray (monochromatic) painted settings, common in the early days of TV, have been replaced by the use of colorfully painted scenery. It is easier and more convenient to paint scenery, and the reaction of the studio personnel and actors to the use of color indicates a psychological advantage. To sum up, the television scene designer combines the four elements — line, space, mass and color — to achieve the setting.

A clarification of the term "setting" is important. The television camera is a limiting factor in design — not in a restrictive sense, but limiting in an emphatic sense. In essence, because each camera shot is different (that is, because the information of each shot is different), we have a different setting for each shot angle. The television camera, through its complement of lenses, limits the amount of information being viewed. A wide-angle shot may reveal, as in the theatre, a great expanse of scenery. Such a shot may permit the designer to utilize all of the design elements available to him. But the next picture we see may be of an object in sharp focus large in the foreground before a blurred, out-of-focus and indistinguishable background.

Or the background may be only a small portion of a large expanse of setting. The viewer will see only the information contained in that one shot at that one moment. The designer, consequently, must think in terms of a setting (background) for every shot used in the program. The information and detail required in a wide-angle view of an expanse of scenery is minimal. Therefore, the designer has the opportunity and the obligation to emphasize those areas of setting which come under the close scrutiny of the TV camera — the close-up shots. In this respect, the TV scene designer has an advantage over both his stage and film counterparts. In the theatre, if the viewer becomes bored he can permit his eyes to wander at will about the setting — unconsciously subjecting the scenery to a great degree of scrutiny. Not so the TV viewer! In the movie theatre, the screen may be 50, 75, 100 or more feet wide. All details are magnified and available in a large scale for the viewer. In television, however, how much can the eye wander over a 23-inch screen? Or a 5½-inch screen? What a pleasure it is for the TV scene designer to devote himself to those details of setting which will be seen!

Kinds and Types of Settings

The four common television program types are illustrative of the most frequently designed television settings: dramatic, interview, news and variety. All four program types originate in the studios of the television networks. Most local TV stations, on the other hand, find television settings restricted to news, interview programs and commercials.

Because most network dramas are filmed, and most local station programming is limited to "bread-and-butter" news and commercials, opportunity for the newcomer to break into scenic design rests presently with the ambitious but economically restricted educational television station. Whereas live programming at the local commercial station constitutes only approximately 12% of the schedule, the ETV stations on the average produce an astonishing near-50% live programming.

Television settings can be classified as: realistic, abstract, or stylized.

The realistic setting, although originally derived from a combination of naturalistic elements, has become highly selective in its composition. The judicious combination of properties and furniture (highly realistic) with the scenic elements (very often painted) results in what today is called a realistic setting. Certainly no one today (as was done on the stage many years ago) would advocate the use of real bricks in brick walls of settings in the TV studio. Why, when the plastic sheet vacuum-formed bricks of today cannot be discerned by the TV camera from the real object? We no longer have directors and actors who can demand natural objects and scenic elements. Realism in TV is found today most faithfully duplicated in dramatic settings, although usually simplified to facilitate the design and construction and to reduce the cost.[1] (See Fig. 1.)

Fig. 1   *Realistic Setting*. A combination of realistic elements to achieve a comfortable conversation area. Eight-foot walls of plywood-covered scenic units provide sufficient height in this scene.

Fig. 2 *Abstract Setting.* A television setting for a music group using abstract shapes set before a scrim cyclorama. Lighting changes permit fully lighted shots or a silhouette effect.

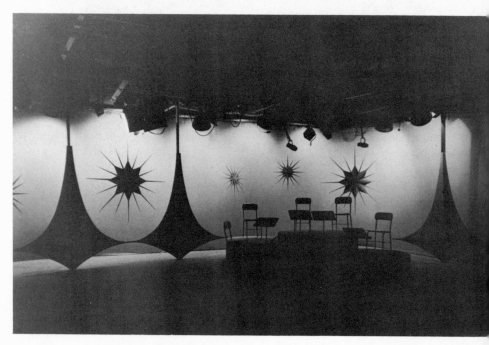

Fig. 3 *Stylized Setting*. A setting for a television program about the painter's art. The realistic artist's clutter in the foreground is framed by a stylization of the traditional garret window and stylized sections of wall as backing for the model.

The use of scenic elements solely as backgrounds has resulted in a strong reliance on abstract forms, shapes or designs to achieve simple, yet attractive settings. Abstract design is particularly popular in music and variety programming. (See Fig. 2). Abstract elements in scenic design are also utilized frequently in ETV stations wherein the settings are simple backgrounds behind the performer or teacher.

Whereas abstract settings are often based solely on elements of design conceived by the artist, symbols or motifs derived from the content of a program or series are usually used by the scene designer as the basis for stylized settings (see Fig. 3).

Design Influences

The television scene designer, in common with the stage and film designer, is influenced by various stimuli in the process of creating settings. A few of the more important factors can be discussed briefly.

The script of a single presentation, or the format of a series, will influence the design as the production demands are indicated. The obvious script requirements are those of time (day, season, year), place (town, country, apartment, terrace), situation (wealth, poverty), and mood (comedy, tragedy). These are the influences which give an initial impetus to the design of a setting. The more subtle determinants are concerned with interpretation of the author's writing. The director or producer selects a style of production which he feels will be successful. The style of the setting may be any one of the three we have previously discussed.

The physical space (studio) within which the presentation is to be produced will determine the size and complexity of the setting(s). The production facilities available within the major. network centers provide equipment and space sufficient to meet the demands of any presentation. For the local station, however, the TV designer must work within the confines of much smaller space. The height of the studio — from floor to the grid arrangement of pipes from which the lighting instruments hang — is a consideration. Satisfactory results for a setting can be achieved with 8′ scenery, if the program is a panel or interview type with limited movement. Shooting patterns differ between a studio with 10 feet of clearance to lights and one with 20 feet of clearance.

Not only must the amount of the floor space available for settings be taken into account, but even the shape of the studio (rectangular or square) is important. The rectangular studio shape can permit two elaborate settings — one at each end — with equipment space in the center or a number of small areas along the walls with equipment space in the middle. (See Figs. 4 and 5.)

The television equipment and the personnel available for production influence design, too. The number of cameras, microphone booms and operators are important factors influencing the size and number of scenic elements. A studio with one perambulator microphone boom must have settings close enough together to enable a short swing of the boom or movement of the perambulator to permit the transition from one setting to another. The settings must be few in number, if the studio equipment includes only two or three cameras, to enable the cameras to maintain a shot sequence.

The lighting capabilities of the studio, including total wattage capacity and instrumentation are all important to the effective visualization of the scenic elements. If the "rule-of-thumb" instrumentation and electrical service of 50 watts per square foot of studio space for black-and-white TV

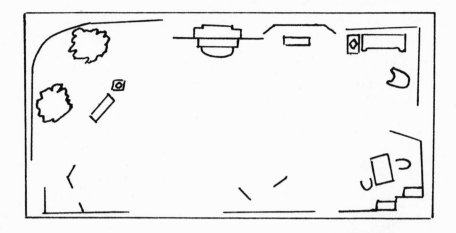

Fig. 4   A rectangular TV studio with small settings spaced along the walls. Space in the center is for cameras and equipment.

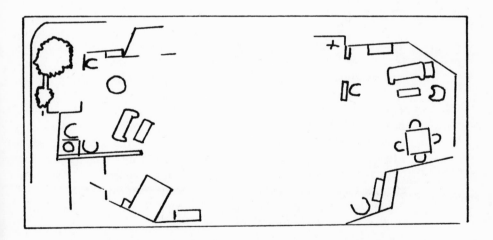

Fig. 5   A rectangular TV studio with settings at the ends of the studio. Space for TV cameras and equipment is in the center of the studio.

prevails, this will be no problem. Although 500 watt fresnel spotlights are adequate for back light in a restricted area studio, they are not satisfactory for "front" light. The 8-inch, 1,000-watt fresnel spot should be the minimum front lighting instrument used in combination with scoops. (See Chapter 2 for description of light equipment.) As already indicated, the height of the light pipes from the floor is a very important consideration for the designer. A low grid height forces the wide angle or cover shot to include either lights or a lot of floor.

In addition to budget limitations which must usually be observed in connection with scenic design, other considerations for the designer are:

1) *Size and kind of audience*. The designer working with settings for a religious program recognizes that the audience is a minority one. Therefore, he must provide a setting suitable to the type of program and to the audience. Programs often are designed for special audiences. Women's shows, sports shows, cultural shows are but a few examples.

2) *Age level* (adult, child, teenager). The settings for "Romper Room" and many "teen-age" bandstands should reflect the taste, habits and fads of that age group. With the young child the elements of fancy, imagination and scale are important ingredients for successful TV design.

3) *Network or local station origination*. Most local station live programming is composed of news and sports shows, live commercials for syndicated shows, and hosts for "movie" shows. In most instances, once designed and constructed, these "bread-and-butter" settings remain in position and are used over and over again. Changes are made after long periods of use or when a different sponsor is obtained. This type of setting, because of its continual re-use, warrants better design and execution. This is not true of the "commercial" settings which change frequently.

4) *Time slot*. If a single studio station is in the position of having live programming "back to back" (one show following another with only a station break or commercial between), design is affected. Such a situation demands either two simple settings easily exchanged, or settings within which replacing a few elements achieves a distinctive change. Ideally, the program schedule will be planned so that this condition does not exist. The problem is considerably simplified if two studios are available for alternate use.

5) *Staff*. The designer must plan on simple sets when the number of personnel available is small. More elaborate settings are possible when more persons are on hand for setting them up.

These factors are all important and must be given due consideration by the scenic designer and all members of the production team in the planning, preparation and presentation of the television program.

Educational Television Station Scenery

Educational television warrants special mention regarding the design of settings because of many considerations distinctive to ETV. Because the *raison d'etre* of the ETV station is to provide educational, instructional and cultural programming to a limited audience, the problems of scenery and design are peculiar.

Educational television scenery must be economical — in terms of size (elaborateness and scale) and in terms of the number of elements or settings. In addition, such settings should be simple, functional and aesthetically pleasing.

1) *Simple.* Time, personnel and money are not available in ETV to permit elaborate, completely detailed settings. The solution is simplicity. The elimination of unnecessary detail, the substitution of one or two elements for multiple units, the planning of shots to reduce the required scenery backgrounds or to simplify them are all part of achieving simple settings. Reducing the number of cover or wide angle shots results in fewer scenery requirements. The judicious use of single elements within the shot composition, and reinforcing the emphasis on the talent or performer will also reduce the need for scenic units.

2) *Functional.* Budgeting influences dictate to the ETV scene designer that all elements of staging must achieve a maximum of flexibility. Flexibility of design here indicates a planned-for multiple use of staging elements. Flexibility of use indicates that most elements are designed for many uses through slight changes. A table base becomes a desk, two-man interview table, conference table, demonstration table by the addition of differently shaped, finished and designed tops. A section of set wall becomes a blackboard, magnet board, display board, rear projection area by the insertion of functional plugs. The hoped-for result of the ETV designer is a series of pieces of furniture, a series of scenic units which will provide imaginative staging personnel the opportunity to combine elements over and over again in almost endless fashion.

3) *Aesthetically Pleasing.* The elimination of excessive detail, of arriving at a setting composed of a few, simple, well-designed, functional scenic elements will achieve, as the primary goal of the ETV designer, a visually pleasing, attractive setting for the performance of the TV production. The low budget simplicity of the ETV situation should produce a product which is both mentally and strongly visually stimulating. ETV cannot compete with commercial TV if transmissions are poorly designed, weakly staged and visually unattractive.

Construction

The basic unit for TV, as for the stage, is the flat. This muslin or can-

vas covered frame of white pine, when properly painted, hinged or rope-
lashed to other flats, becomes the walls and scenic portions of most of the
realistic dramatic settings we see on TV.

The flat is a simple unit to construct. The frame of the typical 10′ flat
is of 1″ x 3″ white pine (#2 white pine or better grade). The two long
pieces (stiles) fit between the ends (rails). At the midpoint in the flat is a
horizontal member (stretcher). The flat is joined at the corners by butt
joints and held in place by corner blocks. The stretcher is held at the joints
by keystones. Corner blocks and keystones are made of ¼″ plywood. (See
Fig. 6.)

The surface of the flat is covered with a heavy unbleached muslin or
light duck, stapled and glued down. The finished paint job is applied over
a prime coat. Canvass covered flats under 3′ in width are called jogs. Some
flats are constructed with window or door openings cut in to accommodate
ready-made doors and windows. A single flat can be easily and quickly
changed by inserting different architectural period styles of doors or windows or by inserting solid plugs to make the opening disappear. A system
of multiple-use units results in a flexible combination of scenic elements.

Television, however, does not rely wholly upon stage construction
techniques. A combination of theatre and movie methods of scene construction are used. In many instances, canvas covered flats may suffice, but the
setting for a continuing drama series may demand plywood and canvas covered solid flats which are more typical of the movie set. Sheet plywood is
nailed and glued to 1″ x 3″ white pine on edge and then covered with
canvas. Because of the 1″ x 3″ edge thickness, it is a simple matter to erect
walls of this type utilizing C-clamps for fasteners. Although this type of
scenery is more rugged and durable, it has disadvantages. It requires more
space for storage; the 1″ x 3″ on edge plus the plywood covering results in
units almost 3″ thick. The space occupied by one such unit will accommodate three "stage" flats. In addition, the plywood units are much heavier
and require more manpower to handle.

Standard scene construction methods are appropriate for most scenic
elements used in the TV studio. It is wise, though, to adopt a standard
height and modular system to enable the interchange of all elements. Plat-
forms, parallels (collapsing or folding units with solid plywood tops) and
step units are easily worked into a modular system.

Painting

The most commonly used paint for the TV studio is a rubber base
(latex) paint. Various techniques exist for breaking up large areas of flat
color. *Scumbling* is accomplished by brushing with various contrast-colors
applied in brief, fairly dry brush strokes in various directions. The blend of
colors and strokes will break up the base color and result in a texture effect.
Spattering, the most frequently used technique, is accomplished over a base

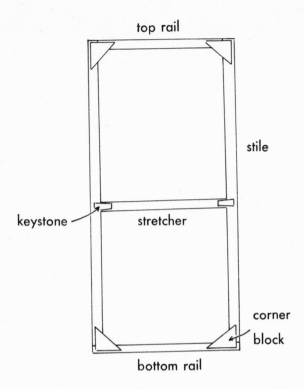

top rail

stile

keystone

stretcher

corner

block

bottom rail

Fig. 6 *Standard flat nomenclature.* Note top rail fits inside stiles. Detail sketches show nailing patterns in cornerblocks and keystones.

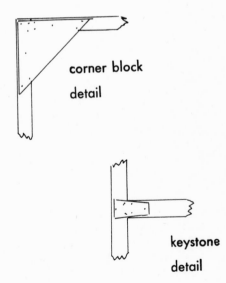

corner block
detail

keystone
detail

coat by striking a paint-laden brush against the hand, causing spatters of paint to land on the base color. *Rolling* is accomplished by taking a piece of heavily textured cloth such as burlap, dipping it into the paint and gently rolling the loosely rolled-up cloth over the painted surface. Interesting textures are acchieved. *Sponging* is the result of dipping sections of sponge (cellulose or natural) into the paint and gently and softly touching the sponge to the surface of the flat. Care must be taken not to fall into repeated rhythm with any of these techniques. A repeated design will be the result of such carelessness. *Spraying* textures can be made by the use of an air compressor and a spray gun. Various sprays can be achieved by adjusting the opening of the gun, from heavy spray to fine mist.

The ease of using pre-painted or pre-finished materials permits plywoods and other surfaces to be used as manufactured. It is possible, therefore, to obtain — at a somewhat higher initial cost — many scenic materials which require no finishing. Many plywood veneers, formicas and linoleums fall into this category.

The Cyclorama

The well equipped television studio should include as a basic scenic element a scrim cyclorama (cyc), an open weave cloth available in 30′ widths and any length which, when dyed a light blue, can be used easily and effectively.[2] The cyc adapted for television use provides a suitable background, when properly lighted and controlled, for scenic elements. Tightly stretched, it becomes an excellent surface for the projection of light patterns and designs to achieve varied and inexpensive backgrounds. With full light the cyc can become a sky or void background. With no light it becomes a dark background suitable for silhouetting scenic elements or for cameo staging (use of simple painted scenic units against a black background).

The scrim cyclorama when hung on carriers on a track along the studio walls can be easily and quickly moved into position behind scenery or scenic elements. One method for blending the scrim cyc in with the floor without a sharp line is to have a foot or more of excess material at the bottom which can be tucked under sections of pipe weighing the cloth down. Bicycle inner tubes threaded over the pipe provide a friction surface. A second method, which demands more floor space, is to utilize a contoured ground row as masking. This method has the advantage of providing a place for lights at the base of the scrim. A skillful paint-job will blend the ground row in with the scrim (see Fig. 7).

Floor Patterns

The restriction of inadequate height in many television studios often forces the TV director to either shoot "lots of floor," or "lights." This choice of shots often requires the scene designer to utilize the floor area and by various means to integrate it into his design. There are several possibilities for decorating the floor to make it visually more attractive.

1) Simple or elaborately painted designs can be applied. Unless adequate floor washing equipment and personnel are available, this is not a satisfactory solution.

2) Interesting effects can be achieved by using patterns of light projected on the visible floor areas. A variety of punched steel patterns are available from the major lighting instrument companies (Kliegl, Century) or may be manufactured on the spot from light aluminum stock. These patterns are used in ellipsoidal reflector spotlights.

3) The use of several sizes of masking tape applied to the floor in perspective lines or in simple patterns is a quick and inexpensive way of breaking up the expanse of floor and of making it part of a designed picture.

4) A supply of 9" x 9" and 12" x 12" rubber or plastic floor tiles in several colors or patterns can be placed upon the floor. Care must be taken to restrict their use to the areas where cameras will not be working.

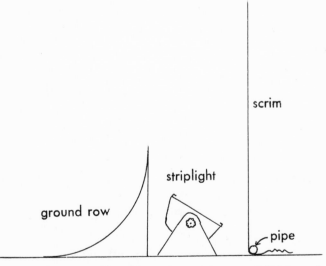

Fig. 7   Sketch of relationship of curved ground row, striplights, and scrim. Note pipe on excess scrim to stretch it tight.

Special Effects

Many special scenic or staging effects are required for effective visualization. Such natural effects as snow, rain, fog, smoke are produced in the studio in various ways.

Snow: the effect of falling snow may be achieved by shooting a drum covered with black paper with white dots on it.[3] Slowly rotating the drum gives an impression of snow falling when supered over a scene. A fast moving drum results in a rain effect. Similarly, it is possible to indicate a moving sky by supering stars over a scene. Care must be exercised to properly spot the stars so they do not travel through objects. A very satisfactory snowfall may be obtained from the use of Styrofoam or plastic snow available at the Christmas trimmings counter of stores, or in bulk from window display supply houses. One method of dropping the snow is to use a snow cradle. Two battens of wood (1″ x 3″ white pine) have a piece of canvas fastened to them. One-third of the canvas is slotted to permit the snow to fall through the slots as the cradle is rocked.

Rain: can be achieved by running water through a pipe drilled to permit the water to run out. Such a pipe hung over and outside a window will give a realistic rain effect. The most difficult part of a realistic rain effect in the studio is getting rid of the water. For large areas, a sheet of plastic, used in home construction as a vapor or condensation barrier, can be banked up to collect the water.

Fog or mist: a piece of gauze (mosquito netting, scrim) or a smoked glass or acetate sheet placed over the camera lens can give a soft diffused effect which can simulate fog. Commercial fog, smoke and dry ice machines are available to achieve these effects.[4]

The success of any special effect is heightened by combining the visual with the aural. The sound of sleigh bells with the snowfall effect will much more quickly establish the desired illusion. Similarly, the foghorn sound with the mist or fog will most quickly create the illusion. The use of recorded sound effects can effectively aid in establishing a mood or atmosphere. This is not a decision of the designer, but he can plan on the use of sound to help in creating an illusion.

PROPERTIES

"Properties" (a carry-over term from the stage and film) is the designation given to furniture and set dressing in the television setting. Properties are of two general kinds, referred to as "hand props" and "set props."

Classification

Hand props are used by the actor or performer during the performance. Some examples of hand props carried or handled by the actor are: firearms, letters, drinking glasses, dishes, packages, billfolds, knives.

Set props (or dressing) include the furnishings of the setting — furniture, floor coverings, wall decorations. Examples of set props are: rugs, pictures on wall, tapestries, other wall hanging decorative devices, table coverings, flowers in vases (unless it is a bouquet carried on by an actor), books in shelves, pillows on furniture, guns on display, lamps.

At times the distinction in classification is determined by how an object is used. If a necklace is worn by an actress as part of a costume, it is classed as costume; if the necklace is displayed on a board on the wall it is a set prop or dressing; if it is carried on set or handled by an actor it is a hand prop.

Arbitrarily, it is possible to classify properties as decorative or functional.

The purpose of *decorative* props is simply that of providing attractive, visually pleasing elements to complete and complement the television setting. Just as a home or room is not "lived-in" without the addition of plants, pictures, knick-knacks, or many other items, the setting is not finished until the set is dressed with many utilitarian and decorative pieces which combine to achieve a complete picture. The decorative props which a designer incorporates into a dramatic setting may importantly affect the viewer. The number of objects in a setting, the tasteful selection of objects displayed, the quality and finish of the furniture can all combine to give a feeling of wealth, luxury, a definite idea of the people who inhabit the setting. In reverse, a room sparsely furnished with tattered wall paper on the walls, cracked windows or mirrors, battered chairs and furniture may immediately indicate a very poor or slum condition. The designer has the opportunity to reveal in the setting and dressing the mood of the play and many of the characteristics of the persons of the drama.

The purpose of the *functional* property is often dictated by the medium. Television, more so than stage or film, has been forced to design and provide many functional properties peculiarly adapted to its shooting patterns and formats. Some of the programs requiring special functional props are panel and audience participation shows such as *What's My Line?, To Tell The Truth, Password, I've Got A Secret* and *The Price Is Right*, and news shows such as *Meet The Press, Face The Nation*, and network and local news programs.

Such programs not only require specifically functional props and settings, but in many instances also need specially designed seating arrangements. For example, Fig. 8 shows a desk designed by the author for a special television program need and which served as a functional and flexible prop.[5] Multiple seating arrangements around this one piece were possible because of its unique design — the centered legs providing leg room on all sides, thus making it available for a variety of uses. In addition, the unusual design makes this desk a distinctive and modern piece of furniture. Flexibility and functional qualities are designed into many unique and attractive elements of television settings, which must be categorized as properties.

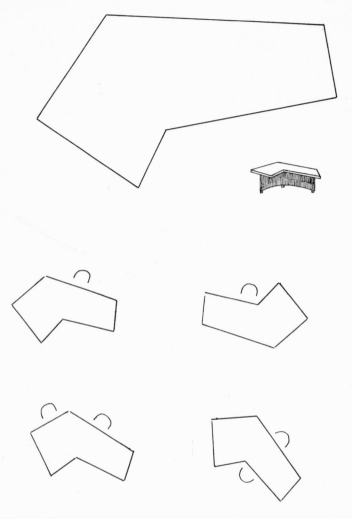

Fig. 8 Top view of specially designed desk-table, and several possible seating arrangements.

Furniture

In selecting furniture, function is most important. Furniture (chairs, sofas, stools) designed for office or commercial uses fits the requirements of non-dramatic TV better than furniture designed for the home, for several reasons: it is an inch or two higher at seat level and usually has firmer or more serviceable upholstery, which makes it easier for the performers to rise and move; it is simpler and cleaner in design, and will combine with many different motifs and styles of settings.

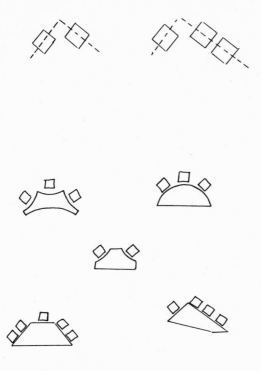

Fig. 9   Inverted "V" and "L" seating arrangements, and variations.

Furniture selected or purchased for permanent use in non-dramatic TV should be simple of design, modern or contemporary of style, functional in use and attractive in appearance.

The most satisfactory seating for TV shot patterns is the open inverted V or L arrangement, illustrated in Fig. 9. There are, of course, many variations possible in the basic V and L shapes to accommodate different numbers of participants.

Although the shot patterns and demands of the program format may dictate the shape of a piece of furniture, the detail, material and finish of the piece are a reflection of the designer and the budget. The not uncommon practice of utilizing, for interview and women's programs, the furnishings and furniture of commercial accounts has helped many TV stations overcome the problems of maintaining a suitable stock of furniture.

TELEVISION LIGHTING

Lighting is influenced by the illumination and the movement requirements of the camera and the microphone. As was pointed out in Chapter 2, there is a minimum amount of light required to produce an acceptable picture. The position and aim of the lighting instruments may also be influenced by the audio pick-up of the microphone and by the necessary movements of the boom. In addition to these technical restrictions, television lighting must achieve aesthetic and artistic goals. Lighting can help to establish time, mood, place and atmosphere. Lighting instruments and mechanical and electrical controls are the tools available to the designer; from experience, he can develop a perceptivity which enables him to visually reach his goals. However, the final determiner is the TV camera. The final result is the picture on the TV monitor.

Functions

The primary functions of television lighting are:

1) *Visibility* — sufficient illumination to activate the camera and to enable the viewer to see all the viewer is supposed to see. The amount of light required to achieve optimum pictures varies considerably with the kind and quality of equipment. It may range from less-than-normal room light to the 250-300 foot-candle[6] reading required for some color TV. It is not sufficient only to create visibility in the studio; TV lighting must insure that the viewer sees well all that he is supposed to see. This means well lighted cover shots as well as properly illuminated fine detail in close-up shots.

2) *Modeling* — sufficient illumination to create shadows and to develop the dimensionality of the object or scene. The human face consists of a number of surfaces (planes). The face in natural light has lighted planes and shadow areas. The TV lighting specialist attempts to light the face and figure just as nature does. In doing so, he develops the shape and form. The lighting instruments are hung at 45° above and in front of the performer to produce a natural look of highlights and shadows. The light, directed on the subject, is aimed, focused, and controlled in intensity in order to effect a natural appearance.

3) *Reality* (illusion) — sufficient illumination to create an illusion of reality in the scene. In attempting to create an illusion of reality, motivated light is used. Light streaming through a window to simulate sunlight is motivated light. The flicker of light from a fire or flame is motivated light. Moonlight, the pool of light beneath a street lamp, light reflected by a mirror through rippling water, all are motivated light — all aid in creating and maintaining an illusion of reality. The proper illusion created by lighting in combination with other visual and aural sensations will result in atmosphere.

4) *Mood* (atmosphere) — sufficient illumination to create, establish and maintain an effect consistent with the intent of the scene. A setting of a forest of trees with patches of sunlight on the grass creates an illusion for the viewer. Add to this the croakings of frogs, the songs of birds, and light, gay music and a mood is established. Take the same setting, subdue the lighting, add to it some wisps of fog or smoke, ominous, eerie music, stillness broken only by the weird hooting of an owl and an entirely different mood is created. Mood is more than an illusion of reality; it combines psychological overtones which act and react to produce in the viewer an atmosphere which is at one moment sweet, light and gay, and the next weird, ominous and mystifying.

5) *Performer* — add beauty and glamour to the face or figure through the use of diffused or soft light. Control features by playing up the good and playing down the bad.

Types of Lighting

The principal illumination on the subject is "key" light and the spotlight is its source. There are two kinds of spotlights used in TV: the fresnel lens and the ellipsoidal reflector spotlight. The general practice is to use fresnel lens spots for key lighting. The fresnel lens provides a soft-edge circle of light in contrast with the sharp-edged light from the ellipsoidal reflector spot. Light from a spotlight is classified as specific or shadow-producing illumination. All spotlights have reflectors and lenses which focus the light rays. Fresnel lens spotlights can be adjusted from a tiny spot position to a broad flood position. Ellipsoidal reflector spotlights emit light rays which are parallel to one another. This feature permits this type of instrument to be used for projecting light patterns or shadows. Focusing this instrument produces little change in size of lighted area.

Light has a characteristic termed quality. Light can be sharp in quality or soft and diffused. Key light is sharp in quality. It may be reduced in intensity, but it is never softened or diffused.

Lighting used to enhance the appearance of a subject or to create effect may be called "modeling," "dimensional," or "accent" lighting. Spotlights are also used for this type of light, the quality of which is usually harsh and undiffused. Other lights are "eye" and "kicker" lights; usually spotlights, they are highly specialized in their use. The eye light is used in a close-up face shot to highlight the eyes or to induce a sparkle of light in the eye. The kicker light is a special light which can be used on any subject to add an emphasis or "kick." Very often a tiny fresnel lens spotlight of 75-150 watts, called an inky-dinky, is used for these purposes. The reason a small instrument is used is because it can be easily concealed within the set.

A flat or even amount of light, often used to eliminate or soften too-black shadows, to fill in dark areas, is called "fill" (base) light. Scoops are usually the source of fill light, the quality of which is soft, with no direction and no shadows. The non-directional, soft light from a scoop is called general illumination. The general illumination instrument has no lens and the distribution of light is controlled only by the shape of the instrument. General illumination is often considered non-shadow producing light. This is achieved by either of two methods: use of a diffusion medium (fiberglass cloth or silk) or an interior quartz-coated lamp. Both methods will produce an almost shadowless picture.

Light used to eliminate shadows on the scenery, to show the scenery or background, or to create silhouette effects is called "background" or "scenery" light. This light is only for the scenery or background, and care must be exercised that the performers remain away from walls or scenery so they do not come into range of this light. If scenery light is separate and controllable, the problem of unwanted shadows can be minimized. The microphone boom is the source of most unwanted shadows. Spotlights producing such shadows can be "barndoored" (one shutter of a barndoor closed in) to remove the shadow. Sometimes a small piece of spun glass can be inserted in the frame holder to reduce or eliminate the undesirable shadow. Scenery or backgrounds may be lighted by scoops or spots from above or, optionally, by strips of light from below. Silhouette effects can be achieved with similar light on a plain, smooth surface. If a translucent surface is available for silhouette, the lights may be placed behind, lighting the surface evenly. Source of background or scenery light may be either scoops or spotlights, and may be harsh or soft in quality as the occasion demands.

Light coming from behind the subject on the axis of the camera, used to separate the subject from the background and to create a halo of light about the head and a rim of light along the top of the shoulders, is called "backlight." Backlight is not a natural light. However, it achieves the effect of giving contour to the figure. It also enhances female performers by highlighting the hair with sparkle and lustre. The spotlight (or reflector lamp) [7] is the source of backlight. Usually a 500-watt, six-inch fresnel lens spotlight is sufficient to add the backlight effect. Care must be taken to attempt at all times to keep the backlight 45° above the floor and 180° from the camera position on an axis with the camera. Backlight is high intensity light, never diffused.

Controllable factors

The distribution of light in the TV studio can be controlled by the number of instruments, the focus (spot or flood), and the use of barndoors on fresnel spotlights and shutters on ellipsoidal reflector spots. For example, if the studio has five 1,000-watt spotlights, a greater distribution of light is possible than with one 5,000-watt spot. The quantity (amount) of light is controllable by the number, type and size of the instruments.

The intensity of TV light can be controlled by use of a dimmer. A commonly used dimmer is the auto-transformer type. In principle, a single transformer coil (primary) around a soft iron core is supplied with full voltage. A portion of this coil between a movable brush and a common neutral constitutes a secondary coil. The brush movement varies the amount of voltage going to the lamp and so dims the light output. This is an efficient type of dimmer which is not too expensive. Other types of dimmers available include electronic and silicon core rectifier dimmers. Innumerable preset features and punch card control are available. The TV studio does not require elaborate lighting controls unless the program schedule includes a variety of programming atypical of the local station operation.

The quality (harshness or softness) of the light is controlled by use of silk over scoops or spun glass (fiberglass) over fresnel lens spotlights. Because of the characteristics of its soft-edge light beam and focus ability, the fresnel spotlight is the most frequently used. The soft-edge light permits areas of light to be blended together. The 500-watt 6" lens fresnel is commonly used for backlight in small studios. The eight-inch 1,000-2,000-watt fresnel usually is used for back light in large studios. Eight-inch, 2,000-watt (deuce) or 5,000-watt (5 kw), 10" or 12" fresnels are used for front (key) light in large network production centers.

The ellipsoidal reflector spots (6", 500-750-watt and 8", 1000-2000-watt) are usually used as light projector instruments.

Application

Television lighting is applied in areas or spaces. Utilizing a minimum of three instruments, any one camera "shot" or position can be lighted. The three basic types of lighting (key, fill and backlight) are used. The inverted Y with the subject at the midpoint is the pattern most frequently used. (See Fig. 10.)

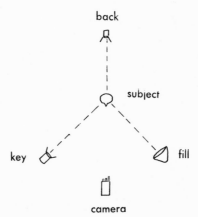

Fig. 10 The instrument, camera and subject positioning for the inverted Y television lighting method.

The spacing of the key and fill instruments is approximately 45° from center, with the backlight on the axis of the taking camera. This lighting arrangement, adapted to multiple positions or to two or three person situations, will satisfy most basic lighting requirements. Additional types of lighting can be added to this basic set-up for accent or scenery emphasis. Subtle controls can be effected in the basic light plot through the use of dimmer circuits or some of the special controllable factor devices. [8]

It is entirely feasible in lighting for TV to address most effort to area lighting. A dramatic scene which includes three positions for an actor would be carefully lighted at the three important areas or positions. The spaces between these important positions are adequately lighted for the cross-movements. While the actor is moving, the viewer will not be able to distinguish detail, nor even expect the lighting polish of the important action areas. On occasion, scoop (fill) light may suffice for the walk-over movements. This technique permits the lighting man to devote his time to completing and polishing the important action areas.

Special Lighting Effects

There are many unusual methods available to the lighting designer of the TV program to achieve special effects. Ellipsoidal reflector spotlights can be used as "pattern" projectors. A metal pattern can be inserted into the focal plane of the instrument and the design projected onto background surfaces — an effective way of adding visual interest to the picture. It is a simple matter to use thin aluminum frozen food pans and to cut unique appropriate designs for such patterns. Cucalorus (cookie) patterns cut out of wood or cardboard may be suspended before a fresnel spot with the lens removed and a pattern can be thus projected. Barndoors, top hats[9] and snoots[10] are available in different sizes and shapes to provide special light patterns. Clouds silk screened on heat resistant glass slides are available for use in ellipsoidal reflector spotlights. The ellipsoidal reflector spot also has framing shutters which can be adjusted to form several light patterns.

Light in this visual medium provides the imaginative, resourceful person with an outlet for creative ideas which can contribute strongly to achieving interesting, attractive and effective pictures.

GRAPHICS

The purpose of any graphic card is to take certain information and convey it in a clear, concise, visually interesting way. The elements which combine to achieve this are: words, ideas and design.

Types

There are two basic types of graphics or visuals common to television: the visual designed to relay *identification*, and the visual designed to relay *information*. Station identification cards, title cards, credits and product identification cards are common to the first classification. Without doubt, the most frequent TV use of the informational visual is in the "super" card.[11] In baseball, for example, the super provides the viewer not only with the name of the batter but, often, also with his batting average.

The production of effective visuals is the responsibility of the graphics designer. This artist, and he must be an artist and craftsman, must be conversant with the visual media. His background and training should include the ability to produce in any drawing medium, including chalk, conté crayon, tempera, pencil and ink. In addition, he should know film techniques, especially slides, slide cameras and Polaroid cameras. Versatility coupled with the knack of speedy work are a prime combination for the graphic artist.

The television picture has an "aspect ratio" of 3:4 — three units high by four units wide. All pictures should be composed with this relationship in mind. The most frequently used card size for television studio graphics is 11 x 14 inches. An 11" x 14" card will provide an information area of 7" x 10". The space between the information area and the edge of the card is called "safety." Safety must be provided on all graphic cards to permit some degree of leeway in "framing" the picture.[12] Usually, the object being televised on any camera is centered in the frame.

The lettering requirements for television graphics are: size, clarity and spacing. *Size* of lettering should be 1/10th the vertical size of the graphic card, or 1/7th the size of the information area of the card. *Clarity* of lettering will be achieved if the graphic artist relies on simple, clean-of-line letters. Elaborate letter styles have a specialized use on TV. Proper *spacing* of the lettering and restricting the width of the type font will remove the liklihood of "smeared" or "streaked" letters running together in the TV picture. The use of "extra-condensed" type styles encourages these problems.

The "gray-scale" guides the graphic artist in his work. The television system reproduces only a 10-step scale — black (step 10), white (step 1) and 8 shades of gray between. All TV pictures are made up of these 10 steps of the gray scale. The use of white lettering on black card is best restricted to supers. Good design and visualization result from wise use of 2-3-step minimum separations of the gray scale in TV graphics.

Although hand lettering lends character to the television visuals, the most frequently used printing device is the "hot press" printer. A less expensive yet quite versatile printing press has the type set and locked in position on bars secured to the layout surface by strong magnets. In addition to a variety of type faces (fonts), each of these two printing presses are capable of re-registration of cards. Simplicity of operation recommends the hot press and the magnetic press to television stations.

Educational television operations place special demands on graphic arts departments because of broadcasts designed for instructional purposes.

Teaching requires greater use of special illustrations, cartoons, maps, graphs and charts. All such two-dimensional materials are the responsibility of the graphic artist. Frequently, teaching programs demand the use of three-dimensional and/or animated visual materials. The graphic and visual requirements of ETV quite often exceed those of the commercial TV station. The ETV graphic artist often must produce working scale or simplified, but functional, models of objects, processes or machines.

Studio Display

Many methods of displaying graphics in the studio are available. The easel with an adjustable ledge is one basic graphic display device. On an easel, graphic cards can be pulled away to the side or flipped down to change. An easel with a ring binder mounted on it provides another easy method of flipping cards for fast, smooth, guided changes. (See Fig. 11.)

Other methods of displaying title cards are available. The parchment scroll device reminiscent of the Middle Ages is one method. The scroll is opened and unrolled slowly, revealing the information. A circular drum with a strip containing the information is slowly turned past the camera lens focused on one area. As the drum turns, the information appears and disappears from view. The information may be printed white on black for superimposition. An electrically operated drum provides flexibility of speed control. (See footnote 3.) A book of blank pages with titles and information can be an effective method of visualizing information. The pages can be turned remotely by affixing very thin wires; it is equally effective to have a hand turn the pages. For a dramatic presentation, the title would be on the cover of the book. A ferris wheel effect can be utilized. The cards, as the wheel is turned, rotate into view. A similar device is a paddle wheel with information displayed on the paddles. Other devices used have included umbrellas with printing on the panels on top, guillotines with lettering on the blade readable when the blade drops into view, trays of water with lettering beneath the surface, and even sand-covered cards from which the sand is blown to reveal information. The imagination of the graphics designer is the only limiting factor in the method of displaying information.

Special Devices

Television production problems, including many relating to graphics, have resulted in many unusual, unique and interesting devices being developed as solutions. The following are a few of the most commonly used special production techniques or devices:

Super pointer. The inability to point or focus attention on film chain-originated pictures can be solved by placing a large black card next to the speaker. Give the performer a pointer (painted dull black) with an arrow or dot of white on the tip. By supering the white tip held before the black card over the film chain camera, the person can, by watching a studio

Fig. 11   Ring binder mounting flip card easel. Cards can be dropped *out of* camera view, or *into* camera view if focus is on the lower card.

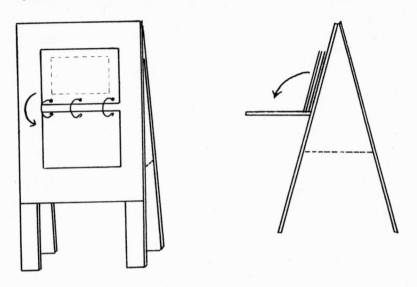

Fig. 12   Side view sketch showing another method of changing a series of graphics ——— they are tipped and floated down to reveal next in sequence. Usually for on-the- air movement.

monitor, indicate any part of the screen with the pointer and emphasize aspects of motion picture film or still pictures (slides) at will.

Pull-up unit. To provide a method of revealing visuals, yet concealing them until the proper moment, the pull-up unit was developed. It is a narrow box which in height is just concealed by a desk. The box has a number of grooves into which individual graphic cards can be slipped. Spring metal leaves against the sides of the cards, when raised into view, hold them in position. A simple lift by the performer reveals the graphic, which, when no longer needed, is pushed down out of sight. A number of visuals can be revealed and concealed in this way.

Spring tension pole. One of the most versatile graphic display devices developed is the spring tension pole, which follows the basic design of the "pole-cat."[13] This pole, extendable from 10'6" to 19'6", can be spotted anywhere in the studio playing area. A number of display devices which can be used on this pole or on the pole-cat have been developed. These devices, all of which are adjustable in height to fit the performer, can be easily produced. Variations on this device permit two visuals to be used on a two-sided holder, or three or four. A further variation constructed with a number of grooves permits a series of graphics to be inserted and pulled to be revealed.

COSTUMING

The purpose of the costume designer is to portray visually, through the costumes of the characters of the drama, the prevailing design of clothing worn in any period of our civilization. The costume designer, utilizing the principles of costume design, selection of fabrics, color and style, achieves in the clothing of the characters visual reinforcement of the dramatist's ideas.

As with all visual aspects of dramatic presentation, television costuming must contribute information about the character for the viewer. The age of a person may be reflected in the cut or style of the clothes. The type and quality of material might indicate his financial standing. The use and selection of color and accessories might indicate a person's taste and refinement — or lack of it. The way the clothes are worn and look may reflect his social standing. What a person wears, how he wears it, are indicators of that person and a reflection of his characterization.

Basic Costume Rules

The typical television station today is rarely concerned with costuming actors. Rather, the concern is with the clothing the performer wears. A list of do's and don't's pertaining to television dress and accessories may provide a basic guide.

1) Test fabrics on camera whenever possible to determine the transposition from the fabric color into the monochrome television gray scale.
2) Avoid flamboyant extremes in contrasts and patterns of cloth.
3) Avoid excessive use of black and white in single costumes. Work as much as possible in 2-3-step gray scale contrast separations.
4) Learn the gray scale. Develop a color sense to be able to transpose from color into the 10-step gray scale.
5) Avoid extremes in accessories. Do not use highly reflective jewelry, pins or similar items.
6) Avoid small repetitive patterns in cloth, which tend to become "busy" before the camera.
7) Avoid hard surface (chintz, glosheen, fiberglass, rayon, sateen), highly reflective costume materials.
8) Advocate the use of off-white or pastel shades of shirts for men.
9) Lapel pins, pens and pencils in breast pockets of coats, and highly reflective tie pins are not desirable for the male performer. The common and often preferred use of a lavalier microphone in television presentations requires the removal of tie pins.
10) Do not expect the performer to follow the basic good sense rules of dress for television — be prepared by judicious use of lighting and video control to compensate for and correct the common costume errors.

11) A good mixture of common sense, good taste and luck will result in a minimum of non-dramatic costuming problems.

MAKE-UP

There are two basic types of make-up application for television — *straight* (non-dramatic) and *dramatic*.

The primary purposes of straight make-up are: to cover the dark beard on male performers; to reduce the reflection of light from the nose, forehead and bald head; when necessary, to "play down" or reduce skin texture. Television pancake make-up is most commonly used. The range of skin tone make-up (from very light to very dark) is available from several manufacturers.[14]

Application of straight make-up for men usually consists of: 1) applying on the beard areas of the face with a moist sponge sufficient pancake to smooth out and cover the face; the make-up should blend down over the jaw and chin line into the upper neck regions; 2) touching up the nose and forehead (head, if bald) to cut shine; 3) if eyebrows are pale, a small touch-up with brown or black eyebrow pencil may be necessary to provide contrast with skin tone; the same slight touch-up may be required on the hairline area on the temples.

Women require special attention in only one area — the lips. Street make-up — providing there is a pancake or powder base make-up — for skin and eyes will usually suffice. Care must be taken in selection of lipstick (lip rouge). Test the street make-up on camera for suitability, especially the lipstick. Many of the popular pale shades of lipstick fail to provide sufficient absorption of light to give the slightly darker lip effect desired for a good picture.

For best results, extremes of straight make-up must be avoided at all times. During the first on-camera rehearsal check for the need of make-up — it may not be required.

Dramatic make-up has as its primary purposes (over and above the uses of straight make-up) the creating and aiding of characterization. The fundamentals of effective stage character make-up are appropriate for television. The techniques, which are an art in themselves, will not be analyzed here. Basically, television requirements differ from those of the stage primarily in emphasis. On the stage it is the projection of the characterization which demands strong, bold and often "contrasty" make-up. The make-up must be effective for the many hundreds of spectators, seated near and far from the actor. Television, on the other hand, is an intimate medium and the make-up must, therefore, be more natural. Greater emphasis is placed upon the subtleties of make-up. The viewer is, in effect, the television camera and very often views the performer from extremely close range.

In all matters of staging, the local commercial station and the educational television station have a special advantage that frequently is not fully utilized. If they are close (in the former case geographically, in the latter case usually administratively) to a dramatic arts or radio and television department of a college or university, they have good sources of advice, materials and assistance in regard to staging, properties, effects, lighting, costuming and make-up.

NOTES

[1] Photos of settings, courtesy of University of Michigan Television Center. Designer: U. J. Moffatt.

[2] Cyclorama is a U-shaped cloth expanse without seams, enclosing three sides of the playing area, used as a sky or void background on the stage.

[3] An automatic rotating drum with variable speed control suitable for this effect and for rolling credits is available from Salescaster Displays Corp., Linden, N. J.

[4] Fog, wind and cobweb machines are available from Mole-Richardson Co., Hollywood, Calif.

[5] See *Staging for TV*, a training film produced by the National Educational Television and Radio Center.

[6] To obtain an accurate foot-candle reading, stand in the position of the subject and read on a light meter scale the level of illumination with the meter pointed toward the camera position. Repeat this procedure for each camera position.

[7] Lamps with glass-shaped and mirror-coated elements as reflectors are available in spot and flood types of reflector lamps. "Birdseye" is one of this type of lamp.

[8] Ordinary screen door wire inserted in the gelatin frame holder of a fresnel spot will cut down the intensity of the light by some 10-15%, but doesn't change the quality of the light.

[9] A top hat is a section of stove pipe or vent pipe spot-welded to a flat metal piece sized to fit the frame holder of a spot. In silhouette shape it resembles a top hat.

[10] A snoot is a conical shaped metal tube fastened to a flat metal piece to fit into the frame holder of a spotlight. The tip of the cone is removed to allow light to pass.

[11] "Super" refers to superimposition, a double exposure providing a background picture with secondary information electronically superimposed over the primary picture.

[12] "Framing" refers to the effective composition of any shot to achieve a pleasing, balanced and effective picture.

[13] See *Staging for TV* film.

[14] Both Max Factor (N series) and Stein's (TV series) manufacture make-up for television use. The author has most frequently used N series (Max Factor) for standard face make-up needs for men.

BIBLIOGRAPHY

Barton, Lucy, *Historic Costume for the Stage*. Boston: Walter H. Baker Co., 1935. Hundreds of sketches illustrating all periods of costume. Additional valuable information on accessories and construction.

Bretz, Rudy, *Techniques of Television Production*. New York: McGraw-Hill, 1962. Excellent, thorough treatment of subject. Technical and detailed for the professional television worker. Well illustrated with pictures and sketches.

Corson, Richard, *Stage Makeup*. New York: Appleton-Century-Crofts, Inc., 1949. Good treatment of basic makeup techniques applicable to television. Good beginning reference book.

Gillette, Arnold S., *Stage Scenery: its construction and rigging*. New York: Harper & Bros., 1959. Very well illustrated text in the construction and rigging of scenery on stage.

Journal of the Society of Motion Pictures and Television Engineers. Articles on lighting, grayscale, color response, and technical information on film and cameras.

Kehoe, Vincent J. R., *The Technique of Film and Television Make-up*. New York: Hastings House, Publishers, Inc., 1957. Excellent reference book for the professional or well informed.

Burris-Meyer, Harold, and Edward C. Cole, *Scenery for the Theatre*. Boston: Little, Brown & Co., 1948. Excellent reference for the standard methods and techniques used in the construction and handling of scenery for the stage.

Parker, W. Oren, and Harvey K. Smith, *Scene Design and Stage Lighting*. New York: Holt, Rinehart, and Winston, Inc., 1963. Brief but good section on properties. Well illustrated. "Drafting the Design" section illustrates a scaled compositional elevation with all props and dressing indicated — an excellent technique.

Philippi, Herbert, *Stagecraft and Scene Design*. New York: Houghton Mifflin Co., 1953.

Wade, Robt. J., *Designing for TV*. New York: Pellegrini and Cudahy, 1952. Good reference for problems of designing and executing the television setting. Well illustrated. Good section on gray scale.

Wade, Robt. J., *Staging TV Programs and Commercials*. New York: Hastings House, Publishers, Inc., 1954. Coverage of visual aspects of television from the scenic and graphic designer's viewpoint. How to plan and execute settings and props. Includes a chapter on graphics.

Wilcox, R. Turner, *The Mode in Costume*. New York: Charles Scribner's Sons, 1948. Well illustrated reference for costumes through the years. Standard reference in costuming.

SUPPLEMENTAL MATERIAL: PERFORMING AND RESEARCH

THIS BOOK is not intended to be exhaustive, either in a given subject area of television or in scope of the field as a whole. This is an introduction to television broadcasting, and there are many other aspects that the beginner eventually may go into, using the material in this book as a base. Among the other areas of study are two worthy of brief mention here: Performing and Research.

PERFORMING

Of the subject areas *not* covered by the preceding chapters of this book, performing probably is that which is most often offered as a course in the educational institution and which is also basic for the beginner. The performer is anyone who appears before the television camera in any capacity. The two most important categories are those of announcing and acting.

Announcing

The television announcer needs the desirable vocal qualities of the radio announcer: control of volume and pitch, pleasant quality, clear diction and accurate pronunciation. The addition of sight, however, necessitates special adaptation. The television announcer's vocal qualities should match his physical appearance — an appropriate, optimum pitch, for example. The announcer must not only know the proper use of the microphone, but also the proper use of the camera. More than anyone, his is the presentational approach — talking directly to the audience, coming directly as a visitor into the home.

In addition to knowing how to "read" well — that is, to present the ideas smoothly and with effective interpretation — a television announcer must have a broad background which enables him to understand the materials with which he deals. This background should include a knowledge of his duties, limitations, and impact on the audience as a part of the television process (see Chapter 1 of this book); his function in relation to the producer and director, and to the artistic and routine processes of production (as described in Chapters 3 and 5); and his place in terms of the technical and staging potentials and needs of the program (as delineated in Chapters 2 and 6). He should also be familiar with the various commercial announcements, forms of presentation and program types to which he might be assigned (see Chapter 4). In addition, inasmuch as television is in great part a medium of news and public affairs, he should have a broad background in the philosophical, historical, social, economic and political influences of our time. In fact, most networks and stations now require a college education or its equivalent as a condition of employing announcers.

Above all, the announcer must remember that he is a guest in someone's home, not portraying a fictional character, but as himself. He must therefore behave with the kind of honesty and sincerity that he would expect from a guest in his own home. Inasmuch as, most of the time, he is persuading people of something to believe or do, he should speak and behave with good taste. He also should be aware that no matter how good and effective his vocal presentation, the slightest disconcerting facial or physical movement, the smallest note of falsity in a gesture may obviate all of his words. Much television commercial announcing is done "voice-over," so in some instances the visual aspects do not apply.

The announcer conveys not only ideas, but feelings and personality. In that respect he is also an actor, and should be thoroughly familiar with the special requirements of television acting for his basic development as an announcer.

Acting

The best training for the television actor is the stage. The basic elements of acting are learned in the theatre and if any talent does exist, it is there that it has a chance to come to the fore. (It is a peculiarity of film technique that although there are many fine actors in that medium, the ability of the medium to edit, create and recreate both visual and sound aspects of any performance permits a person of virtually no acting talent whatsoever to become a successful star.) The stage actor will find that his abilities are transferred to television, insofar as character interpretation and development are concerned, almost in toto. The peculiar characteristics of the medium, however, require special adaptations for most effective use of its potentials and most efficient adjustment to its restrictions.

For the theatre-trained actor, television lacks most importantly an interaction with the audience. The actor cannot feel the audience response and play the subtleties of character delineation accordingly. Everything must be fixed beforehand, in anticipation of what the reaction of the small group watching in front of any given television set likely will be.

Filmed or taped (with film-technique) television production — that is, where the scenes are shot individually, usually out of sequence — prevents the actor from building or maintaining a rising intensity of continuity of character development. On the other hand, live (or live-type taped) television does permit this and, in addition, provides the actor with the continuity of stage acting and the close-up intimacy of the film at the same time. Even here, however, the actor's advantages are complicated by restrictions. Because the sustained performance is in a close-up medium, the actor must never for a second step out of character. He must be acting, or reacting to the other performers, every moment because he cannot know when the camera may pick him up — even when he is supposedly off camera, but still on the set. He must "freeze" in character before his next scene in case the camera comes in a second earlier. We have all watched the embarrassment of an actor who suddenly leaps into the characterization and scene after the camera has unexpectedly come on him. The television actor must always be in the scene, listening, feeling and conveying the feeling — more so, in fact, in live-type continuous television than in any other medium.

The technical needs of television and the necessity of the director to have every shot planned clearly beforehand, with no unwarranted deviations once on the air, require the actor to make frequent compromises in his motivations, interpretations and movements. For example, to meet the requirements of a particular shot, the actor may have to make a movement that is not clearly a part of the character he is portraying. Accordingly, he may then have to adjust his character interpretation to find valid motivation for that particular movement. Usually, this kind of adjustment is made during the rehearsal period. Sometimes it is more difficult. In a *Studio One* television production, actress Mary Ellen Verheyden was supposed to jump out of the armchair in which she was seated and cross the room to her injured husband (Jack Palance). The camera, however, instead of getting the previous close-up on her from a distance with a long lens, as planned, had dollied in with a short lens and was completely blocking her way out of the chair. She had to change her character's motivation and action for that moment to justify her staying in the chair until the camera could be pulled back and an alternate shot pattern ad-libbed by the director.

Because of the impact of television's special characteristics upon the actor, it is important that he become acquainted not only with the director's approaches and problems (see Chapter 5), but with the technical needs and potentials of camera movement, switcher-fader transitions, lighting, sound and special effects (see Chapters 2 and 6). A familiarity with the terminology and uses of equipment and directorial techniques can be of immeasurable help.

Pointers for the Television Actor

The following are some of the more pertinent considerations for the television actor in his attempt to make the most of the medium's potentials and at the same time adjust effectively to its restrictions.

1) The first sign of the professional actor is that he's constantly writing — making clear notes of all the directions given him by the director and making certain that he will be able to execute them with precise detail.

2) Precision is important. Because a specific shot has been prepared by the director, the actor must be able to repeat on cue the exact spatial position and bodily relationships set up during rehearsals. All directions must be memorized even more accurately and fully, if possible, than are the character's lines.

3) Learn to "hit the chalk mark," the term applied to the exact place the actor has been rehearsed to be in for any given shot. The slightest error on the actor's part may throw off the entire composition of the shot. Yet, the actor must hit the mark without being obvious or mechanical about it.

4) Television, as a close-up medium, requires movement, gesture and expression to be both natural and restrained at the same time. The actor must use his face and body with the fullest control, scaling down the entire pattern of movements and conveying all things with the minimum specific motion possible — unless told otherwise by the director. An economy of movement is important and each cross, gesture or move should be purposeful and the actor should clearly validate the reason for it. Make every action count. Excess movements are especially distracting because they are so close to the audience. The slightest facial expression can often serve for what would have to be a gross movement or gesture on the stage. A facial expression that conveys something at all times is important — and so is an avoidance of grimacing. In a close-up, if the audience either gets nothing or too much from your face, then your best solution as an actor may be to try to learn scene designing. Arm and hand movements must be carefully controlled or the gesture may go right off the edge of the television screen. Nose-to-nose playing may be required in two-shots of what may otherwise be natural conversation between two people; on the television screen the distance will look normal. Because of close-ups,

not only must the actor avoid artificial and exaggerated movements, but he must have an ease, a grace and a naturalness, as opposed to giving the audience the feeling that he may be ill at ease, awkward or self-conscious. Even static pictures can be given the essence of movement sometimes by the change of camera angle or distance.

5) Be aware of the mike placement and pick-up patterns so that you can help maintain the proper level of vocal reception while retaining a well-modulated tone. For example, in moving across a set you not only have to walk to the pattern set up for the camera, but you must time and space your vocal delivery to fit the microphone pick-up pattern.

6) Although you must always be aware of the location of the camera (the tally light on a camera tells you that it's the one that's on), never look directly into it unless so ordered by the director, or by the form of the program. Most TV dramas are representational in style; the commercial, the panel show and variety program, among other types, are presentational in nature and demand direct rapport with the cameras. In some instances, in the representational drama, the actor is required to "cheat" — that is, for the purpose of an effective close shot, to turn somewhat away from the character with whom he is performing and toward the camera, so that he still seems to be in direct relationship with the other actor while at the same time the camera can pick up the desired shot of his face or body.

7) Because of the comparatively little rehearsal time in the pressure- and budget-controlled commercial television field, the actor must memorize quickly and adhere to what has been agreed upon.

8) Never drop out of character.

9) Learn to take cues from the floor manager without looking directly at him and without being distracted from the business under way.

10) Remember that the director is always with you — unlike the theatre where, after the curtain goes up, the director is gone. In TV he is still there, calling the shots. Since he controls the cameras, the actor must follow his directions explicitly. If the actor is unhappy with any direction or acting requirement, he must say so during an early rehearsal before the pattern of the show is set.

11) Although the actor in commercial television usually does not have to oversee his own costumes or apply his own make-up, the good actor always works as closely as possible with the costumer to see that his costume fits the needs of his characterization; and he should know enough about make-up to clarify his character's needs to the make-up man or put on his own, if necessary. (Many experienced actors insist on applying their own make-up.) Make-up for television must be extremely light and subtle. Be careful of aging during a show, of beards, wigs and the use of lines. Usually, only a lightly applied base

with light and shadow tones, as opposed to lining, is effective. Avoid
extremes of black and white in costumes. Stick to the middle tones and
avoid clashing colors, striped or wavy lines. (For a clarification of
costume and make-up needs, see Chapter 6.)

12) While the above principles apply primarily to television acting
technique, as exemplified by live or live-type taped television production, many of the points made here are applicable or adaptable to film
acting. Inasmuch as films comprise such a large part of the drama
presentations on television, it is desirable for the potential actor to
familiarize himself fully with film acting requirements as an important
supplement to his knowledge of television acting techniques.

A distinct opportunity for the good television performer is the chance
to utilize, by the very nature of the medium, a combination of both representational and presentational acting techniques. Even as the close-up permits a delineation of the intimate, subjective thoughts and actions of the
character, the opportunity and sometimes the need to work directly to the
camera results in the person-to-person presentational effect. On occasion the
actor is required to combine both techniques virtually at the same time —
a fine means for effective communication to the audience, but a not inconsiderable task.

Concentration is one of the key disciplines of the actor — and probably
the most difficult thing to achieve in television. It is not possible to isolate
oneself as on the stage and use "inspiration" or to "lose" oneself in the
character. Even while having to understand, believe and feel the character's
motivations and actions in the creation of the role, the actor must be aware
of the cameras, the directions, watch the floor manager for cues, look out
for the mass of equipment and numerous technicians running back and
forth, and constantly be ready to adapt motivation and action to the exigencies of a technical medium. The television actor must develop intense concentration and full awareness of his outside surroundings at one and the
same time. The problem is to remain calm and collected — and, sometimes, sane — in the midst of the confusion and mechanism — and mad-
house — of TV.

RESEARCH

Television research is worthy of discussion here, not because it is
necessarily especially popular as a formal course of study, but because it
has grown exceedingly fast in a relatively new academic subject area, and
because it provides broad and intensive bases for the constantly new developments and understandings in the field. Television, as a fusion of so many
of the arts and sciences, is able to utilize all the basic accepted techniques
of formal research as much as any and more than most other academic

disciplines. The following are the six major research approaches, all applicable to television.

1. *Historical Research* — a systematizing of information. Sample research projects might include "A History of Television in North Carolina"; "A Biographical Study of Reginald Rose's Contributions to Television."

2. *Rhetorical, Critical, Literary Analysis* — the establishing of criteria of what are considered good and effective principles of writing or acting or directing or other elements within the creative process of the medium, and then analyzing one or more presentations according to the principles and standards. The following titles are examples of this kind of research: "New Concepts of Dramaturgy for Television as Developed in Television Adaptations of Stage Plays"; "A Critical Analysis of the Television Productions of Sidney Lumet."

3. *Experimental Research*—measuring under controlled circumstances, analyzing and arriving at conclusions utilizing statistical methods. Projects under this category might include "Physiological Correlates of Enjoyment During Television Westerns"; "Some Psychological Factors in Audience Reaction to Television Commercials."

4. *Action Research* — primarily oriented toward educational situations: after setting up the experiment, changing hypotheses as results are obtained, and proceeding further; arriving at generalizations that can be implemented immediately in a given area. This research category includes new inventions, such as the recent dramatic progress in the development of low-cost video tape recorders. A sample title for a project: "The Application of a Quality Control Program to the Television Film Lab with Special Emphasis on the Processing of Color Film for TV Commercials."

5. *Philosophical Research* — setting up a hypothesis and then trying to prove it by the process of reasoning. Examples of this kind of research might be "The Rights of Networks and Stations to Editorialize"; "The Place of the Federal Communications Commission in setting minimum standards and time allocations for public service broadcasting."

6. *Normative Survey* — the obtaining of statistical information, usually of human activities or attitudes, through questionnaires, interviews, observations. The ratings and surveys pertaining to the number of people allegedly watching any given television program are examples of the quantitative survey. Qualitative surveys, those probing in depth, are frequent and include such subjects as "The Habits and Characteristics of the Television Audience in Anytown." Surveys need not deal directly or solely with people, but may include compilations of information from varying sources, such as "A Survey of Trends in Television Education in Colleges and Universities."

A research project in the mass media may, of course, combine more than one research technique and frequently does. Much important research is being conducted today on the impact of television insofar as it affects the political, economic and social attitudes and behavior of peoples in many parts of the world. Some of this kind of research is oriented toward educational or instructional television purposes and programs. In the "impact" research project, historical, critical, experimental, action, philosophical and survey techniques are often combined, or utilized in different areas of one study to provide a comprehensive and valid whole.

Progress in television, as in other fields, depends upon research: the achievement of understanding and the development of new principles, standards and means which will not only permit but will foster continued creativity and enterprise in the mass media's contributions to the advancement of mankind.

R. L. H.

INDEX